Delhi to Kolkata

Vanessa Betts & Victoria McCulloch

Credits

Footprint credits
Managing Editor: Felicity Laughton
Production and layout: Emma Bryers
Maps and cover: Kevin Feeney

Publisher: Patrick Dawson
Advertising: Elizabeth Taylor
Sales and marketing: Kirsty Holmes

Photography credits
Front cover: Shutterstock/Regien Paassen
Back cover: Shutterstock/Byelikova Oksana

Printed in Great Britain by Alphaset,
Surbiton, Surrey

Every effort has been made to ensure that
the facts in this guidebook are accurate.
However, travellers should still obtain advice
from consulates, airlines, etc, about travel
and visa requirements before travelling.
The authors and publishers cannot accept
responsibility for any loss, injury or
inconvenience however caused.

The content of Footprint *Focus Delhi to
Kolkata* has been taken directly from
Footprint's *India Handbook*, which was
researched and written by David Stott,
Vanessa Betts and Victoria McCulloch.

Publishing information
Footprint *Focus Delhi to Kolkata*
1st edition
© Footprint Handbooks Ltd
November 2013

ISBN: 978 1 909268 40 1
CIP DATA: A catalogue record for this book
is available from the British Library

® Footprint Handbooks and the Footprint
mark are a registered trademark of
Footprint Handbooks Ltd

Published by Footprint
6 Riverside Court
Lower Bristol Road
Bath BA2 3DZ, UK
T +44 (0)1225 469141
F +44 (0)1225 469461
footprinttravelguides.com

Distributed in the USA by Globe Pequot
Press, Guilford, Connecticut

Contents

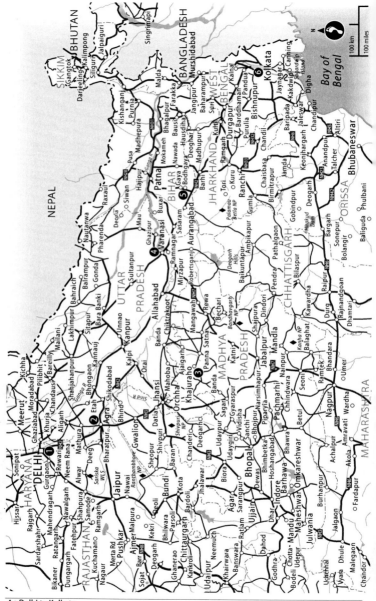

Delhi to Kolkata takes you through the heartlands of India –
the central plains and their rich cultural and spiritual history.
The route heads east from Delhi and Agra into the Ganges plains
and takes in Islamic heritage, Hindu mythology and Buddhist
wisdom. You will find magnificent Sufi shrines in Delhi and
follow the majestic Ganga river at the heart of Hindu mythology;
the state of Uttar Pradesh is also the cultural heartland of Islam
and you will see Mughal architecture at its best in Agra, while in
Gwalior, in neighbouring Madhya Pradesh, you will encounter
magnificent forts and the intricate fusion architecture of the
imambaras. Next there are the stunning temples of Orchha and
the erotic sculptures at Khajuraho.

History is also found in India's ancient jungle land and beautiful
national parks. And the history and precarious future of the Bengal
tigers, a living symbol of India, is nowhere more evident than in
Bandhavgarh and Kanha.

Onwards and northwards, to the ancient city of Varanasi – which
seems older than time itself – where you will witness traditions,
bathing rituals and funeral rites that have gone on for thousands
of years on the banks of the River Ganges. Further east, in
Bodhgaya, you will meet Buddhist monks from all over the world
who have come to the place where Buddha gained enlightenment

Finally, in Kolkata, you'll find a Roman Catholic cathedral, an
Armenian church and the awe-inspiring temple to Kali, goddess
of death and creation. Kolkata is renowned for being the
intellectual capital of India, famous for its colonial buildings
and cultural and artistic life.

Planning your trip

Best time to visit Delhi and Kolkata

By far the best time to visit north central India is from October to April. It is intensely hot, especially on the plains, during May and June and then humidity builds up as the monsoon approaches. The monsoon season lasts from between two and three months, from July to September, with the east seeing the strongest and longest rains when large parts of Kolkata can be knee-deep in water for hours at a time. If you are travelling during the monsoon you need to be prepared for extended periods of torrential rain and disruption to travel. Hot summers are followed by much cooler and clearer winters, and in Delhi the temperatures can plummet to near freezing in January. Some of the region's great festivals such as **Durga Puja** in West Bengal and **Diwali** take place in the autumn and winter.

Getting to Delhi and Kolkata

Air
India is accessible by air from virtually every continent. Most international flights arrive in Delhi or Mumbai. Some carriers permit 'open-jaw' travel, arriving in, and departing from, different cities in India. Some (eg **Air India**, **Jet Airways** or **British Airways**) have convenient non-stop flights from Europe, eg from London to Delhi, takes only nine hours.

You can fly to numerous destinations across India with **Jet Airways**, **Indigo** or **Spicejet**. The prices are very competitive if domestic flights are booked in conjunction with Jet on the international legs.

From Europe Britain remains the cheapest place in Europe for flights to India. From mainland Europe, major European flag carriers including **KLM** and **Lufthansa** fly to Delhi and/or Mumbai from their respective hub airports. In most cases the cheapest flights are with Middle Eastern or Central Asian airlines, transiting via airports in the Gulf. Several airlines from the Middle East (eg **Emirates**, **Gulf Air**, **Kuwait Airways**, **Qatar Airways** and **Oman Air**) offer good discounts to Indian regional capitals from London, but fly via their hub cities, adding to the journey time. Consolidators in the UK can quote some competitive fares, such as: www.skyscanner.net, www.ebookers.com, or **North South Travel** ① *www.northsouthtravel.co.uk (profits to charity)*. In 2013 the cheapest return flights from Delhi to London started at around £500, but leapt to £900+ as you approached the high season of Christmas, New Year and Easter.

From North America From the east coast, several airlines including **Air India**, **Jet Airways**, **Continental** and **Delta** fly direct from New York to Delhi and Mumbai. **American** flies to both cities from Chicago. Discounted tickets on **British Airways**, **KLM**, **Lufthansa**, **Gulf Air** and **Kuwait Airways** are sold through agents although they will invariably fly via their country's capital cities. **Air India** flies from Los Angeles to Delhi and Mumbai, and **Jet Airways** from San Francisco to Mumbai via Shanghai. **Air Canada** operates between Vancouver and Delhi. **Air Brokers International** ① *www.airbrokers.com*, is competitive and reputable. **STA** ① *www.statravel.co.uk*, has offices in many US cities, Toronto and Ontario. Student fares are also available from **Travel Cuts** ① *www.travelcuts.com*, in Canada.

Don't miss...

1 Art galleries, crumbling university and atmospheric cafés of Hauz Khas in South Delhi, page 44.
2 The Taj Mahal from the Yamuna River, page 65.
3 Temple bells and chanting at the Matangesvara Temple in Khajuraho, page 94.
4 Puja on the Ganga, at dawn or dusk, in Varanasi, page 108.
5 Meeting monks from around the globe at the Mahabodhi Temple in Bodhgaya, page 128.
6 The lingering colonial ambiance of Kolkata, page 136.

Numbers relate to the map on page 4.

From Australasia Qantas, Singapore Airlines, Thai Airways, Malaysian Airlines, Cathay Pacific and **Air India** are the principal airlines connecting the continents, although Qantas is the only one that flies direct, with services from Sydney to Mumbai. Singapore Airlines, with subsidiary Silk Air, offers the most flexibility. Low-cost carriers including **Air Asia** (via Kuala Lumpur), **Scoot** and **Tiger Airways** (Singapore) offer a similar choice of arrival airports at substantial savings, though long layovers and possible missed connections make this a slightly more risky venture than flying with the mainstream airlines. **STA** and **Flight Centre** offer discounted tickets from their branches in major cities in Australia and New Zealand.

Airport information The formalities on arrival in India have been streamlined during the last few years and the facilities at the major international airports have greatly improved. However, arrival can still be a slow process and you may well find that there are delays of over an hour at immigration. When departing, note that you'll need to have a printout of your itinerary to get into the airport, and the security guards will only let you into the terminal within three hours of your flight.

Departure tax and passenger fees Rs 500 is payable for all international departures other than those to neighbouring SAARC countries, when the tax is Rs 250. This is normally included in your international ticket; check when buying. Some airports have also begun charging a Passenger Service Fee or User Development Fee to each departing passenger. This is normally included in international tickets, but some domestic airlines have been reluctant to incorporate the charge. Keep some spare cash in rupees in case you need to pay the fee on arriving at the terminal.

Transport in Delhi and Kolkata

Air

India has a comprehensive network linking the major cities of the different states. Deregulation of the airline industry has had a transformative effect on travel within India, with a host of low-budget private carriers offering sometimes unbelievably cheap fares on an ever-expanding network of routes in a bid to woo the train-travelling middle class. Promotional fares as low as Rs 9 (US$0.20) are not unknown, though such numbers are rendered somewhat meaningless by additional taxes and fuel charges – an extra US$30-50 on most flights. On any given day, booking a few days in advance, you can expect to fly between Delhi and Kolkata for around US$100 one way including taxes, while a month's notice and flying with a no-frills airline can reduce the price to US$70-80; regional routes, eg Lucknow to Kolkata, are often cheaper than routes between main cities.

Competition from the efficiently run private sector has, in general, improved the quality of services provided by the nationalized airlines. It also seems to herald the end of the two-tier pricing structure, meaning that ticket prices are now usually the same for foreign and Indian travellers.

The best way to get an idea of the current routes, carriers and fares is to use a third-party booking website such as **www.cheapairticketsindia.com** (toll-free numbers: UK T0800-101 0928, USA T1-888 825 8680), **www.cleartrip.com**, **www.makemytrip.co.in**, **www.travelocity.com**, or **www.yatra.com** although some of these refuse foreign credit cards. Tickets booked on these sites are typically issued as an email ticket or an SMS text message, though they must be converted to a paper ticket at the relevant carrier's airport offices before you will be allowed into the terminal. **Makemytrip.com** and **Travelocity. com** both accept international credit cards.

Rail

Trains can still be the cheapest and most comfortable means of travelling long distances saving you hotel expenses on overnight journeys. It gives access to booking station Retiring Rooms, which can be useful from time to time. Above all, you have an ideal opportunity to meet local travellers and catch a glimpse of life on the ground. See also www.indianrail.gov.in and www.erail.in.

High-speed trains There are several air-conditioned 'high-speed' **Shatabdi** (or 'Century') **Express** for day travel, and **Rajdhani Express** ('Capital City') for overnight journeys. These cover large sections of the network but due to high demand you need to book them well in advance (up to 90 days). Meals and drinks are usually included.

Classes A/c First Class, available only on main routes, is very comfortable with two- or four-berth carpeted sleeper compartments with washbasin. As with all a/c sleeper accommodation, bedding is included, and the windows are tinted to the point of being almost impossible to see through. **A/c Sleeper**, two- and three-tier configurations (known as 2AC and 3AC), are clean and comfortable and popular with middle class families; these are the safest carriages for women travelling alone. **A/c Executive Class**, with wide reclining seats, are available on many Shatabdi trains at double the price of the ordinary **a/c Chair Car** which are equally comfortable. **First Class (non-a/c)** is gradually being phased out, and is now restricted to a handful of routes in the south, but the run-down old carriages still provide a pleasant experience if you like open windows. **Second Class (non-a/c)** two- and three-tier (commonly called **Sleeper**), provides exceptionally cheap and atmospheric travel, with basic padded vinyl seats and open windows that allow the sights and sounds of India (not to mention dust, insects and flecks of spittle expelled by passengers up front) to drift into the carriage. On long journeys Sleeper can be crowded and uncomfortable, and toilet facilities can be unpleasant; it is nearly always better to use the Indian-style squat loos rather than the Western-style ones as they are better maintained. At the bottom rung is **Unreserved Second Class**, with hard wooden benches. You can travel long distances for a trivial amount of money, but unreserved carriages are often ridiculously crowded, and getting off at your station may involve a battle of will and strength against the hordes trying to shove their way on.

Indrail passes These allow travel across the network without having to pay extra reservation fees and sleeper charges but you have to spend a high proportion of your time on the train to make it worthwhile. However, the advantages of pre-arranged reservations and automatic access to 'Tourist Quotas' can tip the balance in favour of the pass for some travellers. Tourists (foreigners and Indians resident abroad) may buy these passes from the tourist sections of principal railway booking offices and pay in foreign currency, major credit cards, traveller's cheques or rupees with encashment certificates. Indrail passes can also conveniently be bought abroad from special agents. For people contemplating a single long journey soon after arriving in India, the half- or one-day pass with a confirmed reservation is worth the peace of mind.

The UK agent is **SDEL** ① *103 Wembley Park Drive, Wembley, Middlesex HA9 8HG, UK, T020-8903 3411, www.indiarail.co.uk*. They make all necessary reservations and offer excellent advice. They can also book **Air India** and **Jet Airways** internal flights.

Cost A/c first class costs about double the rate for two-tier shown below, and non a/c second class about half. Children (aged five to 12) travel at half the adult fare. The young (12-30 years) and senior citizens (65 years and over) are allowed a 30% discount on journeys over 500 km (just show your passport).

Period	US$ A/c 2-tier	Period	US$ A/c 2-tier
½ day	26	21 days	198
1 day	43	30 days	248
7 days	135	60 days	400
15 days	185	90 days	530

Fares for individual journeys are based on distance covered and reflect both the class and the type of train. Higher rates apply on the Mail and Express trains and the air-conditioned Shatabdi and Rajdhani Expresses.

Internet services Much information is available online at www.railtourismindia.com, www.indianrail.gov.in and www.trainenquiry.com, where you can check timetables (which change frequently), numbers, seat availability and even the running status of your train. E-tickets can be bought and printed at www.irctc.in, although the credit card process can be complicated, and at time of writing does not accept credit cards issued outside India. The best option is to use a third-party agent, such as www.makemytrip.com or www.cleartrip.com. An alternative is to seek a local agent who can sell e-tickets, and can save hours of hassle; simply present the printout to the ticket collector.

Note All train numbers now have five digits; in most cases, adding a '1' to the start of an old four-figure number will produce the new number. Otherwise, try your luck with the 'train number enquiry' search at www.indianrail.gov.in/inet_trnno_enq.html.

Tickets and reservations It is now possible to reserve tickets for virtually any train on the network from one of the 1000 computerized reservation centres across India. It is always best to book as far in advance as possible (usually up to 60 days). To reserve a seat on a particular train, note down the train's name, number and departure time and fill in a reservation form while you line up at the ticket window; you can use one form for up to four passengers. At busy stations the wait can take an hour or more. You can save a lot of time and effort by asking a travel agent to get your tickets for a fee of Rs 50-100. If the class you want is full, ask if special 'quotas' are available under any of **Indian Rail**'s special quotas. **Foreign Tourist Quota** (FTQ) reserves a small number of tickets on popular routes for overseas travellers; you need your passport and either an exchange certificate or ATM receipt to book tickets under FTQ. The other useful special quota is **Tatkal**, which releases a last-minute pool of tickets at 1000 on the day before the train departs. If the quota system can't help you, consider buying a 'wait list' ticket, as seats often become available close to the train's departure time; phone the station on the day of departure to check your ticket's status. If you don't have a reservation for a particular train but carry an **Indrail Pass**, you may get one by arriving three hours early. Be wary of touts at the station offering tickets, hotels or exchange.

Timetables Regional timetables are available cheaply from station bookstalls; the monthly *Indian Bradshaw* is sold in principal stations. The handy *Trains at a Glance* (Rs 30) lists popular trains likely to be used by most foreign travellers and is available at stalls at Indian railway stations and in the UK from **SDEL** (see page 9).

Road
Road travel is sometimes the only choice for reaching many of the places of outstanding interest, particularly national parks or isolated tourist sites. For the uninitiated, travel by road can also be a worrying experience because of the apparent absence of conventional traffic regulations. Vehicles drive on the left – in theory. Routes around the major cities are usually crowded with lorry traffic, especially at night, and the main roads are often poor and slow. There are a few motorway-style expressways, but most main roads are single track.

Bus Buses now reach virtually every part of India, offering a cheap, if often uncomfortable, means of visiting places off the rail network. Very few villages are now more than 2-3 km from a bus stop. Services are run by the State Corporation from the State Bus Stand (and private companies, which often have offices nearby). The private companies allow advance reservations, including e-tickets (check www.redbus.in and www.viaworld.in) and, although tickets prices are a little higher, they have fewer stops and are a bit more comfortable. If you travel on a 'sleeper' bus, choose a lower berth near the front of the bus as the upper berths are almost always really uncomfortable on bumpy roads.

 Bus categories Though comfortable for sightseeing trips, apart from the very best 'sleeper coaches' even **air-conditioned luxury coaches** can be very uncomfortable for really long journeys. Often the air conditioning is very cold so wrap up. Journeys over 10 hours can be extremely tiring so it is better to go by train if there is a choice. **Express buses** run over long distances (frequently overnight) and are often called 'video coaches. They can be an appalling experience unless you appreciate loud film music blasting through the night. Ear plugs and eye masks may ease the pain. They rarely average more than 45 kph. **Local buses** are often very crowded, quite bumpy, slow and usually poorly maintained. However, over short distances, they can be a very cheap, friendly and easy way of getting about. Even where signboards are not in English someone will usually give you directions. Many larger towns have **minibus** services which charge a little more than the buses and pick up and drop passengers on request. Again very crowded, and with restricted headroom, they are the fastest way of getting about many of the larger towns.

 Bus travel tips Some towns have different bus stations for different destinations. Booking on major long-distance routes is now computerized. Book in advance where possible and avoid the back of the bus where it can be very bumpy. If your destination is only served by a local bus you may do better to take the Express bus and 'persuade' the driver, with a tip in advance, to stop where you want to get off. You will have to pay the full fare to the first stop beyond your destination but you will get there faster and more comfortably.

Car A car provides a chance to travel off the beaten track, and gives unrivalled opportunities for seeing something of India's great variety of villages and small towns. Until recently, the most widely used hire car was the Hindustan Ambassador. However, except for the newest model, they are often very unreliable, and although they still have their devotees, many find them uncomfortable for long journeys. Ambassadors are gradually giving way to more efficient (and boring) Tata and Toyota models with mod-cons like optional air conditioning – and seat belts. A handful of international agencies offer self-drive car hire (Avis, Sixt), but India's majestically anarchic traffic culture is not for the faint-hearted.

   Car hire Hiring a car and driver is the most comfortable and efficient way to cover short to medium distances, and although prices have increased sharply in recent years car travel in India is still a bargain by Western standards. A car shared by three or four can be very good value. Even if you're travelling on a modest budget a day's car hire can help take the sting out of an arduous journey, allowing you to go sightseeing along the way without looking for somewhere to stash your bags. Local drivers often know their way around an area much better than drivers from other states, so where possible it is a good idea to get a local driver who speaks the state language, in addition to being able to communicate with you. The best way to guarantee a driver who speaks good English is to book in advance with a professional travel agency, either in India or in your home country. You can, if you choose, arrange car hire informally by asking around at taxi stands, but don't expect your driver to speak anything more than rudimentary English.

   On pre-arranged overnight trips the fee you pay will normally include fuel and interstate taxes – check before you pay – and a wage for the driver. Drivers are responsible for their expenses, including meals (and the pervasive servant-master culture in India means that most will choose to sit separately from you at meal times). Some tourist hotels provide rooms for drivers, but they often choose to sleep in the car overnight to save money. In some areas drivers also seek to increase their earnings by taking you to hotels and shops where they earn a handsome commission; these are generally hugely overpriced and poor alternatives to the hotels recommended in this book, so don't be afraid to say no and insist on your choice of accommodation. If you feel inclined, a tip at the end of the tour of Rs 100 per day is perfectly acceptable. Be sure to check carefully the mileage at the beginning and end of the trip.

	Tata Indica non-a/c	Tata Indigo non-a/c	Hyundai Accent a/c	Toyota Innova
8 hrs/80 km	Rs 1200	Rs 1600	Rs 2200	Rs 2500
Extra km	Rs 8	Rs 10	Rs 15	Rs 15
Extra hour	Rs 80	Rs 100	Rs 200	Rs 180
Out of town				
Per km	Rs 8	Rs 10	Rs 15	Rs 15
Night halt	Rs 200	Rs 200	Rs 300	Rs 250

Taxi Taxi travel in India is a great bargain, and in most cities you can take a taxi from the airport to the centre for under US$10. Yellow-top taxis in cities and large towns are metered, although tariffs change frequently. These changes are shown on a fare chart which should be read in conjunction with the meter reading. Increased night-time rates apply in most cities, and there might be a small charge for luggage. Insist on the taxi meter being flagged in your presence. If the driver refuses, the official advice is to contact the police. This may not work, but it is worth trying. When a taxi doesn't have a meter, you will need to fix the fare before starting the journey. Ask at your hotel desk for a guide price. As a foreigner, it is rare to get a taxi in the big cities to use the meter – if they are eager to, watch out as sometimes the meter is rigged and they have a fake rate card. Also, watch out for the David Blaine-style note shuffle: you pay with a Rs 500 note, but they have a Rs 100 note in their hand. This happens frequently at the pre-paid booth outside New Delhi train station too, no matter how small the transaction.

At stations and airports it is often possible to share taxis to a central point. It is worth looking for fellow passengers who may be travelling in your direction and get a pre-paid taxi. At night, always have a clear idea of where you want to go and insist on being taken there. Taxi drivers may try to convince you that the hotel you have chosen 'closed three years ago' or is 'completely full'. Say that you have a reservation.

Rickshaw Auto-rickshaws (autos) are almost universally available in towns across North India and are the cheapest and most convenient way of getting about. It is best to walk a short distance away from a hotel gate before picking up an auto to avoid paying an inflated rate. In addition to using them for short journeys it is often possible to hire them by the hour, or for a half or full day's sightseeing. In some areas younger drivers who speak some English and know their local area well may want to show you around. However, rickshaw drivers are often paid a commission by hotels, restaurants and gift shops so advice is not always impartial. Drivers generally refuse to use a meter, often quote a ridiculous price or may sometimes stop short of your destination. If you have real problems it can help to note down the vehicle licence number and threaten to go to the police. Beware of some rickshaw drivers who show the fare chart for taxis.

Where to stay in Delhi and Kolkata

India has an enormous range of accommodation. You can stay safely and very cheaply by Western standards right across the country. In all the major cities there are also high-quality hotels, offering a full range of facilities; in small centres hotels are much more variable. In Madhya Pradesh, old Maharajas' palaces and forts have been privately converted into comfortable, unusual hotels. The mainstay of the budget traveller is the ubiquitous Indian 'business hotel': walking distance to train and bus stations, anonymous but generally decent value, with en suite rooms of variable cleanliness and a TV showing 110 channels of cricket and Bollywood MTV. At the top end, alongside international chains such as **ITC Sheraton** (ostentatious) and **Radisson Blu** (dependable), India boasts several home-grown hotel chains, best of which are the exceptional heritage and palace hotels operated by the **Taj** group. In the peak season (October to April) bookings can be extremely heavy in popular destinations. It is sometimes possible to book in advance by phone, fax or email, but double check your reservation, and always try to arrive as early as possible in the day.

Hotels
Price categories The category codes used in this book are based on prices of double rooms excluding taxes. They are **not** star ratings and individual facilities vary considerably. The most expensive hotels charge in US dollars only. Modest hotels may not have their

Price codes

Where to stay

$$$$ over US$150	**$$$** US$66-150
$$ US$30-65	**$** under US$30

For a double room in high season, excluding taxes.

Restaurants

$$$ over US$12	**$$** US$6-12	**$** under US$6

For a two-course meal for one person, excluding drinks and service charge.

own restaurant but will often offer 'room service', bringing in food from outside. In temple towns, restaurants may only serve vegetarian food. Many hotels operate a 24-hour checkout system. Make sure that this means that you can stay 24 hours from the time of check-in. Expect to pay more in Delhi and, to a lesser extent, in Kolkata for all categories. Prices away from large cities tend to be lower for comparable hotels.

Large discounts are often made by hotels in all categories out of season. Always ask if any is available. You may also request the 10-15% agent's commission to be deducted from your bill if you book direct. Clarify whether the agreed figure includes all taxes.

Taxes In general most hotel rooms rated at Rs 3000 or above are subject to a tax of 10%. Many states levy an additional luxury tax of 10-25%, and some hotels add a service charge of 10% on top of this. Taxes are not necessarily payable on meals, so it is worth settling your meals bill separately. Most hotels in the **$$** category and above accept payment by credit card. Check your final bill carefully the evening before departure, and keep all receipts.

Hotel facilities You have to be prepared for difficulties which are uncommon in the West. It is best to inspect the room and check that all equipment (air conditioning, TV, water heater, flush) works before checking in at a modest hotel. Don't expect any but the most expensive or tourist-savvy hotels to fit a top sheet to the bed.

In some states **power cuts** are common, or hot water may be restricted to certain times of day. The largest hotels have their own generators but it is best to carry a good torch.

In some regions **water supply** is rationed periodically. Keep a bucket filled to use for flushing the toilet during water cuts. Occasionally, tap water may be discoloured due to rusty tanks. During the cold weather and in hill stations, hot water will be available at certain times of the day, sometimes in buckets, but is usually very restricted in quantity.

Hotels close to temples can be very **noisy**, especially during festivals. Music blares from loudspeakers late at night and from very early in the morning, often making sleep impossible. Mosques call the faithful to prayers at dawn. Some find ear plugs helpful.

Some hotels offer 24-hour checkout, meaning you can keep the room a full 24 hours from the time you arrive – a great option if you arrive in the afternoon and want to spend the morning sightseeing.

Homestays

At the upmarket end, increasing numbers of travellers are keen to stay in private homes and guesthouses, opting not to book large hotel chains that keep you at arm's length from a culture. Instead, travellers get home-cooked meals in heritage houses and learn about a country through conversation with often fascinating hosts. Delhi has many new and smart family-run B&Bs springing up. Tourist offices have lists of families with more modest homestays. Companies specializing in homestays include Home & Hospitality, www.homeandhospitality.co.uk, **MAHout** ① *www.mahoutuk.com* and **Sundale Vacations** ① *www.sundale.com*.

Food and drink in Delhi and Kolkata

Food

You find just as much variety in dishes crossing India as you would on an equivalent journey across Europe. Combinations of spices give each region its distinctive flavour.

The larger hotels, open to non-residents, often offer **buffet** lunches with Indian, Western and sometimes Chinese dishes. These can be good value (Rs 400-500; but Rs 850 in the top grades) and can provide a welcome, comfortable break in the cool. There can, however, be considerable health risks if food is kept warm for long periods, especially if turnover at the buffet is slow.

It is essential to be very careful since food hygiene may be poor, flies abound and refrigeration in the hot weather may be inadequate and intermittent because of power cuts. It is best to eat only freshly prepared food by ordering from the menu (especially meat and fish dishes). Avoid salads and cut fruit, unless the menu advertises that they have been washed in mineral water.

If you are unused to spicy food, go slow. Food is often spicier when you eat with families or at local places. Popular local restaurants are obvious from the number of people eating in them. Try a traditional *thali*, which is a complete meal served on a large stainless steel plate. Several preparations, placed in small bowls, surround the central serving of wholewheat chapati and rice. A vegetarian *thali* would include *dhal* (lentils), two or three curries (which can be quite hot) and crisp poppadums. A variety of pickles are offered – mango and lime are two of the most popular. These can be taken in minute quantities alongside the main dishes. Plain *dahi* (yoghurt), or *raita*, usually acts as a bland 'cooler'. Simple *dhabas* (rustic roadside eateries) are an alternative experience for sampling authentic local dishes.

Many city restaurants and backpacker eateries offer a choice of so-called **European options** such as toasted sandwiches, stuffed pancakes, apple pies, fruit crumbles and cheesecakes. Italian favourites (pizzas, pastas) can be very different from what you are used to, although **ice creams** can be exceptionally good; there are excellent Indian ones as well as some international brands.

India has many delicious tropical **fruits**. Some are seasonal (eg mangoes, pineapples and lychees), while others (eg bananas, grapes and oranges) are available throughout the year. It is safe to eat the ones you can wash and peel.

In cities and larger towns, you will see all types of regional Indian food on the menus, with some restaurants specializing in South Indian food such as *dosas*, *uttapams* and *idlis*. North Indian kebabs and the richer flavoursome cuisine of Lucknow are also worth seeking out. In Bengal, there is an emphasis on fish and seafood, especially river fish, the most popular being *hilsa* and *bekti*. *Bekti* is grilled or fried and is tastier than the fried fish of the west as it has often been marinated in mild spices first. Bengali *mishti* (sweetmeats) are another distinctive feature. Many are milk based. Pale pinkish brown, *mishti doi*, is an excellent sweet yoghurt eaten as a dessert, typically sold in hand-thrown clay pots.

Drink

Drinking water used to be regarded as one of India's biggest hazards. It is still true that water from the tap or a well should never be considered safe to drink since public water supplies are often polluted. Bottled water is now widely available although not all bottled water is mineral water; most are simply purified water from an urban supply. Buy from a shop or stall, check the seal carefully and avoid street hawkers.

There is growing concern over the mountains of plastic bottles that are collecting so travellers are being encouraged to carry their own bottles and take a portable water filter. It is important to use pure water for cleaning teeth.

Tea and **coffee** are safe and widely available. Both are normally served sweet, and with milk. If you wish, say 'no sugar' (*chini nahin*), 'no milk' (*dudh nahin*) when ordering. Alternatively, ask for a pot of tea and milk and sugar to be brought separately. Freshly brewed coffee is a common drink in South India, but in the North, ordinary city restaurants will usually serve the instant variety.

Bottled **soft drinks** such as Coke, Pepsi, Teem, Limca and Thums Up are universally available; always check the seal when you buy from a street stall. There are also several brands of fruit juice sold in cartons, including mango, pineapple and apple – Indian brands are very sweet. Don't add ice cubes as the water source may be contaminated.

Indians rarely drink **alcohol** with a meal. In the past wines and spirits were generally either imported and extremely expensive, or local and of poor quality. Now, the best Indian whisky, rum and brandy (IMFL or 'Indian Made Foreign Liquor') are widely accepted, as are good Champagnoise and other wines from Maharashtra. If you hanker after a bottle of imported wine, you will only find it in the top restaurants or specialist liquor stores for at least Rs 1000.

For the urban elite, refreshing Indian beers are popular when eating out and so are widely available. 'Pubs' have sprung up in the major cities. Elsewhere, seedy, all-male drinking dens in the larger cities are best avoided by women travellers, but can make quite an experience otherwise – you will sometimes be locked into cubicles for clandestine drinking. If that sounds unsavoury then head for the better hotel bars instead. In rural India, local rice, palm, cashew or date juice *toddy* and *arak* is deceptively potent.

Most states have alcohol-free days or enforce degrees of Prohibition. Some upmarket restaurants may serve beer even if it's not listed, so it's worth asking. In some states there are government-approved wine shops where you buy your alcohol through a metal grille. For dry states and liquor permits, see page 23.

Festivals in Delhi and Kolkata

India has a wealth of festivals with many celebrated nationwide, while others are specific to a particular state or community or even a particular temple. Many fall on different dates each year depending on the Hindu lunar calendar so check with the tourist office, or see the thorough calendar of upcoming major and minor festivals at www.drikpanchang.com.

The Hindu calendar

Hindus follow two distinct eras: The *Vikrama Samvat* which began in 57 BC and the *Salivahan Saka* which dates from AD 78 and has been the official Indian calendar since 1957. The *Saka* new year starts on 22 March and has the same length as the Gregorian calendar. The 29½-day lunar month with its 'dark' and 'bright' halves based on the new and full moons, are named after 12 constellations, and total a 354-day year. The calendar cleverly has an extra month (*adhik maas*) every 2½ to three years, to bring it in line with the solar year of 365 days coinciding with the Gregorian calendar of the West.

Some major national and regional festivals are listed below. A few count as national holidays: **26 January**: Republic Day; **15 August**: Independence Day; **2 October**: Mahatma Gandhi's Birthday; **25 December**: Christmas Day.

Major festivals and fairs

Jan New Year's Day (1 Jan) is accepted officially when following the Gregorian calendar but there are regional variations which fall on different dates, often coinciding with spring/harvest time in Mar and Apr.

14 Jan Makar Sankranti marks the end of winter and is celebrated with kite flying.

Feb Vasant Panchami, the spring festival when people wear bright yellow clothes to mark the advent of the season with singing, dancing and feasting.

Feb-Mar Maha Sivaratri marks the night when Siva danced his celestial dance of destruction (*Tandava*), which is celebrated with feasting and fairs at Siva temples, but preceded by a night of devotional readings and hymn singing.

Mar Holi, the festival of colours, marks the climax of spring. The previous night bonfires are lit symbolizing the end of winter (and conquering of evil). People have fun throwing coloured powder and water at each other and in the evening some gamble with friends. If you don't mind getting covered in colours, you can risk going out but celebrations can sometimes get very rowdy (and unpleasant). Some worship Krishna who defeated the demon Putana.

Apr/May Buddha Jayanti, the 1st full moon night in Apr/May marks the birth of the Buddha.

Jul/Aug Raksha (or Rakhi) Bandhan symbolizes the bond between brother and sister, celebrated at full moon. A sister says special prayers for her brother and ties coloured threads around his wrist to remind him of the special bond. He in turn gives a gift and promises to protect and care for her. Sometimes *rakshas* are exchanged as a mark of friendship. **Narial Purnima** on the same full moon. Hindus make offerings of *narial* (coconuts) to the Vedic god Varuna (Lord of the waters) by throwing them into the sea. **15 Aug** is **Independence Day**, a national secular holiday is marked by special events. **Ganesh Chaturthi** was established just over 100 years ago by the Indian nationalist leader Tilak. The elephant-headed God of good omen is shown special reverence. On the last of the 5-day festival after harvest, clay images of Ganesh are taken in procession with dancers and musicians, and are immersed in the sea, river or pond.

Aug/Sep Janmashtami, the birth of Krishna is celebrated at midnight at Krishna temples.

Sep/Oct Dasara has many local variations. Celebrations for the 9 nights (*navratri*) are marked with **Ramlila**, various episodes of the Ramayana story are enacted with particular reference to the battle between the forces of good and evil. In some parts of India it celebrates *Rama*'s victory over the Demon king *Ravana* of Lanka with the help of loyal *Hanuman* (Monkey). Huge effigies of *Ravana* made of bamboo and paper are burnt on the 10th day (*Vijaya dasami*) of **Dasara** in public open spaces. In West Bengal the focus is on Durga's victory over the demon *Mahishasura*, and the festival is known as **Durga Puja** and is celebrated in Kolkata and surrounding towns, culminating with the submersion of the idols into the river on the final night.

Oct/Nov Gandhi Jayanti (2 Oct), Mahatma Gandhi's birthday, is remembered with prayer meetings and devotional singing.

Diwali/Deepavali (*Sanskrit ideepa* lamp), the festival of lights. Some Hindus celebrate Krishna's victory over the demon *Narakasura*, some Rama's return after his 14 years' exile in the forest when citizens lit his way with oil lamps. The festival falls on the dark *chaturdasi* (14th) night (the one preceding the new moon), when rows of lamps or candles are lit in remembrance, and *rangolis* painted on the floor as a sign of welcome. Fireworks have become an integral part of the celebration which are often set off days before Diwali. Equally, Lakshmi, the Goddess of Wealth (as well as Ganesh) is worshipped by merchants and the business community who open the new financial year's account on the day. Most people wear new clothes; some play games of chance.

Guru Nanak Jayanti commemorates the birth of Guru Nanak. **Akhand Path** (unbroken reading of the holy book) takes place and the book itself (*Guru Granth Sahib*) is taken out in procession.

Dec Christmas Day (25 Dec) sees Indian Christians celebrate the birth of Christ in much the same way as in the West; many churches hold services/mass at midnight. There is an air of festivity in city markets which are specially decorated and illuminated. Over **New Year's Eve** (31 Dec) hotel prices peak and large supplements are added for meals and entertainment in the upper category hotels. Some churches mark the night with a Midnight Mass.

Muslim holy days

These are fixed according to the lunar calendar. According to the Gregorian calendar, they tend to fall 11 days earlier each year, dependent on the sighting of the new moon.

Ramadan, known in India as 'ramzan', is the start of the month of fasting when all Muslims (except young children, the very elderly, the sick, pregnant women and travellers) must abstain from food and drink, from sunrise to sunset.

Id ul Fitr is the 3-day festival that marks the end of Ramzan.

Id-ul-Zuha/Bakr-Id is when Muslims commemorate Ibrahim's sacrifice of his son according to God's commandment; the main time of pilgrimage to Mecca (the Hajj). It is marked by the sacrifice of a goat, feasting and alms giving.

Muharram is when the killing of the Prophet's grandson, Hussain, is commemorated by Shi'a Muslims. Decorated *tazias* (replicas of the martyr's tomb) are carried in procession by devout wailing followers who beat their chests to express their grief. Lucknow is famous for its grand *tazias*. Shi'as fast for the 10 days.

Essentials A-Z

Accident and emergency
Contact the relevant emergency service (police T100, fire T101, ambulance T102) and your embassy. Make sure you obtain police/medical reports required for insurance claims.

Customs and duty free
Duty free
Tourists are allowed to bring in all personal effects 'which may reasonably be required', without charge. The official customs allowance includes 200 cigarettes or 50 cigars, 0.95 litres of alcohol, a camera and a pair of binoculars. Valuable personal effects and professional equipment including jewellery, special camera equipment and lenses, laptop computers and sound and video recorders must in theory be declared on a Tourist Baggage Re-Export Form (TBRE) in order for them to be taken out of the country (though in practice it's unlikely that your bags will be inspected beyond a cursory x-ray). It is essential to keep these forms for showing to the customs when leaving India, otherwise considerable delays are very likely at the time of departure.

Prohibited items
The import of live plants, gold coins, gold and silver bullion and silver coins not in current use are either banned or subject to strict regulation. Enquire at consular offices abroad for details.

Drugs
Be aware that the government takes the misuse of drugs very seriously. Anyone charged with the illegal possession of drugs risks facing a fine of Rs 100,000 and a minimum 10 years' imprisonment. Several foreigners have been imprisoned for drugs-related offences in the last decade.

Electricity
India's supply is 220-240 volts AC. Some top hotels have transformers. There may be pronounced variations in the voltage, and power cuts are common. Power back-up by generator or inverter is becoming more widespread, even in humble hotels, though it may not cover a/c. Socket sizes vary so take a universal adaptor; low-quality versions are available locally. Many hotels, even in the higher categories, don't have electric razor sockets. Invest in a stabilizer for a laptop.

Embassies and consulates
For information on visas and immigration, see page 23. For details of Indian embassies and consulates around the world, go to embassy.goabroad.com.

Health
Obviously 5-star travel is going to carry less risk than backpacking on a budget. Health care in India is varied. There are many excellent private and government clinics/hospitals. Your embassy or consulate will be able to tell you where the recommended clinics are. You can also ask about locally recommended medical dos and don'ts. If you do get ill, and you have the opportunity, you should also ask your medical insurer whether they are satisfied that the medical centre/hospital you have been referred to is of a suitable standard.

Before you go
Ideally, you should see your GP or travel clinic at least 6 weeks before your departure for general advice on travel risks, malaria and vaccinations. Make sure you have travel insurance, get a dental check (especially if you are going to be away for more than a month), know your own blood group and if you suffer a long-term condition such as diabetes or epilepsy make sure someone knows or that you have a Medic Alert bracelet/necklace

with this information on it. Remember that it is risky to buy medicinal tablets abroad because the doses may differ and India has a huge trade in counterfeit drugs.

Vaccinations

If you need vaccinations, see your doctor well in advance of your travel. The following vaccinations are recommended: typhoid, polio, tetanus, infectious hepatitis and diptheria. For details of malaria prevention, contact your GP or local travel clinic.

The following vaccinations may also be considered: rabies, possibly BCG (since TB is still common in the region) and in some cases meningitis and diphtheria (if you're staying in the country for a long time). Yellow fever is not required in India but you may be asked to show a certificate if you have travelled from Africa or South America. Japanese encephalitis may be required for rural travel at certain times of the year (mainly rainy seasons). An effective oral cholera vaccine (Dukoral) is now available as 2 doses providing 3 months' protection.

Websites

British Travel Health Association (UK), www.btha.org This is the official website of an organization of travel health professionals. **Fit for Travel, www.fitfortravel.scot. nhs.uk** This site from Scotland provides a quick A-Z of vaccine and travel health advice requirements for each country. **Foreign and Commonwealth Office (FCO) (UK), www.fco.gov.uk** This is a key travel advice site, with useful information on the country, people, climate and lists the UK embassies/consulates.
The Health Protection Agency, www.hpa. org.uk Up-to-date malaria advice guidelines for travel around the world. It gives specific advice about the right drugs for each location. It also has useful information for those who are pregnant, suffering from epilepsy or planning to travel with children. **Medic Alert (UK), www.medicalalert.com** This is the website of the foundation that

produces bracelets and necklaces for those with existing medical problems. **Travel Screening Services (UK), www. travelscreening.co.uk** A private clinic dedicated to integrated travel health. **World Health Organisation, www.who. int** The WHO site has links to the *WHO Blue Book* on travel advice. This lists the diseases in different regions of the world and describes vaccination schedules.

Language

Hindi, spoken as a mother tongue by over 400 million people, is India's official language. The use of English is also enshrined in the Constitution for a wide range of official purposes, notably communication between Hindi and non-Hindi speaking states. The most widely spoken Indo-Aryan languages are: Bengali (8.3%), Marathi (8%), Urdu (5.7%), Gujarati (5.4%), Oriya (3.7%) and Punjabi (3.2%). Among the Dravidian languages Telugu (8.2%), Tamil (7%), Kannada (4.2%) and Malayalam (3.5%) are the most widely used. In West Bengal more than 85% of the population speak Bengali.

English now plays an important role across India. It is widely spoken in towns and cities and even in quite remote villages it is usually not difficult to find someone who speaks at least a little English. Outside of major tourist sites, other European languages are almost completely unknown.

Money

Indian currency is the Indian Rupee (Re/Rs). It is **not** possible to purchase these before you arrive. If you want cash on arrival it is best to get it at the airport bank, although see if an ATM is available as airport rates are not very generous. Rupee notes are printed in denominations of Rs 1000, 500, 100, 50, 20, 10. The rupee is divided into 100 paise. Coins are minted in denominations of Rs 10, 5, Rs 2, Rs 1 and (the increasingly uncommon) 50 paise. **Note** Carry money, mostly as traveller's cheques, in a money belt worn under clothing. Have a small amount in an easily accessible place.

Exchange rates ➔ *UK £1 = Rs 98.3, €1 = Rs 83.4, US$1 = Rs 61.5 (Nov 2013).*

ATMs

By far the most convenient method of accessing money, ATMs are all over India, usually attended by security guards, with most banks offering some services to holders of overseas cards. Banks whose ATMs will issue cash against **Cirrus** and **Maestro** cards, as well as Visa and MasterCard, include **Bank of Baroda, Citibank, HDFC, HSBC, ICICI, IDBI, Punjab National Bank, State Bank of India (SBI), Standard Chartered** and **UTI**. A withdrawal fee is usually charged by the issuing bank on top of the conversion charges applied by your own bank. Fraud prevention measures quite often result in travellers having their cards blocked by the bank when unexpected overseas transactions occur; advise your bank of your travel plans before leaving.

Credit cards

Major credit cards are increasingly acceptable in the main centres, though in smaller cities and towns it is still rare to be able to pay by credit card. Payment by credit card can sometimes be more expensive than payment by cash, whilst some credit card companies charge a premium on cash withdrawals. **Visa** and **MasterCard** have an ever-growing number of ATMs in major cities and several banks offer withdrawal facilities for Cirrus and Maestro cardholders. It is however easy to obtain a cash advance against a credit card. Railway reservation centres in major cities take payment for train tickets by Visa card which can be very quick as the queue is short, although they cannot be used for Tourist Quota tickets.

Currency cards

If you don't want to carry lots of cash, prepaid currency cards allow you to preload money from your bank account, fixed at the day's exchange rate. They look like a credit or debit card and are issued by specialist money changing companies, such as **Travelex** and **Caxton FX**. You can top up and check your balance by phone, online and sometimes by text.

Traveller's cheques (TCs)

TCs issued by reputable companies (eg **Thomas Cook, American Express**) are widely accepted. They can be easily exchanged at small local travel agents and tourist internet cafés but are rarely used directly for payment. Try to avoid changing at banks, where the process can be time consuming; opt for hotels and agents instead, take large denomination cheques and change enough to last for some days.

Changing money

The **State Bank of India** and several others in major towns are authorized to deal in foreign exchange. Some give cash against Visa/MasterCard (eg ANZ). American Express cardholders can use their cards to get either cash or TCs in Delhi. The larger cities have licensed money changers with offices usually in the commercial sector. Changing money through unauthorized dealers is illegal. Premiums on the currency black market are very small and highly risky. Large hotels change money 24 hrs a day for guests, but banks often give a substantially better rate of exchange. It is best to exchange money on arrival at the airport bank or the Thomas Cook counter. Many international flights arrive during the night and it is generally far easier and less time consuming to change money at the airport than in the city. You should be given a foreign currency encashment certificate when you change money through a bank or authorized dealer; ask for one if it is not automatically given. It allows you to change Indian rupees back to your own currency on departure. It also enables you to use rupees to pay hotel bills or buy air tickets for which payment in foreign exchange may be required. The certificates are only valid for 3 months.

Cost of travelling

Most food, accommodation and public transport, especially rail and bus, is exceptionally cheap, although the price of basic food items such as rice, lentils, tomatoes and onions has skyrocketed. There is a widening range of moderately priced but clean hotels and restaurants outside the big cities, making it possible to get a great deal for your money. Budget travellers sharing a room, taking public transport, avoiding souvenir stalls, and eating nothing but rice and *dhal* can get away with a budget of Rs 400-600 a day. This sum leaps up if you drink alcohol (still cheap by European standards at about Rs 80 for a pint), smoke foreign-brand cigarettes or want to have your own wheels (you can expect to spend between Rs 150 and 200 to hire a Honda per day). Those planning to stay in fairly comfortable hotels and use taxis sightseeing should budget at US$50-80 a day. Then again you could always check into **Imperial Hotel** or the **Oberoi Amarvilas** for Christmas and notch up an impressive US$600 bill on your B&B alone. India can be a great place to pick and choose, save a little on basic accommodation and then treat yourself to the type of meal you could only dream of affording back home. Also, be prepared to spend a fair amount more in Delhi, where not only is the cost of living significantly higher but where it's worth coughing up extra for a half-decent room; you can penny-pinch in places like Varanasi where, you'll be spending precious little time indoors anyway. A newspaper costs Rs 5 and breakfast for 2 with coffee can come to as little as Rs 100 in a basic 'hotel', but if you intend to eat banana pancakes or pasta in a backpacker restaurant, you can expect to pay more like Rs 100-150 a plate.

Opening hours

Banks are open Mon-Fri 1030-1430, Sat 1030-1230. Top hotels sometimes have a 24-hr money-changing service. **Post offices** open Mon-Fri 1000-1700, often shutting for lunch, and Sat mornings. **Government offices** Mon-Fri 0930-1700, Sat 0930-1300 (some open on alternate Sat only). **Shops** open Mon-Sat 0930-1800. Bazars keep longer hours.

Safety
Personal security

In general the threats to personal security for travellers in India are remarkably small. However, incidents of petty theft and violence directed specifically at tourists have been on the increase so care is necessary in some places, and basic common sense needs to be used with respect to looking after valuables. Follow the same precautions you would when at home. There have been much-reported incidents of severe sexual assault in Delhi, Kolkata and some more rural areas in 2013. Avoid wandering alone outdoors late at night in these places. During daylight hours be careful in remote places, especially when alone. If you are under threat, scream loudly. Be cautious before accepting food or drink from casual acquaintances, as it may be drugged – though note that Indians on a long train journey will invariably try to share their snacks with you, and balance caution with the opportunity to interact.

The left-wing Maoist extremist Naxalites are active in east central India. They have a long history of conflict with state and national authorities, including attacks on police and government officials. The Naxalites have not specifically targeted Westerners, but have attacked symbolic targets including Western companies. As a general rule, travellers are advised to be vigilant in the lead up to and on days of national significance, such as Republic Day (26 Jan) and Independence Day (15 Aug) as militants have in the past used such occasions to mount attacks.

Travel advice

It is better to seek advice from your consulate than from travel agencies. Before you travel you can contact: **British Foreign & Commonwealth Office Travel Advice Unit**, T0845-850 2829 (Pakistan desk T020-7270 2385), www.fco.gov.uk. **US State Department's Bureau of Consular Affairs**, Overseas Citizens Services, Room 4800, Department of State, Washington, DC 20520-4818, USA, T202-647 1488, http://travel.state.gov. **Australian Department of Foreign Affairs Canberra**, Australia, T02-6261 3305, www.smartraveller.gov.au. Canadian official advice is on www.voyage.gc.ca.

Theft

Theft is not uncommon. It is best to keep TCs, passports and valuables with you at all times. Don't regard hotel rooms as being automatically safe; even hotel safes don't guarantee secure storage. Avoid leaving valuables near open windows even when you are in the room. Use your own padlock in a budget hotel when you go out. Pickpockets and other thieves operate in the big cities. Crowded areas are particularly high risk. Take special care of your belongings when getting on or off public transport.

If you have items stolen, they should be reported to the police as soon as possible. Keep a separate record of vital documents, including passport details and numbers of TCs. Larger hotels will be able to assist in contacting and dealing with the police. Dealings with the police can be very difficult and in the worst regions, such as Bihar, even dangerous. The paperwork involved in reporting losses can be time consuming and irritating and your own documentation (eg passport and visas) may be demanded.

In some states the police occasionally demand bribes, though you should not assume that if procedures move slowly you are automatically being expected to offer a bribe. Traffic police have the right to make on-the-spot fines for speeding and illegal parking. If you face a fine, insist on a receipt. If you have to go to a police station, try to take someone with you.

Confidence tricksters are particularly common where people are on the move, notably around railway stations or places where budget tourists gather.

Telephone

The international code for India is +91. International Direct Dialling is widely available in privately run call booths, usually labelled on yellow boards with the letters 'PCO-STD-ISD'. You dial the call yourself, and the time and cost are displayed on a computer screen. Cheap rate (2100-0600) means long queues may form outside booths. Telephone calls from hotels are usually more expensive (check price before calling), though some will allow local calls free of charge. Internet phone booths, usually associated with cybercafés, are the cheapest way of calling overseas.

Directory enquiries, T197, can be helpful but works only for the local area code.

Mobile phones are for sale everywhere, as are local SIM cards that allow you to make calls within India and overseas at much lower rates than using a 'roaming' service from your normal provider at home – sometimes for as little as Rs 0.5 per min. **Univercell**, www.univercell.in, and **The Mobile Store**, www.themobilestore.in, are 2 widespread and efficient chains selling phones and SIM cards.

India is divided into a number of 'calling circles' or regions, and if you travel outside the region where your connection is based, eg from Delhi into Uttar Pradesh, you will pay higher 'roaming' charges for making and receiving calls.

Time

India doesn't change its clocks, so from the last Sun in Oct to the last Sun in Mar the time is GMT +5½ hrs, and the rest of the year it's +4½ hrs (USA, EST +10½ and +9½ hrs; Australia, EST -5½ and -4½ hrs).

Tipping

A tip of Rs 10 to a bellboy carrying luggage in a modest hotel (Rs 20 in a higher category) would be appropriate. In upmarket restaurants, a 10% tip is acceptable when service is not already included, while in places serving very cheap meals, round off the bill with small change. Indians don't normally tip taxi drivers but a small extra is welcomed. Porters at airports and railway stations often have a fixed rate displayed but will usually press for more. Ask fellow passengers what a fair rate is.

Tourist information

There are **Government of India** tourist offices in the state capitals, as well as state tourist offices (sometimes **Tourism Development Corporations**) in the Delhi and some towns and places of tourist interest. They produce their own tourist literature, either free or sold at a nominal price, and some also have lists of city hotels and paying guest options. The quality of material is improving though maps are often poor. Many offer tours of the city, neighbouring sights and overnight and regional packages. Some run modest hotels and midway motels with restaurants and may also arrange car hire and guides. The staff in the regional and local offices are usually helpful.

Visas and immigration

For embassies and consulates, see page 18. Virtually all foreign nationals, including children, require a visa to enter India. Nationals of Bhutan and Nepal only require a suitable means of identification. The rules regarding visas change frequently and arrangements for application and collection also vary from town to town so it is essential to check details and costs with the relevant embassy or consulate. These remain closed on Indian national holidays. Many consulates and embassies are currently outsourcing the visa process; it's best to find out in advance how long it will take. Note that visas are valid from the date granted, not from the date of entry.

Recently the Indian government has decided to issue 'visas on arrival' for some 40 countries (including the UK, the USA, France and Germany), as well as for citizens of all countries who are over the age of 60. The exact time frame for the change is not yet clear, so check the latest situation online before travelling.

No foreigner needs to register within the 180-day period of their tourist visa. All foreign visitors who stay in India for more than 180 days need to get an income tax clearance exemption certificate from the Foreign Section of the Income Tax Department in Delhi, Mumbai, Kolkata or Chennai.

Applications for visa extensions should be made to the Foreigners' Regional Registration Offices at New Delhi or Kolkata, or an office of the Superintendent of Police in the District Headquarters. After 6 months, you must leave India and apply for a new visa – the Nepal office is known to be difficult. Anyone staying in India for a period of more than 180 days (6 months) must register at a convenient Foreigners' Registration Office.

Liquor permits

Periodically some Indian states have tried to enforce prohibition. To some degree it is in force in Gujarat, Manipur, Mizoram and Nagaland. When applying for your visa you can ask for an All India Liquor Permit. Foreigners can also get the permit from any Government of India Tourist Office in Delhi or the state capitals. Instant permits are issued by some hotels.

Weights and measures

Metric is in universal use in the cities. In remote areas local measures are sometimes used. One lakh is 100,000 and 1 crore is 10 million.

Contents

Delhi

Delhi can take you aback with its vibrancy and growth. Less than 60 years ago the spacious, quiet and planned city of New Delhi was still the pride of late colonial British India, while to its north, the lanes of Old Delhi resonated with the sounds of a bustling medieval market. Today, both worlds have been overtaken by the rush of modernization. As Delhi's population surges, its tentacles have spread in all directions – from both the ancient core of Shahjahan's city in the north and the late British capital of New Delhi to its south.

Close to New Delhi Railway Station, the cheap hotels and guesthouses of Paharganj squeeze between cloth merchants and wholesalers. In Old Delhi, further north, with the Red Fort and Jama Masjid, the old city is still a dense network of narrow alleys and tightly packed markets and houses. Your senses are bombarded by noise, bustle, smells and apparent chaos. A 'third city' comprises the remorselessly growing squatter settlements (*jhuggies*), which provide shelter for more than a third of Delhi's population. To the south is another, newer, chrome-and-glass city, the city of the modern suburbs and urban 'farms', where the rural areas of Gurgaon have become the preserve of the prosperous, with shopping malls, banks and private housing estates. Old and new, simple and sophisticated, traditional and modern, East and West are juxtaposed. Whatever India you are looking for, the capital has it all – getting lost in warrens of crowded streets, wandering through spice markets, eating kebabs by the beautiful Jama Masjid, lazing among Mogul ruins, listening to Sufi musicians by a shrine at dusk or shopping in giant shining malls, drinking cocktails in glitzy bars and travelling on the gleaming Metro.

Arriving in Delhi

Getting there

Delhi is served by **Indira Gandhi International (IGI) Airport**, which handles both international and domestic traffic. The new T3 (International Terminal) has one of the longest runways in Asia and is connected to the city centre by Metro. It is about 23 km from the centre. During the day, it can take 30-45 minutes from the Domestic Terminal and 45 minutes to an hour from the International Terminal to get to the centre. With the Metro, it should take 20 minutes. A free shuttle runs between the terminals. To get to town take a pre-paid taxi (see Transport, page 59) or an airport coach, or ask your hotel to collect you.

The **Inter State Bus Terminus (ISBT)** is at Kashmere Gate, near the Red Fort, about 30 minutes by bus from Connaught Place. Local buses connect it to the other ISBTs.

There are three main railway stations. The busy **New Delhi Station**, a 10-minute walk north of Connaught Place, can be maddeningly chaotic; you need to have all your wits about you. The quieter **Hazrat Nizamuddin** (which has some south-bound trains) is 5 km southeast of Connaught Place. The overpoweringly crowded **Old Delhi Station** (2 km north of Connaught Place) has a few important train connections. ▶▶ *See Transport, page 59.*

Getting around

The new Metro is making the sprawling city very navigable: it's now possible to get from Connaught Place to Old Delhi in a cool five minutes; while Connaught Place to Qutb Minar is about 30 minutes, and all the way down to the final stop in Gurgaon is about one hour. It is a strange experience to go from air-conditioned high tech to the bustling streets of Chandi Chowk. There is a women-only carriage at the front of each train, clearly marked inside and on the platform – this prevents women from having to succumb to the crush of the other carriages. There is a fine of Rs 250 for men ignoring all the signs in pink and, in early 2011, a posse of women made men do sit-ups on the train for trespassing into the pink zone! Like any city Metro service, try and avoid rush hour if you can. At each Metro station you have to go through airport-like security and have your bag x-rayed, etc.

Auto-rickshaws and taxis are widely available, and new rate cards mean that drivers will now use their meters, even with foreigners. It's best to use pre-paid stands at stations, airport terminals and at the junction of Radial Road 1 and Connaught Place if possible. The same applies to cycle rickshaws, which ply the streets of Old Delhi. City buses are usually packed and have long queues. Be on your guard from thieves around New Delhi Station. State Entry Road runs from the southern end of Platform 1 to Connaught Place. This is a hassle-free alternative to the main Chelmsford Road during the day (gate closed at night). Also watch your change or cash interactions even at the pre-paid booths – sometimes they do a switch of a Rs 100 note for a Rs 10 for example. Fleets of Radio Taxis are the newest additions to the city's transport options. These include: **Delhi Cab** ① *T011-4433 3222*; **Easy Cab** ① *T011-4343 4343*; **Mega Cabs** ① *T011-4141 4141* and **Quick Cab** ① *T011-4533 3333*. ▶▶ *See Transport, page 59.*

Orientation

The **Red Fort** and **Jama Masjid** are the focal point of Old Delhi, 2 km northeast of Connaught Place. Chandni Chowk, the main commercial area, heads west from the fort. Around this area are narrow lanes packed to the rafters with all different types of wares for sale. To the southeast are **New Delhi Railway Station** and the main backpackers' area, **Paharganj**, with **Connaught Place**, the notional 'centre' of New Delhi, about 1 km south.

Running due south of Connaught Place is **Janpath** with small shops selling craft products, and hotels like the **Imperial**. Janpath is intersected by **Rajpath** with all the major state buildings at its western end. Immediately south is the diplomatic enclave, **Chanakyapuri**. Most of the upmarket hotels are scattered across the wide area between Connaught Place and the airport to the southwest. As Delhi's centre of gravity has shifted southwards, a series of new markets has grown up to serve extensive housing colonies such as **South Extension**, **Greater Kailash** and **Safdarjang Enclave**. This development has brought one of the major historic sites, the **Qutb Minar**, within the limits of the city, about half an hour by taxi south of Connaught Place. **Gurgaon** which is strictly not in Delhi but in Haryana, is the new business hub with many shopping malls to boot.

Tourist information

Most tourist offices are open Monday-Friday 1000-1800, www.delhitourism.com. **The Government of India Tourist Office** ① *88 Janpath, T011-332 0005, Mon-Sat 0900-1800; also at the international airport*, is helpful and issues permits for visits to Rashtrapati Bhavan and gardens. There are several branches of **Delhi Tourism** ① *N-36 Connaught Pl, T011-2331 5322 (touts pester you to use one of many imposters; the correct office is directly opposite 'Competent House')*; the branch at **Coffee Home Annexe** ① *Baba Kharak Singh Marg, T011-336 5358*, offers hotel, transport and tour bookings (T011-2462 3782, 0700-2100). There are also branches at the airport terminals; the Inter-State Bus Terminal; **New Delhi Railway Station** ① *T011-2373 2374*; and **Nizamuddin Railway Station** ① *T011-2251 1083*. Also contact the **India Tourism Development Corporation (ITDC)** ① *L-1 Connaught Circus, T011-2332 0331*.

Best time to visit

October to March are the best months to visit, but December and January can get quite cold and foggy at night. Pollution can affect asthma sufferers – in fact a lot of people develop respiratory problems and sore throats if they spend more than a few days in Delhi; echinacea can help. Monsoon lasts from the end of June to mid-September. May and June are very hot and dry and, with the whole city switching on its air-condioning units, power cuts are suffered more frequently at this time. Even the malls in Saket were having to keep their air conditioning on low during the summer of 2012.

Background

In the modern period, Delhi has only been India's capital since 1911. It is a city of yo yo-ing fortunes and has been repeatedly reduced to rubble. There have been at least eight cities founded on the site of modern Delhi.

According to Hindu mythology, Delhi's first avatar was as the site of a dazzlingly wealthy city, Indraprastha, mentioned in the Mahabharata and founded around 2500 BC. The next five cities were to the south of today's Delhi. First was Lalkot, which, from 1206, became the capital of the Delhi Sultanate under the Slave Dynasty. The story of the first Sultan of Delhi, Qutb-ud-din Aybak, is a classic rags-to-riches story. A former slave, he rose through the ranks to become a general, a governor and then Sultan of Delhi. He is responsible for building Qutb Minar, but died before its completion.

The 1300s were a tumultuous time for Delhi, with five cities built during the century. Siri, the first of these, has gruesome roots. Legend has it that the city's founder, Ala-ud-din, buried the heads of infidels in the foundation of the fort. Siri derives its name from the

Hindi word for 'head'. After Siri came Tughlaqabad, whose existence came to a sudden end when the Sultan of Delhi, Muhammad Tughlaq, got so angry about a perceived insult from residents, he destroyed the city. The cities of Jahanpanah and Ferozebad followed in quick succession. Delhi's centre of gravity began to move northwards. In the 1500s Dinpanah was constructed by Humayun, whose wonderful tomb (1564-1573) graces Hazrat Nizamuddin. Shahjahanabad, known today as Old Delhi, followed, becoming one of the richest and most populous cities in the world. The Persian emperor Nadir Shah invaded, killing as many as 120,000 residents in a single bloody night and stealing the Kohinoor Diamond (now part of the British royal family's crown jewels).

The next destroyers of Delhi were the British, who ransacked the city in the wake of the Great Uprising/Mutiny of 1857. The resulting bloodbath left bodies piled so high that the victors' horses had to tread on them. For the next 50 years, while the port cities of Calcutta and Bombay thrived under the British, Delhi languished. Then, in 1911, King George, on a visit to India, announced that a new city should be built next to what remained of Delhi, and that this would be the new capital of India. The British architect Edwin Lutyens was brought in to design the city. You could argue that the building hasn't stopped since ...

The central part of New Delhi is an example of Britain's imperial pretensions. The government may have been rather more reticent about moving India's capital, if it had known that in less than 36 years time, the British would no longer be ruling India. Delhi's population swelled after the violence of partition, with refugees flooding to the city. In 10 years the population of Delhi doubled, and many well-known housing colonies were built during this period.

The economic boom that began in the 1990s has lead to an explosion of construction and soaring real estate prices. Delhi is voraciously eating into the surrounding countryside. It is a city changing at such breakneck speed that shops, homes and even airports seem to appear and disappear almost overnight.

Places in Delhi

The sites of interest are grouped in three main areas. In the centre is the British-built capital of **New Delhi**, with its government buildings and wide avenues. The heart of **Shahjahanabad** (Old Delhi) is about 2 km north of Connaught Circus. Some 10 km to the south is the **Qutb Minar** complex, with the old fortress city of **Tughluqabad**, 8 km to its east. Across the Yamuna River is the remarkable new Akshardham Temple. You can visit each separately, or link routes together into a day-tour to include the most interesting sites.

Old Delhi → For listings, see pages 49-62.

Shah Jahan (ruled 1628-1658) decided to move back from Agra to Delhi in 1638. Within 10 years the huge city of **Shahjahanabad**, now known as Old Delhi, was built. The plan of Shah Jahan's new city symbolized the link between religious authority enshrined in the Jama Masjid to the west, and political authority represented by the Diwan-i-Am in the Fort, joined by Chandni Chowk, the route used by the emperor. The city was protected by rubble-built walls, some of which still survive. These walls were pierced by 14 main gates. The **Ajmeri Gate**, **Turkman Gate** (often referred to by auto-rickshaw wallahs as 'Truckman Gate'), **Kashmere Gate** and **Delhi Gate** still survive.

Chandni Chowk

Shahjahanabad was laid out in blocks with wide roads, residential quarters, bazars and mosques. Its principal street, Chandni Chowk, had a tree-lined canal flowing down its centre which became renowned throughout Asia. The canal is long gone, but the jumble of shops, alleys crammed with craftsmen's workshops, food stalls, mosques and temples, cause it to retain some of its magic. A cycle rickshaw ride gives you a good feel of the place. Make sure you visit **Naughara Street**, just off Kinari Bazar; it's one of the most atmospheric streets in Delhi, full of brightly painted and slowly crumbling *havelis*.

The impressive red sandstone façade of the **Digambar Jain Mandir** (temple) standing at the eastern end of Chandni Chowk, faces the Red Fort. Built in 1656, it contains an image of Adinath. The charity bird hospital (www.charitybirdshospital.org) within this compound releases the birds on recovery instead of returning them to their owners; many remain within the temple precincts. Beyond Shahjahanabad to the north lies Kashmiri Gate, Civil lines and the Northern Ridge. The siting of the railway line which effectively cut Delhi into two unequal parts was done deliberately. The line brought prosperity, yet it destroyed the unity of the walled city forever. The Northern Ridge was the British cantonment and Civil Lines housed the civilians. In this area the temporary capital of the British existed from 1911-1931 until New Delhi came. The Northern Ridge is a paradise for birds and trees. Follow the **Mutiny Trail** by visiting Flagstaff Tower, Pir Ghaib, Chauburj, Mutiny Memorial. Around Kashmire Gate and Civil Lines, you can discover the Old Residency, St James Church, Nicholson's Cemetery and Qudsia Bagh.

Red Fort (Lal Qila)

ⓘ *Tue-Sun sunrise to sunset, Rs 250 foreigners, Rs 10 Indians, allow 1 hr. The entrance is through the Lahore Gate (nearest the car park) with the admission kiosk opposite; keep your ticket as you will need to show it at the Drum House. There are new toilets inside, best to avoid* the ones in Chatta Chowk. You must remove shoes and cover all exposed flesh from your shoulders to your legs.

Between the new city and the River Yamuna, Shah Jahan built a fort. Most of it was built out of red *lal* (sandstone), hence the name **Lal Qila** (Red Fort), the same as that at Agra on which the Delhi Fort is modelled. Begun in 1639 and completed in 1648, it is said to have cost Rs 10 million, much of which was spent on the opulent marble palaces within. In recent years much effort has been put into improving the fort and gardens, but visitors may be saddened by the neglected state of some of the buildings, and the gun-wielding soldiers lolling around do nothing to improve the ambience. However, despite the modern development of roads and shops and the never-ending traffic, it's an impressive site.

The approach The entrance is by the Lahore Gate. The defensive barbican that juts out in front of it was built by Aurangzeb (see page 65). A common story suggests that Aurangzeb built the curtain wall to save his nobles and visiting dignitaries from having to walk – and bow – the whole length of Chandni Chowk, for no one was allowed to ride in the presence of the emperor. When the emperor sat in the Diwan-i-Am he could see all the way down the chowk, so the addition must have been greatly welcomed by his courtiers. The new entrance arrangement also made an attacking army more vulnerable to the defenders on the walls.

Chatta Chowk and the Naubat Khana Inside is the **Covered Bazar**, which was quite exceptional in the 17th century. In Shah Jahan's time there were shops on both upper and lower levels. Originally they catered for the Imperial household and carried stocks of silks, brocades, velvets, gold and silverware, jewellery and gems. There were coffee shops too for nobles and courtiers.

The **Naqqar Khana** or **Naubat Khana** (Drum House or music gallery) marked the entrance to the inner apartments of the fort. Here everyone except the princes of the royal family had to dismount and leave their horses or *hathi* (elephants), hence its other name of **Hathi Pol** (Elephant Gate). Five times a day ceremonial music was played on the kettle drum, *shahnais* (a kind of oboe) and cymbals, glorifying the emperor. In 1754 Emperor Ahmad Shah was murdered here. The gateway with four floors is decorated with floral designs. You can still see traces of the original panels painted in gold or other colours on the interior of the gateway.

Diwan-i-Am Between the first inner court and the royal palaces at the heart of the fort, stood the **Diwan-i-Am** (Hall of Public Audience), the furthest point a normal visitor would reach. It has seen many dramatic events, including the destructive whirlwind of the Persian Nadir Shah in 1739 and of Ahmad Shah the Afghan in 1756, and the trial of the last 'King of Delhi', **Bahadur Shah II** in 1858.

The well-proportioned hall was both a functional building and a showpiece intended to hint at the opulence of the palace itself. In Shah Jahan's time the sandstone was hidden behind a very thin layer of white polished plaster, *chunam*. This was decorated with floral motifs in many colours, especially gilt. Silk carpets and heavy curtains hung from the canopy rings outside the building; such interiors were reminders of the Mughals' nomadic origins in Central Asia, where royal durbars were held in tents.

At the back of the hall is a platform for the emperor's throne. Around this was a gold railing, within which stood the princes and great nobles separated from the lesser nobles inside the hall. Behind the throne canopy are 12 marble panels inlaid with motifs

1 Old Delhi

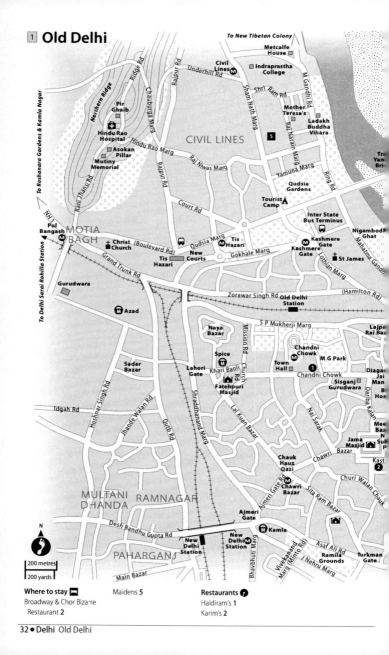

Where to stay 🛏
Broadway & Chor Bizarre
Restaurant **2**

Maidens **5**

Restaurants 🍴
Haldiram's **1**
Karim's **2**

➡ **Delhi maps**
3 Old Delhi, page 32
4 New Delhi, page 38
5 Connaught Place, page 41

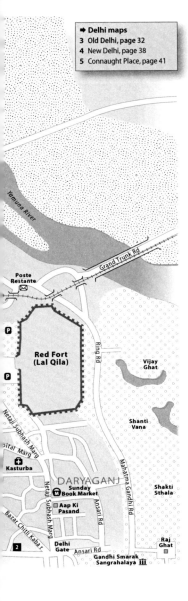

of fruiting trees, parrots and cuckoos. Figurative workmanship is very unusual in Islamic buildings, and these panels are the only example in the Red Fort.

As well as matters of official administration, Shah Jahan would listen to accounts of illness, dream interpretations and anecdotes from his ministers and nobles. Wednesday was the day of judgement. Sentences were often swift and brutal and sometimes the punishment of dismemberment, beating or death was carried out on the spot. The executioners were close at hand with axes and whips. On Friday, the Muslim holy day, there would be no business.

Inner palace buildings Behind the Diwan-i-Am is the private enclosure of the fort. Along the east wall, overlooking the River Yamuna, Shah Jahan set six small palaces (five survive). Also within this compound are the Harem, the Life-Bestowing Garden and the Nahr-i-Bihisht (Stream of Paradise).

Life-Bestowing Gardens (Hayat Baksh Bagh) The original gardens were landscaped according to the Islamic principles of the Persian *char bagh*, with pavilions, fountains and water courses dividing the garden into various but regular beds. The two pavilions **Sawan** and **Bhadon**, named after the first two months of the rainy season (July-August), reveal something of the character of the garden. The garden used to create the effect of the monsoon and contemporary accounts tell us that in the pavilions – some of which were especially erected for the **Teej** festival, which marks the arrival of the monsoon – the royal ladies would sit in silver swings and watch the rains. Water flowed from the back wall of the pavilion through a slit above the marble shelf and over the niches in the wall. Gold and silver pots of flowers were placed in these alcoves during the day whilst at night candles were lit to create a glistening and colourful effect.

Shahi Burj From the pavilion next to the Shahi Burj (**Royal Tower**) the canal known as the **Nahr-i-Bihisht** (Stream of Paradise) began its journey along the Royal Terrace. The three-storey octagonal tower was seriously damaged in 1857 and is still unsafe. In Shah Jahan's time the Yamuna lapped the walls. Shah Jahan used the tower as his most private office and only his sons and a few senior ministers were allowed with him.

Moti Masjid To the right are the three marble domes of Aurangzeb's 'Pearl Mosque' (shoes must be removed). Bar the cupolas, it is completely hidden behind a wall of red sandstone, now painted white. Built in 1662 of polished white marble, it has some exquisite decoration. All the surfaces are highly decorated in a fashion similar to rococo, which developed at the same time as in Europe. Unusually the prayer hall is on a raised platform with inlaid outlines of individual *musallas* ('prayer mats') in black marble. While the outer walls were aligned to the cardinal points like all the other fort buildings, the inner walls were positioned so that the mosque would correctly face Mecca.

Hammam The **Royal Baths** have three apartments separated by corridors with canals to carry water to each room. The two flanking the entrance, for the royal children, had hot and cold baths. The room furthest away from the door has three basins for rose water fountains.

Diwan-i-Khas Beyond is the single-storeyed **Hall of Private Audience**, topped by four Hindu-style *chhattris* and built completely of white marble. The *dado* (lower part of the wall) on the interior was richly decorated with inlaid precious and semi-precious stones. The ceiling was silver but was removed by the Marathas in 1760. Outside, the hall used to have a marble pavement and an arcaded court. Both have gone.

This was the Mughal office of state. Shah Jahan spent two hours here before retiring for a meal, siesta and prayers. In the evening he would return to the hall for more work before going to the harem. The hall's splendour moved the 14th-century poet Amir Khusrau to write the lines inscribed above the corner arches of the north and south walls: "*Agar Firdaus bar rue Zamin-ast/Hamin ast o Hamin ast o Hamin ast*" (If there be a paradise on earth, it is here, it is here, it is here).

Royal palaces Next to the Diwan-i-Khas is the three-roomed **Khas Mahal** (Private Palace). Nearest the Diwan-i-Khas is the **Tasbih Khana** (Chamber for the Telling of Rosaries) where the emperor would worship privately with his rosary of 99 beads, one for each of the mystical names of Allah. In the centre is the **Khwabgah** (Palace of Dreams) which gives on to the octagonal **Mussaman Burj** tower. Here Shah Jahan would be seen each morning. A balcony was added to the tower in 1809 and here George V and Queen Mary appeared in their Coronation Durbar of 1911. The **Tosh Khana** (Robe Room), to the south, has a beautiful marble screen at its north end, carved with the scales of justice above the filigree grille. If you are standing with your back to the Diwan-i-Khas you will see a host of circulating suns (a symbol of royalty), but if your back is to the next building (the Rang Mahal), you will see moons surrounding the scales. All these rooms were sumptuously decorated with fine silk carpets, rich silk brocade curtains and lavishly decorated walls. After 1857 the British used the Khas Mahal as an officer's mess and sadly it was defaced.

The **Rang Mahal** (Palace of Colours), the residence of the chief *sultana*, was also the place where the emperor ate most of his meals. It was divided into six apartments. Privacy and coolness were ensured by the use of marble *jali* screens. Like the other palaces it was beautifully decorated with a silver ceiling ornamented with golden flowers to reflect the water in the channel running through the building. The north and south apartments were both known as **Sheesh Mahal** (Palace of Mirrors) since into the ceiling were set hundreds of small mirrors. In the evening when candles were lit a starlight effect would be produced.

Through the palace ran the **Life-bestowing Stream** and at its centre is a lotus-shaped marble basin which had an ivory fountain. As might be expected in such a cloistered and cosseted environment, the ladies sometimes got bored. In the 18th century the **Empress of Jahandar Shah** sat gazing out at the river and remarked that she had never seen a boat sink. Shortly afterwards a boat was deliberately capsized so that she could be entertained by the sight of people bobbing up and down in the water crying for help.

The southernmost of the palaces, the **Mumtaz Mahal** (Palace of Jewels) ① *Tue-Sun 1000-1700*, was also used by the harem. The lower half of its walls are of marble and it contains six apartments. After the Mutiny of 1857 it was used as a guardroom and since 1912 it has been a museum with exhibits of textiles, weapons, carpets, jade and metalwork as well as works depicting life in the court. It should not be missed.

Spice market

Outside the Red Fort, cycle rickshaws offer a trip to the spice market, Jama Masjid and back through the bazar. You travel slowly westwards down Chandni Chowk passing the town hall. Dismount at Church Road and follow your guide into the heart of the market on Khari Baoli where wholesalers sell every conceivable spice. Ask to go to the roof for an excellent view over the market and back towards the Red Fort. The ride back through the bazar is equally fascinating – look up at the amazing electricity system. The final excitement is getting back across Netaji Subhash Marg. Panic not, the rickshaw wallahs know what they are doing. Negotiate for one hour and expect to pay about Rs 100. The spice laden air may irritate your throat. Also ask a cycle rickshaw to take you to Naughara Street, just off Kinari Bazar, a very pretty street amidst the chaos of Old Delhi.

Jama Masjid (Friday Mosque)

① *Visitors welcome from 30 mins after sunrise until 1215; and from 1345 until 30 mins before sunset, free, still or video cameras Rs 150, tower entry Rs 20.*

The magnificent Jama Masjid is the largest mosque in India and the last great architectural work of Shah Jahan, intended to dwarf all mosques that had gone before it. With the fort, it dominates Old Delhi. The mosque is much simpler in its ornamentation than Shah Jahan's secular buildings – a judicious blend of red sandstone and white marble, which are interspersed in the domes, minarets and cusped arches.

The gateways Symbolizing the separation of the sacred and the secular, the threshold is a place of great importance where the worshipper steps to a higher plane. There are three huge gateways, the largest being to the east. This was reserved for the royal family who gathered in a private gallery in its upper storey. Today, the faithful enter through the east gate on Fridays and for **Id-ul-Fitr** and **Id-ul-Adha**. The latter commemorates Abraham's (Ibrahim's) sacrificial offering of his son Ishmael (Ismail). Islam (unlike the Jewish and Christian tradition) believes that Abraham offered to sacrifice Ishmael, Isaac's brother.

The courtyard The façade has the main *iwan* (arch), five smaller arches on each side with two flanking minarets and three bulbous domes behind, all perfectly proportioned. The *iwan* draws the worshippers' attention into the building. The minarets have great views from the top; well worth the climb for Rs 10 (women may not be allowed to climb alone).

The **hauz**, in the centre of the courtyard, is an ablution tank placed as usual between the inner and outer parts of the building to remind the worshipper that it is through the ritual of baptism that one first enters the community of believers. The **Dikka**, in front of the ablution tank, is a raised platform. Muslim communities grew so rapidly that by the eighth century it sometimes became necessary to introduce a second *muballigh* (prayer leader) who stood on this platform and copied the postures and chants of the *imam* inside to relay them to a much larger congregation. With the introduction of the loudspeaker and amplification, the *dikka* and the *muballigh* became redundant. In the northwest corner of the mosque there is a small shed. For a small fee, the faithful are shown a hair from the beard of the prophet, as well as his sandal and his footprint in rock.

New Delhi → For listings, see pages 49-62.

Delhi's present position as capital was only confirmed on 12 December 1911, when George V announced at the Delhi Durbar that the capital of India was to move from Calcutta to Delhi. The new city, New Delhi, planned under the leadership of British architect Edwin Lutyens with the assistance of his friend Herbert Baker, was inaugurated on 9 February 1931.

The city was to accommodate 70,000 people and have boundless possibilities for future expansion. The king favoured something in form and flavour similar to the Mughal masterpieces but fretted over the horrendous expense that this would incur. A petition signed by eminent public figures such as Bernard Shaw and Thomas Hardy advocated an Indian style and an Indian master builder. Herbert Baker had made known his own views even before his appointment when he wrote "first and foremost it is the spirit of British sovereignty which must be imprisoned in its stone and bronze". Lutyens himself despised Indian architecture. "Even before he had seen any examples of it", writes architectural historian Giles Tillotson, "he pronounced Mughal architecture to be 'piffle', and seeing it did not disturb that conviction". Yet in the end, Lutyens was forced to compromise.

India Gate and around
A tour of New Delhi will usually start with a visit to India Gate. This war memorial is situated at the eastern end of **Rajpath**. Designed by Lutyens, it commemorates more than 70,000 Indian soldiers who died in the First World War. Some 13,516 names of British and Indian soldiers killed on the Northwest Frontier and in the Afghan War of 1919 are engraved on the arch and foundations. Under the arch is the Amar Jawan Jyoti, commemorating Indian armed forces' losses in the Indo-Pakistan War of 1971. The arch (43 m high) stands on a base of Bharatpur stone and rises in stages. Similar to the Hindu *chhattri* signifying regality, it is decorated with nautilus shells symbolizing British maritime power. Come at dusk to join the picnicking crowds enjoying the evening. You may even be able to have a pedalo ride if there's water in the canal.

National Gallery of Modern Art
ⓘ *Jaipur House, near India Gate, T011-2338 4640, www.ngmaindia.gov.in, Tue-Sun 1000-1700, Rs 150 foreigners, Rs 10 Indians.*
There is now a new air-conditioned wing of this excellent gallery and select exhibits in the old building housed in a former residence of the Maharaja of Jaipur. The '*In the Seeds of Time...*' exhibition traces the trajectory of modern Indian art. Artists include: Amrita Shergil, with over 100 exhibits, synthesizing the flat treatment of Indian painting with a realistic tone; Rabindranath Tagore (ground floor) has examples from a brief but intense

spell in the 1930s; The Bombay School or Company School (first floor) includes Western painters who documented their visits to India. Realism is reflected in Indian painting of the early 19th century represented by the schools of Avadh, Patna, Sikkim and Thanjavur; The Bengal School (the late 19th-century Revivalist Movement) showcases artists such as Abanindranath Tagore and Nandalal Bose have their works exhibited here. Western influence was discarded in response to the nationalist movement. Inspiration derived from Indian folk art is evident in the works of Jamini Roy and YD Shukla. Prints from the gallery shop are incredibly good value – up to Rs 80 for poster-size prints of famous works.

National Museum
ⓘ Janpath, T011-2301 9272, www.nationalmuseumindia.gov.in, daily 1000-1700, foreigners Rs 300 (including audio tour), Indians Rs 10, camera Rs 300; free guided tours 1030, 1130, 1200, 1400, films are screened every day (1430), marble squat toilets, but dirty.

The collection was formed from the nucleus of the Exhibition of Indian Art, London (1947). Now merged with the Asian Antiquities Museum it displays a rich collection of the artistic treasure of Central Asia and India including ethnological objects from prehistoric archaeological finds to the late Medieval period. Replicas of exhibits and books on Indian culture and art are on sale. There is also a research library.

Ground floor Prehistoric: seals, figurines, toy animals and jewellery from the Harappan civilization (2400-1500 BC). **Maurya Period**: terracottas and stone heads from around the third century BC include the *chaturmukha* (four-faced) *lingam*. **Gandhara School**: stucco heads showing the Graeco Roman influence. **Gupta terracottas** (circa AD 400): including two life-size images of the river goddesses Ganga and Yamuna and the four-armed bust of Vishnu from a temple near Lal Kot. **South Indian sculpture**: from Pallava and early Chola temples and relief panels from Mysore. Bronzes from the Buddhist monastery at Nalanda. Some of Buddha's relics were placed in the Thai pavilion in 1997.

First floor Illustrated manuscripts: include the *Babur-i-nama* in the emperor's own handwriting and an autographed copy of Jahangir's memoirs. **Miniature paintings**: include the 16th-century Jain School, the 18th-century Rajasthani School and the Pahari schools of Garhwal, Basoli and Kangra. **Aurel Stein Collection** consists of antiquities recovered by him during his explorations of Central Asia and the western borders of China at the turn of the 20th century.

Second floor Pre-Columbian and Mayan artefacts: anthropological section devoted to tribal artefacts and folk arts. **Sharad Rani Bakkiwal Gallery of Musical Instruments**: displays over 300 instruments collected by the famous *sarod* player.

Rashtrapati Bhavan and Nehru Memorial Museum
Once the Viceroy's House, Rashtrapati Bhavan is the official residence of the President of India. The Viceroy's House, New Delhi's centrepiece of imperial proportions, was 1 km around the foundations, bigger than Louis XIV's palace at Versailles. It had a colossal dome surmounting a long colonnade and 340 rooms in all. It took nearly 20 years to complete, similar to the time it took to build the Taj Mahal. In the busiest year, 29,000 people were working on the site and buildings began to take shape. The project was surrounded by controversy from beginning to end. Opting for a fundamentally classical structure, both Baker and Lutyens sought to incorporate Indian motifs, many entirely superficial. While

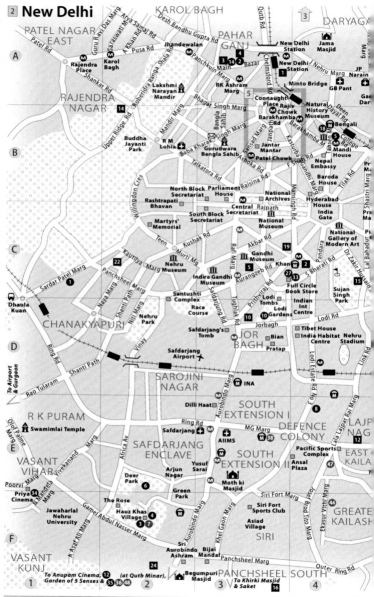

KAROL BAGH

DARYAGA

PATEL NAGAR EAST

PAHAR GANJ

New Delhi Station

Jama Masjid

Jhandewalan

New Delhi Station

JP Narain

Rajendra Place

Karol Bagh

Minto Bridge

GB Pant

RK Ashram Marg

Gal Dar

RAJENDRA NAGAR

Lakshmi Narayan Mandir

Connaught Place

Natural Dayal Rd

Rajiv Chowk

Natural History Museum

Bengali

Buddha Jayanti Park

R M Lohia

Gurudwara Bangla Sahib

Jantar Mantar

Mandi House

Patel Chowk

Nepal Embassy

Baroda House

North Block Secretariat

Parliament House

Raisina Rd

Hyderabad House

Rashtrapati Bhavan

Central Secretariat

National Archives

India Gate

South Block Secretariat

Rajpath

National Museum

Martyrs' Memorial

National Gallery of Modern Art

Nehru Museum

Gandhi Museum

Khan

Indira Gandhi Museum

Full Circle Book Store

Sujan Singh Park

Dhaula Kuan

CHANAKYAPURI

Santushti Complex

Race Course

Lodi Tombs

Lodi Gardens

Indian Int Centre

Nehru Park

Safdarjang's Tomb

JOR BAGH

Bian Pratap

Tibet House

India Habitat Centre

Nehru Stadium

Safdarjang Airport

SAROJINI NAGAR

INA

To Airport & Gurgaon

Dilli Haat

SOUTH EXTENSION I

DEFENCE COLONY

LAJP NAG

R K PURAM

Swamimlai Temple

Safdarjang

SAFDARJANG ENCLAVE

AIIMS

SOUTH EXTENSION II

Pacific Sports Complex

Ansal Plaza

EAST KAILA

VASANT VIHAR

Arjun Nagar

Yusuf Sarai

Moth ki Masjid

Deer Park

Green Park

Priya Cinema

The Rose

Hauz Khas Village

Siri Fort Sports Club

Asiad Village

SIRI

GREATE KAILASH

Jawaharlal Nehru University

Sri Aurobindo Ashram

Bijai Mandal

PANCHSHEEL SOUTH

VASANT KUNJ

To Anupam Cinema, Garden of 5 Senses &

(at Qutb Minar),

Begumpuri Masjid

To Khirki Masjid & Saket

➡ **Delhi maps**
3 Old Delhi, page 32
4 **New Delhi, page 38**
5 Connaught Place, page 41

700 metres
700 yards

Where to stay 🛏
Amarya Haveli **24** *F2*
Claridges **5** *C3*
Jyoti Mahal **1** *A3*
K One One **28** *D4*
Life Tree **12** *E4*
Lutyens Bungalow **10** *D3*
Manor **13** *E5*
Master **14** *B2*
Oberoi **15** *C4*
Prince Polonia **3** *A3*
Rak Internacional **4** *A3*
Taj Mahal **19** *C3*
Tree of Life **16** *F3*
Vivanta by Taj **2** *C4*
Youth Hostel **22** *C2*

Restaurants 🍴
Baci **21** *C4*
Bukhara **1** *C1*
Café Sim Tok **2** *A3*
Dum Pukht **1** *C1*
Grey Garden **3** *F2*
Indian Accent **13** *D5*
Kainoosh **34** *E1*
Khan Cha Cha **33** *C4*
Latitude **27** *C3*
Lodi **10** *D3*

Magique **35** *F2*
Naivedyam & Elma's **4** *F2*
Nathu's & Bengali Sweet
House **18** *B4*
Oh! Calcutta **16** *F5*
Olive at the Qutb **12** *F2*
Park Baluchi **6** *E2*
Sagar Ratna **8** *E4*
Tadka **14** *A3*
Triveni Tea Terrace **5** *B4*

Bars & clubs 🍸
Blue Frog **36** *F2*
Café Morrisons **38** *E3*
Living Room **7** *F2*
Shalom **44** *F4*
Stone **45** *D4*
Urban Pind **47** *E4*
Zoo **48** *F2*

Metro Stops (Yellow Line) Ⓜ
Metro Stops (Videt Line) Ⓜ

some claim that Lutyens achieved a unique synthesis of the two traditions, Tillotson asks whether "the sprinkling of a few simplified and classicized Indian details (especially *chhattris*) over a classical palace" could be called a synthesis. The Durbar Hall, 23 m in diameter, has coloured marble from all parts of India.

To the south is **Flagstaff House**, formerly the residence of the commander-in-chief. Renamed Teen Murti Bhawan it now houses the **Nehru Memorial Museum** ⓘ *T011-2301 4504, Tue-Sun 1000-1500, planetarium Mon-Sat 1130-1500, library Mon-Sat 0900-1900, free*. Designed by Robert Tor Russell, in 1948 it became the official residence of India's first prime minister, Jawaharlal Nehru. Converted after his death (1964) into a national memorial, the reception, study and bedroom are intact. A *Jyoti Jawahar* (torch) symbolizes the eternal values he inspired and a granite rock is carved with extracts from his historic speech at midnight on 14 August 1947; an informative and vivid history of the Independence Movement.

The **Martyr's Memorial**, at the junction of Sardar Patel Marg and Willingdon Crescent, is a magnificent 26-m-long, 3-m-high bronze sculpture by DP Roy Chowdhury. The 11 statues of national heroes are headed by Mahatma Gandhi.

Eternal Gandhi Multimedia Museum

ⓘ *Birla House, 5 Tees Jan Marg (near Claridges Hotel), T011-3095 7269, www.eternal gandhi.org, closed Mon and 2nd Sat, 1000-1700, free, film at 1500.*

Gandhi's last place of residence and the site of his assassination, Birla House has been converted into a whizz-bang display of 'interactive' modern technology. Over-attended by young guides eager to demonstrate the next gadget, the museum seems aimed mainly at those with a critically short attention span, and is too rushed to properly convey the story of Gandhi's life. However, a monument in the garden marking where he fell is definitely worth a visit. Other museums in the city related to Gandhi include: **National Gandhi Museum** ⓘ *opposite Raj Ghat, T011-2331 1793, www.gandhimuseum.org, Tue-Sat 0930-1730*, with five pavilions – sculpture, photographs and paintings of Gandhi and the history of the *Satyagraha* movement (the philosophy of non-violence); **Gandhi Smarak Sangrahalaya** ⓘ *Raj Ghat, T011-2301 1480, Fri-Wed 0930-1730*, displays some of Gandhi's personal belongings and a small library includes recordings of speeches; and the **Indira Gandhi Museum** ⓘ *1 Safdarjang Rd, T011-2301 0094, Tue-Sun 0930-1700, free*, charting the phases of her life from childhood to the moment of her death. Exhibits are fascinating, if rather gory – you can see the blood-stained, bullet-ridden sari she was wearing when assassinated.

Parliament House and around

Northeast of the Viceroy's House is the **Council House**, now **Sansad Bhavan**. Baker designed this based on Lutyens' suggestion that it be circular (173 m diameter). Inside are the library and chambers for the Council of State, Chamber of Princes and Legislative Assembly – the **Lok Sabha**. Just opposite the Council House is the **Rakabganj Gurudwara** in Pandit Pant Marg. This 20th-century white marble shrine, which integrates the late Mughal and Rajasthani styles, marks the spot where the headless body of Guru Tegh Bahadur, the ninth Sikh Guru, was cremated in 1657. West of the Council House is the **Cathedral Church of the Redemption** (1927-1935) and to its north the Italianate Roman Catholic **Church of the Sacred Heart** (1930-1934), both conceived by Henry Medd.

Connaught Place and Connaught Circus

Connaught Place and its outer ring, Connaught Circus (now officially named **Rajiv Chowk** and **Indira Chowk**, but still commonly referred to by their old names), comprise two-storey arcaded buildings, arranged radially around a circular garden that was

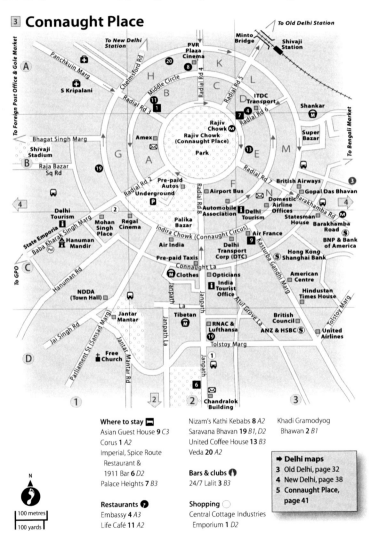

3 **Connaught Place**

Where to stay 🛏
Asian Guest House **9** C3
Corus **1** A2
Imperial, Spice Route
  Restaurant &
  1911 Bar **6** D2
Palace Heights **7** B3

Restaurants 🍴
Embassy **4** A3
Life Café **11** A2

Nizam's Kathi Kebabs **8** A2
Saravana Bhavan **19** B1, D2
United Coffee House **13** B3
Veda **20** A2

Bars & clubs 🍸
24/7 Lalit **3** B3

Shopping ◯
Central Cottage Industries
  Emporium **1** D2

Khadi Gramodyog
  Bhawan **2** B1

➡ **Delhi maps**
3 Old Delhi, page 32
4 New Delhi, page 38
5 Connaught Place,
  page 41

N

100 metres
100 yards

completed after the Metro line was installed. Designed by Robert Tor Russell, they have become the main commercial and tourist centre of New Delhi. Sadly, the area also attracts bands of insistent touts.

Lakshmi Narayan Mandir

To the west of Connaught Circus is the Lakshmi Narayan **Birla Temple** in Mandir Marg. Financed by the prominent industrialist Raja Baldeo Birla in 1938, this is one of the most popular Hindu shrines in the city and one of Delhi's few striking examples of Hindu architecture. Dedicated to Lakshmi, the goddess of well-being, it is commonly referred to as **Birla Mandir**. The design is in the Orissan style with tall curved *sikharas* (towers) capped by large *amalakas*. The exterior is faced with red and ochre stone and white marble. Built around a central courtyard, the main shrine has images of Narayan and his consort Lakshmi while two separate cells have icons of Siva (the Destroyer) and Durga (the 10-armed destroyer of demons). The temple is flanked by a *dharamshala* (rest house) and a Buddhist *vihara* (monastery).

Gurudwara Bangla Sahib

ⓘ *Baba Kharak Singh Rd, free.*

This is a fine example of Sikh temple architecture, featuring a large pool reminiscent of Amritsar's Golden Temple. The 24-hour reciting of the faith's holy book adds to the atmosphere, and there's free food on offer, although don't be surprised if you're asked to help out with the washing up! You must remove your shoes and cover your head to enter – suitable scarves are provided if you arrive without.

Further northeast on Baba Kharak Singh Marg is **Hanuman Mandir**. This small temple was built by Maharaja Jai Singh II of Jaipur. **Mangal haat** (Tuesday Fair) is a popular market.

Jantar Mantar

Just to the east of the Hanuman Mandir in Sansad Marg (Parliament Street) is Jai Singh's **observatory** (Jantar Mantar) ⓘ *sunrise to sunset, Rs 100 foreigners, Rs 5 Indians.* The Mughal Emperor Mohammad Shah (ruled 1719-1748) entrusted the renowned astronomer Maharaja Jai Singh II with the task of revising the calendar and correcting the astronomical tables used by contemporary priests. Daily astral observations were made for years before construction began and plastered brick structures were favoured for the site instead of brass instruments. Built in 1725 it is slightly smaller than the later observatory at Jaipur.

Memorial Ghats

Beyond Delhi Gate lies the **Yamuna River**, marked by a series of memorials to India's leaders. The river itself, a kilometre away, is invisible from the road, protected by a low rise and banks of trees. The most prominent memorial, immediately opposite the end of Jawaharlal Nehru Road, is that of Mahatma Gandhi at **Raj Ghat**. To its north is **Shanti Vana** (Forest of Peace), landscaped gardens where Prime Minister Jawaharlal Nehru was cremated in 1964, as were his grandson Sanjay Gandhi in 1980, daughter Indira Gandhi in 1984 and elder grandson, Rajiv, in 1991. To the north again is **Vijay Ghat** (Victory Bank) where Prime Minister Lal Bahadur Shastri was cremated.

South Delhi ➜ *For listings, see pages 49-62.*

South Delhi is often overlooked by travellers. This is a real pity as it houses some of the city's most stunning sites, best accommodation, bars, clubs and restaurants, as well as some of its most tranquil parks. However be warned, South Delhi can be hell during rushhour when the traffic on the endless flyovers comes to a virtual standstill. But with the Metro, you can explore all the way down to Gurgaon with relative ease.

Lodi Gardens

These beautiful gardens, with mellow stone tombs of the 15th- and 16th-century Lodi rulers, are popular for gentle strolls and jogging. In the middle of the garden facing the east entrance from Max Mueller Road is **Bara Gumbad** (Big Dome), a mosque built in 1494. The raised courtyard is provided with an imposing gateway and *mehman khana* (guest rooms). The platform in the centre appears to have had a tank for ritual ablutions.

The **Sheesh Bumbad** (Glass Dome, late 15th century) is built on a raised incline north of the Bara Gumbad and was once decorated with glazed blue tiles, painted floral designs and Koranic inscriptions. The façade gives the impression of a two-storeyed building, typical of Lodi architecture. **Mohammad Shah's Tomb** (1450) is that of the third Sayyid ruler. It has sloping buttresses, an octagonal plan, projecting eaves and lotus patterns on the ceiling. **Sikander Lodi's Tomb**, built by his son in 1517, is also an octagonal structure decorated with Hindu motifs. A structural innovation is the double dome which was later refined under the Mughals. The 16th-century **Athpula** (Bridge of Eight Piers), near the northeastern entrance, is attributed to Nawab Bahadur, a nobleman at Akbar's court.

Safdarjang's Tomb
ⓘ *Sunrise to sunset, Rs 100 foreigners, Rs 5 Indians.*
Safdarjang's Tomb, seldom visited, was built by Nawab Shuja-ud-Daulah for his father Mirza Mukhim Abdul Khan, entitled Safdarjang, who was Governor of Oudh (1719-1748), and Wazir of his successor (1748-1754). Safdarjang died in 1754. With its high enclosure walls, *char bagh* layout of gardens, fountain and central domed mausoleum, it follows the tradition of Humayun's tomb. Typically, the real tomb is just below ground level. Flanking the mausoleum are pavilions used by Shuja-ud-Daulah as his family residence. Immediately to its south is the battlefield where Timur and his Mongol horde crushed Mahmud Shah Tughluq on 12 December 1398.

Hazrat Nizamuddin
ⓘ *Dress ultra-modestly if you don't want to feel uncomfortable or cause offence.*
At the east end of the Lodi Road, Hazrat Nizamuddin Dargah (Nizamuddin 'village') now tucked away behind the residential suburb of Nizamuddin West, off Mathura Road, grew up around the shrine of Sheikh Nizamuddin Aulia (1236-1325), a Chishti saint. This is a wonderfully atmospheric place. *Qawwalis* are sung at sunset after *namaaz* (prayers), and are particularly impressive on Thursdays – be prepared for crowds. Highly recommended.

West of the central shrine is the *Jama-at-khana Mosque* (1325). Its decorated arches are typical of the Khalji design also seen at the Ala'i Darwaza at the Qutb Minar. South of the main tomb and behind finely crafted screens is the grave of princess Jahanara, Shah Jahan's eldest and favourite daughter. She shared the emperor's last years when he was imprisoned at Agra Fort. The grave, open to the sky, is in accordance with the epitaph written by her: "Let naught cover my grave save the green grass, for grass suffices as the covering of the lowly".

Pilgrims congregate at the shrine twice a year for the **Urs** (fair) held to mark the anniversaries of Hazrat Nizamuddin Aulia and his disciple Amir Khusrau, whose tomb is nearby.

Humayun's Tomb

ⓘ *Sunrise to sunset, Rs 250 foreigners, Rs 10 Indians, video cameras Rs 25, located in Nizamuddin, 15-20 mins by taxi from Connaught Circus, allow 45 mins.*

Eclipsed later by the Taj Mahal and the Jama Masjid, this tomb is the best example in Delhi of the early Mughal style of tomb. Superbly maintained, it is well worth a visit, preferably before visiting the Taj Mahal. Humayun, the second Mughal emperor, was forced into exile in Persia after being heavily defeated by the Afghan Sher Shah in 1540. He returned to India in 1545, finally recapturing Delhi in 1555. The tomb was designed and built by his senior widow and mother of his son Akbar, Hamida Begum. A Persian from Khurasan, after her pilgrimage to Mecca she was known as Haji Begum. She supervised the entire construction of the tomb (1564-1573), camping on the site.

The approach The tomb enclosure has two high double-storeyed gateways: the entrance to the west and the other to the south. A *baradari* occupies the centre of the east wall, and a bath chamber that of the north wall. Several Moghul princes, princesses and Haji Begum herself lie buried here. During the 1857 Mutiny Bahadur Shah II, the last Moghul emperor of Delhi, took shelter here with his three sons. Over 80, he was seen as a figurehead by Muslims opposing the British. When captured he was transported to Yangon (Rangoon) for the remaining four years of his life. The tomb to the right of the approach is that of Isa Khan, Humayun's barber.

The dome Some 38 m high, the dome does not have the swell of the Taj Mahal and the decoration of the whole edifice is much simpler. It is of red sandstone with some white marble to highlight the lines of the building. There is some attractive inlay work, and some *jalis* in the balcony fence and on some of the recessed keel arch windows. The interior is austere and consists of three storeys of arches rising up to the dome. The emperor's tomb is of white marble and quite plain without any inscription. The overall impression is that of a much bulkier, more squat building than the Taj Mahal. The cavernous space under the main tombs is home to great colonies of bats.

Hauz Khas

ⓘ *1-hr cultural show, 1845, Rs 100 (check with Delhi Tourism, see page 28).*

South of Safdarjang's Tomb, and entered off either Aurobindo Marg on the east side or Africa Avenue on the west side, is Hauz Khas. Ala-ud-din Khalji (ruled 1296-1313) created a large tank here for the use of the inhabitants of Siri, the second capital city of Delhi founded by him. Fifty years later Firoz Shah Tughluq cleaned up the silted tank and raised several buildings on its east and south banks which are known as Hauz Khas or Royal Tank.

Firoz Shah's austere tomb is found here. The multi-storeyed wings, on the north and west of the tomb, were built by him in 1354 as a *madrasa* (college). The octagonal and square *chhattris* were built as tombs, possibly to the teachers at the college. Hauz Khas is now widely used as a park for early-morning recreation – walking, running and yoga *asanas*. Classical music concerts, dance performances and a *son et lumière* show are held in the evenings when monuments are illuminated by thousands of earthen lamps and torches. Wandering the streets of Haus Khaz village, you can almost forget that you are in

India. Labyrinthine alleys lead to numerous galleries, boutiques and restaurants. There are a lot of little design studios here and a more boho vibe.

Qutb Minar Complex

ⓘ *Sunrise to sunset, Rs 250 foreigners, Rs 10 Indians. The Metro goes to Qutb Minar. Bus 505 from New Delhi Railway Station (Ajmeri Gate), Super Bazar (east of Connaught Circus) and Cottage Industries Emporium, Janpath. Auto Rs 110, though drivers may be reluctant to take you. This area is also opening up as a hub for new chic restaurants and bars.*

Muhammad Ghuri conquered northwest India at the very end of the 12th century. The conquest of the Gangetic plain down to Benares (Varanasi) was undertaken by Muhammad's Turkish slave and chief general, Qutb-ud-din-Aibak, whilst another general took Bihar and Bengal. In the process, temples were reduced to rubble, the remaining Buddhist centres were dealt their death blow and their monks slaughtered. When Muhammad was assassinated in 1206, his gains passed to the loyal Qutb-ud-din-Aibak. Thus the first sultans or Muslim kings of Delhi became known as the **Slave Dynasty** (1026-1290). For the next three centuries the Slave Dynasty and the succeeding Khalji (1290-1320), Tughluq (1320-1414), Sayyid (1414-1445) and Lodi (1451-1526) dynasties provided Delhi with fluctuating authority. The legacy of their ambitions survives in the tombs, forts and palaces that litter Delhi Ridge and the surrounding plain. Qutb-ud-din-Aibak died after only four years in power, but he left his mark with the **Qutb Minar** and his **citadel**. Qutb Minar, built to proclaim the victory of Islam over the infidel, dominates the countryside for miles around. Visit the *minar* first.

Qutb Minar In 1199 work began on what was intended to be the most glorious tower of victory in the world and was to be the prototype of all *minars* (towers) in India. Qutb-ud-din-Aibak had probably seen and been influenced by the brick victory pillars in Ghazni in Afghanistan, but this one was also intended to serve as the minaret attached to the Might of Islam Mosque. From here the muezzin could call the faithful to prayer. Later every mosque would incorporate its minaret.

As a mighty reminder of the importance of the ruler as Allah's representative on earth, the Qutb Minar (literally 'axis minaret') stood at the centre of the community. A pivot of Faith, Justice and Righteousness, its name also carried the message of Qutb-ud-din's (Axis of the Faith) own achievements. The inscriptions carved in Kufi script tell that "the tower was erected to cast the shadow of God over both east and west". For Qutb-ud-din-Aibak it marked the eastern limit of the empire of the One God. Its western counterpart is the Giralda Tower built by Yusuf in Seville.

The Qutb Minar is 73 m high and consists of five storeys. The diameter of the base is 14.4 m and 2.7 m at the top. Qutb-ud-din built the first three and his son-in-law Iltutmish embellished these and added a fourth. This is indicated in some of the Persian and Nagari (North Indian) inscriptions which also record that it was twice damaged by lightning in 1326 and 1368. While repairing the damage caused by the second, Firoz Shah Tughluq added a fifth storey and used marble to face the red and buff sandstone. This was the first time contrasting colours were used decoratively, later to become such a feature of Mughal buildings. Firoz's fifth storey was topped by a graceful cupola but this fell down during an earthquake in 1803. A new one was added by a Major Robert Smith in 1829 but was so out of keeping that it was removed in 1848 and now stands in the gardens.

The original storeys are heavily indented with different styles of fluting, alternately round and angular on the bottom, round on the second and angular on the third. The beautifully carved honeycomb detail beneath the balconies is reminiscent of the Alhambra Palace in Spain. The calligraphy bands are verses from the Koran and praises to its patron builder.

Quwwat-ul-Islam Mosque The Quwwat-ul-Islam Mosque (The Might of Islam Mosque), the earliest surviving mosque in India, is to the northwest of the Qutb Minar. It was begun in 1192, immediately after Qutb-ud-din's conquest of Delhi and completed in 1198, using the remains of no fewer than 27 local Hindu and Jain temples.

The architectural style contained elements that Muslims brought from Arabia, including buildings made of mud and brick and decorated with glazed tiles, *squinches* (arches set diagonally across the corners of a square chamber to facilitate the raising of a dome and to effect a transition from a square to a round structure), the pointed arch and the true dome. Finally, Muslim buildings came alive through ornamental calligraphy and geometric patterning. This was in marked contrast to indigenous Indian styles of architecture. Hindu, Buddhist and Jain buildings relied on the post-and-beam system in which spaces were traversed by corbelling, ie shaping flat-laid stones to create an arch. The arched screen that runs along the western end of the courtyard beautifully illustrates the fact that it was Hindu methods that still prevailed at this stage, for the 16-m-high arch uses Indian corbelling, the corners being smoothed off to form the curved line.

Screens Qutb-ud-din's screen formed the façade of the mosque and, facing in the direction of Mecca, became the focal point. The sandstone screen is carved in the Indo-Islamic style, lotuses mingling with Koranic calligraphy. The later screenwork and other extensions (1230) are fundamentally Islamic in style, the flowers and leaves having been replaced by more arabesque patterns. Indian builders mainly used stone, which from the fourth century AD had been intricately carved with representations of the gods. In their first buildings in India the Muslim architects designed the buildings and local Indian craftsmen built them and decorated them with typical motifs such as the vase and foliage, tasselled ropes, bells and cows.

Iltutmish's extension The mosque was enlarged twice. In 1230 Qutb-ud-din's son-in-law and successor, Shamsuddin Iltutmish, doubled its size by extending the colonnades and prayer hall – 'Iltutmish's extension'. This accommodated a larger congregation, and in the more stable conditions of Iltutmish's reign, Islam was obviously gaining ground. The arches of the extension are nearer to the true arch and are similar to the Gothic arch that appeared in Europe at this time. The decoration is Islamic. Almost 100 years after Iltutmish's death, the mosque was enlarged again, by Ala-ud-din Khalji. The conductor of tireless and bloody military campaigns, Ala-ud-din proclaimed himself 'God's representative on earth'. His architectural ambitions, however, were not fully realized, because on his death in 1316 only part of the north and east extensions were completed.

Ala'i Minar and the Ala'i Darwaza To the north of the Qutb complex is the 26-m **Ala'i Minar**, intended to surpass the tower of the Qutb, but not completed beyond the first storey. Ala-ud-din did complete the south gateway to the building, the **Ala'i Darwaza**; inscriptions testify that it was built in 1311 (Muslim 710 AH). He benefited from events in Central Asia: since the early 13th century, Mongol hordes from Central Asia fanned out east and west, destroying the civilization of the Seljuk Turks in West Asia, and refugee artists, architects, craftsmen and poets fled east. They brought to India features and techniques that had developed in Byzantine Turkey, some of which can be seen in the Ala'i Darwaza.

Iltutmish's Tomb Built in 1235, Iltutmish's Tomb lies in the northwest of the compound, midway along the west wall of the mosque. It is the first surviving tomb of a Muslim ruler in India. Two other tombs also stand within the extended Might of Islam Mosque. The idea of a tomb was quite alien to Hindus, who had been practising cremation since around 400 BC. Blending Hindu and Muslim styles, the outside is relatively plain with three arched and decorated doorways. The interior carries reminders of the nomadic origins of the first Muslim rulers. Like a Central Asian *yurt* (tent) in its decoration, it combines the familiar Indian motifs of the wheel, bell, chain and lotus with the equally familiar geometric arabesque patterning. The west wall is inset with three *mihrabs* that indicate the direction of Mecca.

Tughluqabad

① *Sunrise to sunset, foreigners Rs100, Indians Rs 5, video camera Rs 25, allow 1 hr for return rickshaws, turn right at entrance and walk 200 m. The site is often deserted so don't go alone. Take plenty of water.*

Tughluqabad's ruins, 7.5 km east from Qutb Minar, still convey a sense of the power and energy of the newly arrived Muslims in India. From the walls you get a magnificent impression of the strategic advantages of the site. **Ghiyas'ud-Din Tughluq** (ruled 1321-1325), after ascending the throne of Delhi, selected this site for his capital. He built a massive fort around his capital city which stands high on a rocky outcrop of the Delhi Ridge. The fort is roughly octagonal in plan with a circumference of 6.5 km. The vast size, strength and obvious solidity of the whole give it an air of massive grandeur. It was not until Babur (ruled 1526-1530) that dynamite was used in warfare, so this is a very defensible site.

East of the main entrance is the rectangular **citadel**. A wider area immediately to the west and bounded by walls contained the **palaces**. Beyond this to the north lay the **city**. Now marked by the ruins of houses, the streets were laid out in a grid fashion. Inside the citadel enclosure is the **Vijay Mandal tower** and the remains of several halls including a long underground passage. The fort also contained seven tanks.

A causeway connects the fort with the tomb of Ghiyas'ud-Din Tughluq, while a wide embankment near its southeast corner gave access to the fortresses of **Adilabad** about 1 km away, built a little later by Ghiyas'ud-Din's son Muhammad. The tomb is very well preserved and has red sandstone walls with a pronounced slope (the first Muslim building in India to have sloping walls), crowned with a white marble dome. This dome, like that of the Ala'i Darwaza at the Qutb, is crowned by an *amalaka*, a feature of Hindu architecture. Also Hindu is the trabeate arch at the tomb's fortress wall entrance. Inside are three cenotaphs belonging to Ghiyas'ud-Din, his wife and son Muhammad.

Ghiyas'ud-Din Tughluq quickly found that military victories were no guarantee of lengthy rule. When he returned home after a victorious campaign the welcoming pavilion erected by his son and successor, Muhammad-bin Tughluq, was deliberately collapsed over him. Tughluqabad was abandoned shortly afterwards and was thus only inhabited for five years. The Tughluq dynasty continued to hold Delhi until Timur sacked it and slaughtered its inhabitants. For a brief period Tughluq power shifted to Jaunpur near Varanasi, where the Tughluq architectural traditions were carried forward in some superb mosques.

Baha'i Temple (Lotus Temple)

① *1 Apr-30 Sep 0900-1900, 1 Oct-31 Mar Tue-Sun 0930-1730, free entry and parking, visitors welcome to attend services, at other times the temple is open for silent meditation and prayer. Audio-visual presentations in English are at 1100, 1200, 1400 and 1530, remove shoes before* entering. Bus 433 from the centre (Jantar Mantar) goes to Nehru Place, within walking distance (1.5 km) of the temple at Kalkaji, or take a taxi or auto-rickshaw.

Architecturally the Baha'i Temple is a remarkably striking building. Constructed in 1980-1981, it is built out of white marble and in the characteristic Baha'i temple shape of a lotus flower – 45 lotus petals form the walls – which internally creates a feeling of light and space (34 m high, 70 m in diameter). It is a simple design, brilliantly executed and very elegant in form. All Baha'i temples are nine-sided, symbolizing 'comprehensiveness, oneness and unity'. The Delhi Temple, which seats 1300, is surrounded by nine pools, an attractive feature also helping to keep the building cool. It is particularly attractive when flood-lit. Baha'i temples are "dedicated to the worship of God, for peoples of all races, religions or castes. Only the Holy Scriptures of the Baha'i Faith and earlier revelations are read or recited".

East of the Yamuna → For listings, see pages 49-62.

Designated as the site of the athletes' village for the 2010 Commonwealth Games, East Delhi has just one attraction to draw visitors across the Yamuna.

Swaminarayan Akshardham

ⓘ www.akshardham.com, Apr-Sep Tue-Sun 1000-1900, Oct-Mar Tue-Sun 0900-1800, temple free, Rs 170 for 'attractions', musical fountain Rs 20, no backpacks, cameras or other electronic items (bag and body searches at entry gate). Packed on Sun; visit early to avoid crowds.

Opened in November 2005 on the east bank of the Yamuna, the gleaming Akshardham complex represents perhaps the most ambitious construction project in India since the foundation of New Delhi itself. At the centre of a surreal 40-ha 'cultural complex' complete with landscaped gardens, cafés and theme park rides, the temple-monument is dedicated to the 18th-century saint Bhagwan Swaminarayan, who abandoned his home at the age of 11 to embark on a lifelong quest for the spiritual and cultural uplift of Western India. It took 11,000 craftsmen, all volunteers, no less than 300 million hours to complete the temple using traditional building and carving techniques.

If this is the first religious site you visit in India, the security guards and swarms of mooching Indian tourists will hardly prepare you for the typical temple experience. Yet despite this, and the boat rides and animatronic shows which have prompted inevitable comparisons to a 'spiritual Disneyland', most visitors find the Akshardham an inspiring, indeed uplifting, experience, if for no other reason than that the will and ability to build something of its scale and complexity still exist.

The temple You enter the temple complex through a series of intricately carved gates. The Bhakti Dwar (Gate of Devotion), adorned with 208 pairs of gods and their consorts, leads into a hall introducing the life of Swaminarayan and the activities of BAPS (Bochasanwasi Shri Akshar Purushottam Swaminarayan Sanstha), the global Hindu sect-cum-charity which runs Akshardham. The main courtyard is reached through the Mayur Dwar (Peacock Gate), a conglomeration of 869 carved peacocks echoed by an equally florid replica directly facing it.

From here you get your first look at the central monument. Perfectly symmetrical in pink sandstone and white marble, it rests on a plinth encircled by 148 elephants, each sculpted from a 20-tonne stone block, in situations ranging from the literal to the mythological: mortal versions grapple with lions or lug tree trunks, while Airavatha, the eight-trunked mount of Lord Indra, surfs majestically to shore after the churning of the oceans at the dawn of Hindu creation. Above them, carvings of deities, saints and *sadhus* cover every inch of the walls and columns framing the inner sanctum, where a gold-plated *murti* (idol) of Bhagwan Swaminarayan sits attended by avatars of his spiritual successors, beneath a staggeringly intricate marble dome. Around the main dome are eight smaller domes, each carved in hypnotic fractal patterns, while paintings depicting Swaminarayan's life of austerity and service line the walls (explanations in English and Hindi).

Surrounding the temple is a moat of holy water supposedly taken from 151 sacred lakes and rivers visited by Swaminarayan on his seven-year barefoot pilgrimage. 108 bronze *gaumukhs* (cow heads) representing the 108 names of God spout water into the tank, which is itself hemmed in by a 1-km-long *parikrama* (colonnade) of red Rajasthani sandstone.

Delhi listings

For hotel and restaurant price codes and other relevant information, see pages 12-15.

🛏 Where to stay

Avoid hotel touts. Airport taxis may pretend not to know the location of your chosen hotel so give full details and insist on being taken there. Around Paharganj particularly, you might be followed around by your driver trying to eek a commission out of the guesthouse once you have checked in. It really saves a lot of hassle if you make reservations. Even if you change hotel the next day, it is good to arrive with somewhere booked especially if you are flying in late at night. Hotel prices in Delhi are significantly higher than in most other parts of the country. Smaller **$$** guesthouses away from the centre in **South Delhi** (eg Kailash, Safdarjang) or in **Sunder Nagar**, are quieter and often good value but may not provide food. **$** accommodation is concentrated around **Janpath** and **Paharganj** (New Delhi), and **Chandni Chowk** (Old Delhi) – well patronized but basic and usually cramped yet good for meeting other backpackers. Signs in some hotels warn against taking drugs as this is becoming a serious cause for concern. Police raids are frequent.

Old Delhi and beyond *p30, map p32*
$$$$ Maidens, 7 Sham Nath Marg, T011-2397 5464, www.maidenshotel.com. 54 large well-appointed rooms, restaurant (slow), barbecue nights are excellent, coffee shop, old-style bar, attractive colonial style in quiet area, spacious gardens with excellent pool, friendly welcome, personal attention. One of Delhi's oldest hotels. Recommended.
$$$ Broadway, 4/15A Asaf Ali Rd, T011-4366 3600, www.hotelbroadwaydelhi.com. 36 rooms, some wonderfully quirky. Interior designer Catherine Levy has designed some of the rooms in a quirky kitsch style, brightly coloured with psychedelic bathroom tiles. The other rooms are classic design. **Chor Bizarre** restaurant and bar is highly regarded, as is the 'Thugs' pub. Walking tours of Old Delhi. Easily one of the best options.

New Delhi *p36, maps p38 and p41*
Connaught Place
$$$$ Imperial, Janpath, T011-2334 1234, www.theimperialindia.com. Quintessential Delhi. 230 rooms and beautiful 'deco suites' in supremely elegant Lutyens-designed 1933 hotel. Unparalleled location, great bar, antiques and art everywhere, beautiful gardens with spa and secluded pool, amazing **Spice Route** restaurant. Highly recommended.
$$$ Hotel Corus, B-49 Connaught Pl, T011-4365 2222, www.hotelcorus.com. Comfortable hotel right at the heart of things. Good value rooms. You get 15% discount in their onsite **Life Caffe**.
$$$ Palace Heights, D26-28 Connaught Pl, T011-4358 2610, www.hotelpalace heights.com. Recently given a complete

facelift, the bright, modern rooms with good attention to detail, represent the best choice in Connaught Pl in this price bracket. There's also an attractive glass-walled restaurant overlooking the street.
$ Asian Guest House, 14 Scindia House, off Kasturba Gandhi Marg, the sign is hidden behind petrol pump, T011-2331 0229, www.asianguesthouse.com. Friendly faces greet you here, although it's a tricky to find – call ahead for directions. Great central location. Clean basic rooms, some with a/c, some with TV.

Paharganj
Parharganj is where backpackers congregate. Sandwiched between the main sights and near the main railway station, it's noisy, dirty and a lot of hassle.
$$$$-$$$ Jyoti Mahal, 2488 Nalwa St, behind Imperial Cinema, T011-2358 0524, www.jyotimahal.net. An oasis in Paharganj with large and atmospheric rooms in a beautiful converted *haveli* and new deluxe rooms in stylish new wing. Top-notch rooftop restaurant serving continental and Indian dishes. It's a very atmospheric place to dine. Nice boutique Pink Safari too. Highly recommended.
$$ Prince Polonia, 2325-26 Tilak Gali (behind Imperial Cinema), T011-4762 6600, www.hotelprincepolonia.com. Very unusual for Paharganj in that it has a rooftop pool (small, but good for a cool down). Breezy rooftop café. Attracts a slightly more mature crowd. Safe, clean. Recently refurbished.
$ Rak International. 820 Main Bazar, Chowk Bowli, T011-2358 6508, www.hotelrak international.com. 27 basic but clean rooms. Professionally run. Quiet, friendly hotel with a rooftop restaurant and water feature.

Karol Bagh and Rajendra Nagar
$$$-$$ Master Guest House, R-500 New Rajendra Nagar (Shankar Rd and GR Hospital Rd crossing), T011-2874 1089, www.master bedandbreakfast.com. 3 beautiful rooms, a/c, Wi-Fi, rooftop for breakfast, *thalis*,

warm welcome, personal attention, secure, recommended. Each room has the theme of a different god, complete with appropriate colour schemes. Very knowledgeable, caring owners run excellent tours of 'hidden Delhi'. They make Delhi feel like home. Recommended.

South Delhi *p43*
Most of the city's smartest hotels are located south of Rajpath, in a broad rectangle between Chanakyapuri and Humayun's Tomb.
$$$$ Claridges, 12 Aurangzeb Rd, T011-3955 5000, www.claridges.com. 138 refurbished, classy rooms, art deco-style interiors, colonial atmosphere, attractive restaurants (Jade Garden is good), slick Aura bar, impeccable service, more atmosphere than most. Recommended.
$$$$ Manor, 77 Friends Colony, T011-2692 5151, www.themanordelhi.com. Contemporary boutique hotel with 10 stylish rooms, heavenly beds, polished stone surfaces and chrome, relaxing garden, a haven. Beautiful artwork and relaxed vibe. Acclaimed restaurant Indian Accent. Charming service.
$$$$ Oberoi, Dr Zakir Hussain Marg, T011-2436 3030, www.oberoihotels.com. 300 rooms and extremely luxurious suites overlooking golf club, immaculate, quietly efficient, beautiful touches, carved Tree of Life in lobby, all 5-star facilities including 2 pools and spa, superb business centre, good restaurants – 360° gets rave reviews.
$$$$ Taj Mahal, 1 Mansingh Rd, T011-2302 6162, www.tajhotels.com. 1 of 3 Taj hotels in Delhi. 300 attractive rooms, comfortable, new club levels outstanding, excellent restaurants and service, lavishly finished with 'lived-in' feel, friendly 1920s-style bar. There is also a Vivanta by Taj hotel close to Khan Market with a more business mood.
$$$$-$$$ Amarya Haveli, P5 Hauz Khas Enclave, T011-4175 9268, www.amarya group.com. Luxury, boutique, hip guesthouse, run by 2 Frenchmen. Unique, bright, en suite rooms, with TV, Wi-Fi.

Fantastic roof garden. Great home cooked food. Book ahead. They have a sister property **Amarya Villa** in Safdarjung Enclave – the decor there is inspired by *Navratna* (nine gems) – both properties are effortlessly chic. Highly recommended.

$$$ K One One, K11, Jangpura Extn, 2nd floor, T011-4359 2583, www.pari gold.com. Homely guesthouse in quiet, central residential area. Run by wonderful ex-TV chef, who also gives cooking lessons. All rooms en suite with a/c, minibar, Wi-Fi, some with balconies. Wonderful roof terrace with views of Humayan's Tomb. Rooftop room is lovely. Book ahead.

$$$ Lutyens Bungalow, 39 Prithviraj Rd, T011-2469 4523, www.lutyensbungalow. co.in. Private guesthouse in a bungalow that has been running for over 35 years – it's looking a little faded around the edges. Eccentric, rambling property with 15 a/c rooms, a wonderful pool and beautiful gardens with a garden accessory shop on-site. Free airport pickup/drop off, full services, used for long-stays by NGOs and foreign consultants.

$$$-$$ Tree of Life B&B, D-193, Saket, T(0)9810-277699, www.tree-of-life.in. Stylish B&B with beautifully decorated rooms, simple but chic. Kitchen access, excellent on-site reflexology and yoga – really good atmosphere. The owner also runs **Metropole Tourist Service** (page 61). Close to Saket Metro station and to **PVR** cinema and malls.

$$ Life Tree, G 14 Lajpat Nagar Part II, T(0)9910-460898, lifetreebnb@gmail.com. A more simple but charming B&B from the **Tree of Life** family – well located for Khan Market and centre.

$ Youth Hostel, 5 Naya Marg, Chanakyapuri, T011-2611 6285, www.yhaindia.org. Wide range of room from a/c doubles to a basic dorm (a/c dorms much better). Meals available at restaurant if ordered in advance. Soulless but clean and comfortable. Great location. You need YHA membership to stay (Rs 250 foreigners, Rs 100 Indians).

Airport

Unless you can afford a 5-star, hotels around the airport are overpriced and best avoided.

$$$-$$ Sam's Snooze at My Space T3 IGI Airport, opposite Gate 17, T(0)8800-230013, www.newdelhiairport.in. You can book a snooze pod for $9 per hr – only if you are flying out of T3. There's Wi-Fi, TV and DVD, work stations.

? Restaurants

The larger hotel restaurants are often the best for cuisine, decor and ambience. Buffets (lunch or dinner) cost Rs 700 or more. Sun buffets are becoming quite the thing in the top-notch hotels. Others may only open around 1930 for dinner; some close on Sun. Alcohol is served in most top hotels, but only in some

non-hotel restaurants eg Amber, Ginza and Kwality.

The old-fashioned 'tea on the lawn' is still served at the Imperial and in Claridges (see Where to stay, pages 49 and 50). Aapki Pasand, at 15 Netaji Subhash Marg, offers unusual tea-tasting in classy and extremely professional surroundings; it's quite an experience.

Old Delhi *p30, map p32*

In Paranthewali Gali, a side street off Chandni Chowk, stalls sell a variety of *paranthas* including *kaju badam* (stuffed with dry fruits and nuts). Other good places to try local foods like *bedmi aloo puri* with spiced potato are Mahalaxmi Misthan Bhandhar at 659 Church Mission St and Natraj Chowk 1396 Chandni Chowk for *dahi balli* and *aloo tikki*. For sweets you have to seek out Old Famous Jalebi Wala, 1797 Dariba Corner, Chandni Chowk – as they are old and famous.

$$$-$$ Chor Bizarre, Broadway Hotel (see Where to stay, page 49), T011-4366 3600. Tandoori and Kashmiri cuisine (Wazwan, Rs 500). Fantastic food, quirky decor, including salad bar that was a vintage car. Well worth a visit.

$ Haldiram's, 1454/2 Chandni Chowk. Stand-up counter for excellent snacks and sweets on the run (try *dokhla* with coriander chutney from seller just outside), and more elaborate sit-down restaurant upstairs.

$ Karim's, Gali Kababiyan (south of Jama Masjid), Mughlai. Authentic, busy, plenty of local colour. The experience, as much as the food, makes this a must. Not a lot to tempt vegetarians though.

New Delhi *p36, maps p38 and p41*
Connaught Place and around

$$$ Sevilla, Claridges Hotel (see Where to stay, page 50). Beautiful restaurant with lots of outdoor seating serving up specialities like tapas and paella as well as wood fired pizza and the dangerous house special sangria.

$$$ Spice Route, Imperial Hotel (see Where to stay, page 49). Award-winning restaurant charting the journey of spices around the world. Extraordinary temple-like surroundings (took 7 years to build), Kerala, Thai, Vietnamese cuisines, magical atmosphere but food doesn't always thrill.

$$$ Veda, 27-H, T011-4151 3535, www. vedarestaurants.com. Owned by fashion designer Rohit Bal with appropriately beautiful bordello-style decor, done out like a Rajasthani palace with high-backed leather chairs and candles reflecting from mirror work on ceilings. Food is contemporary Indian. Great atmosphere at night. There is another branch at DLF Vasant Kunj.

$$$-$$ Life Caffe, Hotel Corus (see Where to stay, page 49), B49 Connaught Pl, T011-4365 2240. Tranquil garden, imaginative, good-value food. Perfect for when you want to escape the noise of CP.

$$ Embassy, D-11, T011-2341 6434. International food. Popular with artistic-intellectual-political crowd, good food, long-standing local favourite.

$$ United Coffee House, E-15 Connaught Pl, T011-2341 1697. Recommended more for the colonial-era cake-icing decor than for the fairly average food. Often someone waxing lyrical over a Casio keyboard. Always attracts a mixed crowd, well worth a visit.

$ Nathu's, and **Bengali Sweet House**, both in Bengali Market (east of Connaught Pl). Sweet shops also serving vegetarian food. Good dosa, *iddli*, *utthapam* and North Indian *chana bathura*, *thalis*, clean, functional. Try *kulfi* (hard blocks of ice cream) with *falooda* (sweet vermicelli noodles).

$ Nizam's Kathi Kebabs, H-5 Plaza, T011-2371 3078. Very good, tasty filled *parathas*, good value, clean, excellent '3-D toilets' (note the emergency button!).

$ Saravana Bhavan, P-15/90, near McDonalds, T011-2334 7755; also at 46 Janpath. Chennai-based chain, light and wonderful South Indian, superb chutneys, unmissable *kaju anjeer* ice cream with figs and nuts. Can take hours to get a table at night or at weekends. Highly recommended.

$ Triveni Tea Terrace, Triveni Kala Sangam, 205 Tansen Marg, near Mandi House Metro station (not Sun). Art galleries, an amphitheatre and this little café in quite an unusual building close to CP – the tea terrace is a bit of an institution.

Paharganj
The rooftop restaurants at **Jyoti Mahal** and **Shelton** are great locations for a bite to eat.
$$-$ Café Sim Tok, Tooti Chowk, above Hotel Navrang, near **Hotel Rak**, T(0)9810-386717. Tucked away little gem of a Korean restaurant. No signage, ask for **Hotel Navrang** and keep going up stairs to find delicious *kimbab* (Korean sushi), *kimchi* and all sorts of soups, in a sweet little café.
$ Tadka, off Main Bazar. Good option for tasty food in this area. Great range of all the usual Indian favourites, with nice decor, friendly staff and good hygiene levels.

South Delhi *p43*
$$$ Baci, 23 Sunder Nagar Market, near HDFC Bank, T011-4150 7445. Classy, top-quality Italian food, run by gregarious Italian-Indian owners. There are also branches of her cheaper café **Amici** springing up in Khan Market and Hauz Khas.
$$$ Bukhara, ITC Maurya Sheraton, Sardar Patel Marg, T011-2611 2233. Stylish Northwest Frontier cuisine amidst rugged walls draped with rich rugs (but uncomfortable seating). Outstanding meat dishes and dhal. Also tasty vegetable and *paneer* dishes, but vegetarians will miss out on the best food.
$$$ Dum Pukht, ITC Maurya Sheraton, Sardar Patel Marg, T011-2611 2233, www.itcwelcomgroup.com. Open evenings; lunch only on Sun. Voted one of the best restaurants in the world, it marries exquisite tastes and opulent surroundings.
$$$ Grey Garden, 13a Hauz Khaz Village, near the lake, T011-2651 6450. New kid on the block in the lovely Hauz Khaz village, this boho

chic little number serves up a small menu but with great attention to detail. Delicious banana-wrapped fish or thin-crust pizzas, lotus stem chips and other assorted goodies. Book ahead at weekends. Highly recommended.
$$$ Indian Accent, at The Manor, 77 Friends Colony West, T011-4323 5151. With a menu designed by Manish Mehotra, who runs restaurants in Delhi and London, this acclaimed restaurant offers up Indian food with a modern twist. Your *dosas* will reveal masala morel mushrooms, rather than the traditional Goan prawns *balchao* here you will find it with roasted scallops. Or how about toffee *chyawanprash* cheesecake with badam milk (*chyawanprash* is a health elixir from the amla fruit)? The menu reflects the changing of the seasons and there is live fusion music on Sat. Highly recommended.
$$$ Kainoosh, 122-124 DLF Promenade Mall, Vasant Kunj, T(0)9560-715544. Under the watchful eye of celebrity chef Marut Sikka, delicious *thalis* marry the traditional and modern faces of Indian food. This is *thali* with a difference – bespoke with giant morel mushrooms, sea bass mousse and chicken cooked in orange juice and saffron in a terracotta pot.
$$$ Latitude, 9 Khan Market, above Good Earth, T011-2462 1013. Like sitting in someone's very posh, very chic living room and getting served delicious Italian numbers like bruschetta, yummy salads and pastas. Topped off with top-notch coffees.
$$$ Lodi, Lodi Gardens, T011-2465 5054. Continental lunch, Indian dinner menu in pleasant, Mediterranean-style surroundings, nice terrace and garden. Come more for the setting than the food which can be mediocre.
$$$ Magique, Gate No 3, Garden of 5 Senses, Mehrauli Badarpur Rd, T97175-35533. High-class quality food, in a magical setting. Sit outside among the candles and fairy lights. One of Delhi's most romantic restaurants.
$$$ Olive at the Qutb, T011-2957 4444, www.olivebarand kitchen.com. Branch of

the ever popular Mumbai restaurant and some people say the Delhi version wins hands down. Serving up delicious platters of Mediterranean food and good strong cocktails. Or head to their sister restaurant in the Diplomat Hotel – Olive Beach especially for their legendary blow-out Sun brunches: for Rs 2195 you get open access to a mind-boggling buffet and as many martini's as you can drink.

$$$ Park Baluchi, inside Deer Park, Hauz Khas Village, T011-2685 9369. Atmospheric dining in Hauz Khas Deer Park. The lamb wrapped in chicken served on a flaming sword comes highly recommended. Can get crowded, book ahead.

$$ Elma's, 24/1 Hauz Khas Village, T011-2652 1020. Lovely little cafe serving up all manner of tea and cakes and more hearty options like shepherds pie! Mismatched china and funky furniture make this a great little hang-out. Also check out their little brother **Edwards** downstairs offering more posh deli-style food.

$$ Naivedyam, Hauz Khas Village, T011-2696 0426. Very good South Indian, great service and very good value in a very beautiful restaurant. Highly recommended.

$$ Oh! Calcutta, E-Block, ground floor, International Trade Towers, Nehru Pl, T011-2646 4180. Authentic Bengali cuisine, with excellent vegetarian and fish options, somewhat odd location but not far from the Baha'i temple.

$ Khan Cha Cha, Khan Market, 75 Middle Lane. This no-frills joint serves some of the best kebabs in the city from a window in the middle lane of Khan Market. Fantastic value. You can recognize the place from the crowd clamouring at the counter.

$ Sagar Ratna, 18 Defence Colony Market, T011-2433 3110. Other branches in Vasant Kunj, Malviya Nagar and NOIDA. Excellent South Indian. Cheap and "amazing" thalis and coffee, very hectic (frequent queues). One of the best breakfasts in Delhi.

🎧 Bars and clubs

Many national holidays are 'dry' days. Delhi's bar/club scene has exploded over the last few years. Expect to pay a lot for your drinks and, when in doubt, dress up; some clubs have strict dress codes. Delhi's 'in' crowd is notoriously fickle; city magazines (Time Out, First City) will point you towards the flavour of the month. For more insight into Delhi check out the website www.bringhomestories.com.

New Delhi p36, maps p38 and p41
Connaught Place
1911, Imperial Hotel (see Where to stay). Elegantly styled colonial bar, good snacks.

South Delhi p43
24/7, Lalit Hotel, Barakhamba Av, Connaught Pl. Boasting molecular mixology with their cocktails and regular turns by prominent DJs and more alternative acts, 24/7 is putting itself in the scene.

Blue Frog, near Qutb Minar, www.blue frog.co.in. For years, **Blue Frog** has been the best venue in Mumbai with supreme live acts and star DJs doing a turn and now it's coming to Delhi.

Café Morrisons, Shop E-12, South Extension Part II, T011-2625 5652. Very popular rock bar. Come for live bands or to mosh to the DJ.

The Living Room, 31 Haus Khaz, T011-4608 0533, www.tlrcafe.com. Recently done-up, this place has a funky laid-back atmosphere day and night over 3 floors. By day there's cosy armchairs and sofas. By night, things kick up a gear with live music, open mics and DJs spinning electronica and dubstep, and all manner of themed nights. Recommended.

Rick's, Taj Mahal Hotel, 1 Mansingh Rd, T011-2302 6162, www.tajhotels.com. Suave Casablanca-themed bar with long martini list, a long-time fixture on Delhi's social scene.

Shalom, 'N' Block Market, Greater Kailash 1, T011-4163 2280. Comfortable, stylish lounge bar serving Lebanese cuisine; the resident DJ plays ambient music.

Urban Pind, N4, N-block market, GK1, T011-3951 5656. Multi-level bar, with large roof terrace, popular. Hosts a controversial expat/journalist night on Thu with an 'all-you-can-drink' entry fee, unsurprisingly this normally features a lot of drunk foreigners.

Zoo, at Magique (see Restaurants, page 53), one of the latest and most popular places on the scene serving up big portions of beats in a beautiful location.

🎭 Entertainment

Delhi *p26, maps p32, p38 and p41*
For advance notice of upcoming events see www.delhievents.com. Current listings and reviews can be found in *First City* (monthly, Rs 50), *Time Out* (fortnightly, Rs 50), *Delhi City Info* (fortnightly, free) and *Delhi Diary* (weekly). For programmes see cinema listings in the daily *Delhi Times*. Also check out www.bringhomestories.com for inspiration on what to do in Delhi.

Music, dance and culture

Goethe Institute, 3 Kasturba Gandhi Marg, T011-2332 9506. Recommended for arts, film festivals, open-air cinema, plays and events.
India Habitat Centre, Lodi Rd, T011-2468 2222. Good programme of lectures, films, exhibitions, concerts, excellent restaurant.
Indian International Centre, 40 Lodhi Estate, Max Mueller Marg, T011-2461 9431, www.iicdelhi.nic.in. Some fantastic debates and performances, well worth checking the 'forthcoming programmes' section of their website.
Kingdom of Dreams, Great Indian Nautanki Company Ltd. Auditorium Complex, Sector 29, Gurgaon, Metro IFFCO, T0124-452 8000, www.kingdomofdreams.in. Ticket prices Rs 750-3000 depending on where you sit and more pricey at the weekend. The highlight is a much acclaimed all-singing, all-dancing Bollywood style performance. A little like an Indian Disneyland showcasing Indian tastes, foods, culture, dress and dance all in one a/c capsule, but done impeccably.
Triveni Kala Sangam, 205 Tansen Marg (near Mandi House Metro station), T011-2371 8833. Strong programme of photography and art exhibitions, plus an excellent North Indian café.

Son et lumière

Red Fort (see page 30), Apr-Nov 1800-1900 (Hindi), 1930-2030 (English). Entry Rs 50. Tickets available after 1700. Take mosquito cream.

🎊 Festivals

Delhi *p26, maps p32, p38 and p41*
For exact dates consult the weekly *Delhi Diary* available at hotels and many shops and offices around town.

Muslim festivals of **Ramadan**, **Id-ul-Fitr**, **Id-ul-Zuha** and **Muharram** are celebrated according to the lunar calendar.

January

26 Jan Republic Day Parade, Rajpath. A spectacular fly-past and military march-past, with colourful pageants and tableaux from every state, dances and music. Tickets through travel agents and most hotels, Rs 100. You can see the full dress preview free, usually 2 days before; week-long celebrations during which government buildings are illuminated.
29 Jan Beating the Retreat, Vijay Chowk, a stirring display by the armed forces' bands marks the end of the Republic Day celebrations.
30 Jan Martyr's Day, Marks the anniversary of Mahatma Gandhi's death; devotional *bhajans* and Guard of Honour at Raj Ghat.
Kite Flying Festival, Makar Sankranti above Palika Bazar, Connaught Pl.

February

2 Feb Vasant Panchami, celebrates the 1st day of spring. The Mughal Gardens are opened to the public for a month.

Thyagaraja Festival, South Indian music and dance, Vaikunthnath Temple.

April
Amir Khusrau's Birth Anniversary, a fair in Nizamuddin celebrates this with prayers and *qawwali* singing.

August
Janmashtami, celebrates the birth of the Hindu god Krishna. Special *puja*, Lakshmi Narayan Mandir.
15 Aug **Independence Day**, Impressive flag-hoisting ceremony and prime ministerial address at the Red Fort.

October-November
2 Oct **Gandhi Jayanti**, Mahatma Gandhi's birthday; devotional singing at Raj Ghat.
Dasara, with over 200 Ramlila performances all over the city recounting the *Ramayana* story.
Ramlila Ballet, the ballet, which takes place at Delhi Gate (south of Red Fort) and Ramlila Ground, is performed for a month and is most spectacular. Huge effigies of Ravana are burnt on the 9th night; noisy and flamboyant.
Diwali, the festival of lights; lighting of earthen lamps, candles and firework displays.
National Drama Festival, Rabindra Bhavan.
Oct/Nov **Dastkar Nature Bazaar**, working with over 25,000 crafts people from across India, **Dastkar's** main objective is to empower rural artisans and keep alive the traditional crafts of India. They hold many events each year, but this is the pinnacle. Knowing that shopping here will bring a difference to the lives of rural people.

December
25 Dec **Christmas**. Special Christmas Eve entertainments at major hotels and restaurants; midnight mass and services at all churches.

⊙ Shopping

Delhi *p26, maps p32, p38 and p41*
There are several state emporia around Delhi including the Cottage Industries Emporium (CIE), a huge department store of Indian handicrafts, and those along Baba Kharak Singh Marg (representing crafts from most states of India). In this stretch, there are several places selling products from women's collectives or rural artisans, like **Mother Earth** and Hansiba). Shops generally open 1000-1930 (winter 1000-1900). Food stores and chemists stay open later. Most shopping areas are closed on Sun.

Art galleries
Galleries exhibiting contemporary art are listed in *First City*.
Delhi Art Gallery, Hauz Khas Village. A newly expanded gallery with a good range of moderately priced contemporary art.
Nature Morte, A-1 Neethi Bagh, near Kamla Nehru College, www.naturemorte. com. With a twin gallery in Berlin, you can expect the most profound and inspiring of contemporary art here.
Photo Ink, Hyundai MGF building, 1 Jhandewalan Faiz Rd, www.photoink.net. Close to Paharganj, this gallery offers up top notch contemporary photography.

Books and music
Serious bibliophiles should head to the Sun book market in Daryaganj, Old Delhi, when 2 km of pavement are piled high with books – some fantastic bargains to be had.
Central News Agency, P 23/90, Connaught Pl. Carries national and foreign newspapers and journals.
Full Circle, 5 B, Khan Market, T011-2465 5641. Helpful knowledgeable staff. Sweet café upstairs for a quick drink – food is hit and miss though.
Kabaadi Bazaar, Netaji Subhash Marg, Old Delhi. Sun market with thousands of very cheap used books, great for browsing.

Manohar, 4753/23 Ansar Rd, Daryaganj, Old Delhi. A real treasure trove for books on South Asia and India especially, most helpful, knowledgeable staff. Highly recommended.
Munshiram Manoharlal, Nai Sarak, Chandni Chowk. Books on Indology.
New Book Depot, 18B, Connaught Pl. Highly recommended.
Rikhi Ram, G Block Connaught Circus, T011-2332 7685. This is the place to come if you've wondered about how easy it is to learn to play and travel with a sitar. Has a range of guitars and other stringed instruments too.

Carpets
Carpets can be found in shops in most top hotels and a number round Connaught Pl, not necessarily fixed price. If you are visiting Agra, check out the prices here first.

Clothing
For designer wear, try **Ogaan** and for more contemporary, less budget blowing try **Grey Garden** both in **Hauz Khas Village**, **Sunder Nagar Market** near the Oberoi hotel, or the Crescent arcade near the Qutab Minar.

For inexpensive (Western and Indian) clothes, try shops along Janpath and between Sansad Marg and Janpath; you can bargain down 50%.

The **Central Cottage Industries Emporium** (see below) has a good selection of clothing and fabrics. The **Khadi shop** (see Emporia, below) has Indian-style clothing. **Fab India**, 14N-Gt Kailash I (also in B-Block Connaught Pl, Khan Market and Vasant Kunj). Excellent shirts, Nehru jackets, *salwar kameez*, linen, furnishing fabrics and furniture. The most comprehensive collection is in N block.

Earthenware
Unglazed earthenware *khumba matkas* (water pots) are sold round New Delhi Railway Station (workshops behind main road).

Emporia
Most open 1000-1800 (close 1330-1400).
Central Cottage Industries Emporium, corner of Janpath and Tolstoy Marg. Offers hassle-free shopping, gift wrapping, will pack and post overseas; best if you are short of time.
Dilli Haat, opposite INA Market. Rs 15, open 1100-2200. Well-designed open-air complex with rows of brick alcoves for craft stalls from different states; local craftsmen's outlets (bargaining obligatory), occasional fairs (tribal art, textiles, etc). Also good regional food – hygienic, safe, weighted towards non-vegetarian. Pleasant, quiet, clean (no smoking) and uncrowded, not too much hassle.
Khadi Gramodyog Bhawan, near the Regal building, Baba Kharak Singh Marg. For inexpensive homespun cotton *kurta pajama* (loose shirt and trousers), cotton/silk waistcoats, fabrics and Jaipuri paintings.
Khazana, Taj Mahal and Taj Palace hotels (daily 0900-2000). High class.

Jewellery
Traditional silver and goldsmiths in Dariba Kalan, off Chandni Chowk (north of Jama Masjid). Cheap bangles and along Janpath; also at Hanuman Mandir, Gt Kailash I, N-Block. Also Sunder Nagar market. Bank St in Karol Bagh is recommended for gold.
Amrapali, Khan Market has an exceptional collection from affordable to mind-blowing.
Ashish Nahar, 1999 Naughara St, Kinari Bazaar, Chandni Chowk, T011-2327 2801. On quite possibly the prettiest street in Delhi, full of brightly painted and slowly crumbling *havelis*, you will find a little gem of a jewellery shop.

Markets and malls
Beware of pickpockets in markets and malls.
Hauz Khas village, South Delhi. Authentic, old village houses converted into designer shops selling handicrafts, ceramics, antiques and furniture in addition to luxury wear. Many are expensive, but some are good value. A

good place to pick up old Hindi film posters with many art galleries and restaurants.

Khan Market, South Delhi. Great bookshops, cafés, restaurants and boutiques. Full of expats so expect expat prices.

Sarojini Nagar, South Delhi. Daily necessities as well as cheap fabric and clothing. Come for incredible bargains. This is where a lot of the Western brands dump their export surplus or end-of-line clothes. Haggle hard.

Select City Walk, Saket. An enormous, glitzy mall for the ultimate in upmarket shopping. Lots of chains, cinemas, etc.

Shahpur Jat, is a new up and coming shopping area, south of **South Extension**.

Tibetan Market, North Delhi. Stalls along Janpath have plenty of curios – most are new but rapidly aged to look authentic.

Souvenirs

Aap ki Pasand, opposite Golcha cinema, Netaji Subhash Marg, Old Delhi. Excellent place to taste and buy Indian teas.

Dastkari Haat, 39 Khan Market, www.indian craftsjourney.in. Charming selection of conscious crafts from around India working with rural artisans and women's collectives.

Gulabsingh Johrimal Perfumers, 467 Chandni Chowk, T011-2326 3743. Authentic *attars* (sandalwood based perfumes), perfumes and incense. High-quality oils are used.

Haldiram's, Chandni Chowk near Metro. Wide selection of sweet and salty snack foods.

Khazana India, 50A Hauz Khaz Village. Little treasure trove of Bollywood posters, old photographs and all sorts of interesting bric-a-brac.

People Tree, 8 Regal Building, Connaught Pl. Handmade clothing, mostly T-shirts with arty and people conscious slogans. Great posters made up of all those weird signs that you see around India and wide-range of ecological books. A real find.

Playclan, F51 Select Citywalk, Saket, www. the playclan.com. Fantastic shop selling all manner of clothes, notebooks, lighters and pictures with great colourful cartoon designs created by a collective of animators

and designers – giving a more animated view of India's gods, goddesses, gurus, Kathakali dancers and the faces of India.

Purple Jungle, 16 Hauz Khaz Village, T(0)9650-973039, www.purple-jungle.com. Offering up kitsch India with bollywood pictures and curious road signs refashioned onto bags, clothes, cushions, etc.

◎ What to do

Body and soul

The Yoga Studio, Hauz Khaz, www.the yogastudio.info. Regular yoga classes with Seema Sondhi, author of several yoga books, and her team

Integral Yoga, Sri Aurobindo Ashram, Aurobindo Marg, T011-2656 7863. Regular yoga classes (Tue-Thu and Sat 0645-0745 and 1700-1800) in *asana* (postures), *pranayama* (breathing techniques) and relaxation.

Laughter Club of Delhi, various locations, T011-2721 7164. Simple yogic breathing techniques combined with uproarious laughter. Clubs meet early morning in parks throughout the city.

Sari School, Jangpura Extension, near Lajpat Nagar, T011-4182 3297. Author of *Saris in India* Rta Christi Kapur holds classes every Sat in different styles of sporting a sari.

Tree of Life Reflexology, T(0)9810-356677. Reflexology with acclaimed teacher Suruchi. She also does private and group yoga classes on the roof and in the park.

Yogalife, Shapur Jat main market, T(0)9811-863332, www.yogalife.org. Closed Mon. Bright, friendly centre.

Tours and tour operators
Delhi Tourism tours

Departs from **Delhi Tourism**, Baba Kharak Singh Mg near State Govt Emporia, T011-2336 3607, www.delhitourism.nic.in. Book a day in advance. Check time.

Evening Tour (Tue-Sun 1830-2200): Rajpath, India Gate, Kotla Firoz Shah, Purana Qila, *son et lumière* (Red Fort). Rs 150.

New Delhi Tour (0900-1400): Jantar Mantar, Qutb Minar, Lakshmi Narayan Temple, Baha'i Temple (Safdarjang's Tomb on Mon only). **Old Delhi Tour** (1415-1715): Jama Masjid, Red Fort, Raj Ghat, Humayun's Tomb. Both Rs 100 plus entry fees.

ITDC Tours

Guides are generally good but tours are rushed, T011-2332 0331. Tickets booked from **Hotel Indraprastha**, T011-2334 4511.
New Delhi Tour: departs from L-1 Connaught Circus and **Hotel Indraprastha** (0800-1330), Rs 125 (a/c coach): Jantar Mantar, Lakshmi Narayan Temple, India Gate, Nehru Pavilion, Pragati Maidan (closed Mon), Humayun's Tomb, Qutb Minar.
Old Delhi Tour: departs **Hotel Indraprastha**. (1400-1700), Rs 100: Kotla Firoz Shah, Raj Ghat, Shantivana, Jama Masjid and Red Fort.

Taj Mahal tours

Many companies offer coach tours to Agra (eg **ITDC**, from L1 Connaught Circus, Sat-Thu 0630-2200, Rs 600, a/c coach). However, travelling by road is slow and uncomfortable; by car, allow at least 4 hrs each way. Train is a better option: either *Shatabdi* or *Taj Express*, but book early.

Walking tours

Chor Bizarre, Hotel Broadway, T011-2327 3821. Special walking tours of Old Delhi, with good lunch, 0930-1330, 1300-1630, Rs 350 each, Rs 400 for both.
Delhi Metro Walks, T(0)9811-330098, www. delhimetrowalks.com. With the charismatic Surekha Narain guiding your every step, informative heritage walks around Delhi.
Master Guest House (see Where to stay, page 50). Highly recommended walking tours for a more intimate experience.
Salaam Baalak Trust, T(0)9873-130383, www.salaambaalaktrust.com. NGO-run tours of New Delhi station and the streets around it, guided by Javed, himself a former street child. Your Rs 200 goes to support the charity's work with street children.

Tour operators

There are many operators offering tours, ticketing, reservations, etc, for travel across India. Many are around Connaught Circus, Parharganj, Rajendra Pl and Nehru Pl. Most belong to special associations (IATA, PATA) for complaints.
Ibex Expeditions, 30 Community Centre East of Kailash, New Delhi, T011-2646 0244, www.ibexpeditions.com. Offers a wide range of tours and ticketing, all with an eco pledge. Recommended.
Kunzum Travel Café, T-49 Hauz Khaz Village, T011-2651 3949. Unusual travel centre and meeting place for travellers. Free Wi-Fi, walls lined with photos, magazines, and buzzing with people. Also hosts photography workshops and travel writing courses.
Namaste Voyages, I-Block 28G/F South City, 2 Gurgaon, 122001, T0124-221 9330, www. namastevoyages.com. Specializes in tailor-made tours, tribal, treks, theme voyages.
Paradise Holidays, 312 Ansal Classique Tower, J block, Rajouri Garden, T011-4552 0736, www.paradiseholidays.com. Value for money. Highly recommended.
Shanti Travel, F-189/1A Main Rd Savitri Nagar, T011-4607 7800, www.shantitravel. com. Tailor-made tours throughout India.

⊖ Transport

Air

All international flights arrive at the shiny new terminal of **Indira Gandhi International Airport**, 20 km south of Connaught Pl. Terminal 1 (Domestic) enquiries T011-2567 5126, www.newdelhiairport.in; Terminal 3 (International) T0124-377 6000. At check-in, be sure to tag your hand luggage, and make sure it is stamped after security check, otherwise you will be sent back at the gate to get it stamped.

The domestic air industry is in a period of massive growth, so check a 3rd-party site such as www.cleartrip.com or www.makemytrip.com for the latest flight schedules and prices.

The most extensive networks are with **Indian Airlines**, T140/T011-2562 2220, www.airindia.com; and **Jet Airways**, T011-3989 3333, airport T011-2567 5404, www.jetairways.com. **Indigo**, T(0)9910-383838, www.goindigo.in, has the best record for being on time etc, and **Spicejet**, T(0)9871-803333, www.spicejet.com.

For a complete list of international airline offices see *First City* magazine.

Transport to and from the airport

The Metro us up and running and it is now possible to travel from New Delhi train station to the airport in 20 mins. There is a booth just outside 'Arrivals' at the International and Domestic terminals for the **bus** services. It is a safe, economical option. A free **shuttle** runs between the 2 terminals every 30 mins during the day. Some hotel buses leave from the Domestic terminal. **Bus 780** runs between the **airport** and **New Delhi Railway Station**.

The International and Domestic terminals have **pre-paid taxi** counters outside the baggage hall (3 price categories) which ensure that you pay the right amount (give your name, exact destination and number of items of luggage). Most expensive are white 'DLZ' **limousines** and then white 'DLY' **luxury taxis**. Cheapest are 'DLT' **ordinary Delhi taxis** (black with yellow top Ambassador/Fiat cars and vans, often very old). 'DLY' taxis charge 3 times the DLT price. A 'Welcome' desk by the baggage reclamation offers expensive taxis only. Take your receipt to the ticket counter outside to find your taxi and give it to the driver when you reach the destination; you don't need to tip, although they will ask. From the International terminal DLT taxis charge about Rs 240 for the town centre (Connaught Pl area); night charges double 2300-0500.

Bus
Local
The city bus service run by the **Delhi Transport Corporation** (DTC) connects all important points in the city and has more than 300 routes. Information is available at www.dtc.nic.in, at DTC assistance booths and at all major bus stops. Don't be afraid to ask conductors or fellow passengers. Buses are often hopelessly overcrowded so only use off-peak.

Long distance
Delhi is linked to most major centres in North India. Services are provided by **Delhi Transport Corporation** (DTC) and State Roadways of neighbouring states from various **Inter-State Bus Termini** (ISBT). Allow at least 30 mins for buying a ticket and finding the right bus. If any of the numbers below have changed since writing check www.delhitourism.gov.in.

Kashmere Gate, north of Old Delhi, T011-2296 0290 (general enquiries), is the main terminus, with a restaurant, left luggage, bank (Mon-Fri 1000-1400; Sat 1000-1200), post office (Mon-Sat 0800-1700) and telephones (includes international calls). The following operators run services to neighbouring states from here: Delhi Transport Corp, T011-2386 5181. Haryana Roadways, T011-2296 1262; daily to **Agra** (5-6 hrs, quicker by rail), **Varanasi** and many others.

Sarai Kale Khan Ring Rd, smaller terminal near Nizamuddin Railway Station, T011-2469 8343 (general enquiries), for buses to Haryana, Rajasthan and UP: Haryana Roadways, T011-2296 1262. Rajasthan Roadways, T011-2291 9537. For **Agra**, **Gwalior**, etc.

Anand Vihar, east side of Yamuna River, T011-2215 2431, for buses to Uttar Pradesh, Uttarakhand and Himachal Pradesh.

Car hire
The main roads out of Delhi are very heavily congested; the best time to leave is in the very early morning.

Hiring a car is an excellent way of getting about town either for sightseeing or if you have several journeys to make.

Full day local use with driver (non a/c) Rs 900 and for (a/c) is about Rs 13-1600, 80 km/8 hrs, driver overnight *bata* Rs 150 per day; to Jaipur, about Rs 6 to 8000 depending on size of car The **Tourist Office**, 88 Janpath, has a list of approved agents. We highly recommend **Metropole** see below.

Cozy Travels, N1 BMC House, Middle Circle, Connaught Pl, T011-4359 4359, cozytravels@vsnl.net.com.

Metropole Tourist Service, 224 Defence Colony Flyover Market (Jangpura Side), New Delhi, T011-2431 2212, T(0)9810-277699, www.metrovista. co.in. Car/jeep (US$45-70 per day), safe, reliable and recommended, also hotel bookings and can help arrange homestays around Delhi. Highly recommended.

Metro

The sparkling new Metro system (T011-2436 5202, www.delhimetrorail.com) is set to revolutionize transport within Delhi. For travellers, the yellow line is the main aorta and useful as it stops Chandni Chowk, Connaught Pl and Qutb Minar. The blue line connects to Paharganj. The violet line for Khan Market. And the Orange Line linking airport to New Delhi train station.

Line 1 (Red) Running northwest to east, of limited use to visitors; from Rithala to Dilshad Garden.

Line 2 (Yellow) Running north–south through the centre from Jahangipuri to Huda City via Kashmere Gate, Chandni Chowk, New Delhi Station, Connaught Pl (Rajiv Chowk), Hauz Khaz, Qutb Minar and Saket – probably the most useful line for visitors.

Line 3 (Blue) From Dwarka 21 to Valshall or City Centre (splits after Yamuna Bank) Intersecting with Line 2 at Rajiv Chowk and running west through Paharganj (RK Ashram station) and Karol Bagh.

Line 4 (Orange) Just 4 stations for now including I.G.I Airport to New Delhi Train Station.

Line 5 (Green) From Mundka to Inderlok.

Line 6 (Violet) From Central Secretariat to Badarpur, including Khan Market and Lajpat Nagar. Useful.

Trains run 0600-2200. Fares are charged by distance: tokens for individual journeys cost Rs 6-19. **Smart Cards**, Rs 100, Rs 200 and Rs 500, save queuing and money. **Tourist Cards** valid for 1 or 3 days (Rs 70/200) are useful if you plan to make many journeys. Luggage is limited to 15 kg; guards may not allow big backpacks on board. Look out for the women-only carriages at the front of each train, clearly marked in pink. For an insight into the construction of the Metro, there is a Metro museum at **Patel Chowk** on the yellow line.

Motorcycle hire

Chawla Motorcycles, 1770, Shri Kissan Dass Marg, Naiwali Gali, T(0)9811-888918. Very reliable, trustworthy, highly recommended for restoring classic bikes.

Ess Aar Motors, Jhandewalan Extn, west of Paharganj, T011-2367 8836, www.essaarmotors.com. Recommended for buying Enfields, very helpful.

Also for scooter rentals **U Ride**, T(0)9711-701932, find them on facebook.

Rickshaw

Auto-rickshaws Widely available at about half the cost of taxis. Normal capacity for foreigners is 2 people (3rd person extra); the new fare system is encouraging rickshaw wallahs to use the meter. Expect to pay Rs 30 for the shortest journeys. Allow Rs 150 for 2 hrs' sightseeing/shopping. It is best to walk away from hotels and tourist centres to look for an auto.

Cycle-rickshaws Available in the Old City. Be prepared to bargain: Chandni Chowk Metro to Red Fort. They are not allowed into Connaught Pl.

Taxi

Yellow-top taxis, which run on compressed natural gas, are readily available at taxi stands or you can hail one on the road. Meters should start at Rs 13; ask for the conversion card. Add 25% at night (2300-0500) plus Rs 5 for each piece of luggage over 20 kg. **Easy Cabs**, T011-4343 4343. Runs clean a/c cars and claim to pick up anywhere within 15 mins; Rs 20 per km (night Rs 25 per km). Waiting charges Rs 50/30mins.

Train
Delhi stations from which trains originate have codes: **OD** – Old Delhi, **ND** – New Delhi, **HN** – Hazrat Nizamuddin, **DSR** – Delhi Sarai Rohilla. The publication *Trains at a Glance'* (Rs 30) lists important trains across India, available at some stations, book shops and newsagents,

New Delhi Railway Station and Hazrat Nizamuddin Station (500 m north and 5 km southeast of Connaught Pl respectively) connect Delhi with most major destinations. The latter has many important southbound trains. Old Delhi Station, 6 km north of the centre, has broad and metre-gauge trains. Delhi Sarai Rohilla, northeast of CP, serves Rajasthan.

Train enquiries T131. Reservations T1330. Each station has a computerized reservation counter where you can book any Mail or Express train in India.

International Tourist Bureau (ITB), 1st floor, Main Building, New Delhi Station, T011-2340 5156, Mon-Fri 0930-1630, Sat 0930-1430, provides assistance with planning and booking journeys, for foreigners only; efficient and helpful if slow. You need your passport; pay in US$, or rupees (with an encashment certificate/ ATM receipt). Those with Indrail passes should confirm bookings here. At the time of writing the station was under renovation, so the layout may change, but be wary of rickshaw drivers/ travel agents who tell you the ITB has closed or moved elsewhere. (There are also counters for foreigners and NRIs at Delhi Tourism, N-36 Connaught Pl, 1000-1700, Mon-Sat, and at the airport; quick and efficient.)

New Delhi and Hazrat Nizamuddin stations have pre-paid taxi and rickshaw counters with official rates per km posted: expect to pay around Rs 25 for 1st km, Rs 8 each km after. Authorized *coolies* (porters), wear red shirts and white *dhotis;* agree the charge, there is an official rate, before engaging one. For left luggage, you need a secure lock and chain.

For the purpose of this guide, some useful services are: **Agra:** *Shatabdi Exp 12002,* ND, 0600, 2 hrs; *Taj Exp 12280,* HN, 0710, 2¾ hrs. **Kolkata:** *Rajdhani Exp 12314,* ND, 1630, 17½ hrs. **Varanasi:** *Swatantrta S Ex 12562,* ND, 2040, 12 hrs.

Directory

Delhi *p26, maps p32, p38 and p41*
Embassies and consulates Most are in the diplomatic enclave/Chanakyapuri. For details, go to embassy.goabroad.com.
Medical services Ambulance (24 hrs): T102. Hospitals: Embassies and high commissions have lists of recommended doctors and dentists. Doctors approved by IAMAT (International Association for Medical Assistance to Travellers) are listed in a directory. Casualty and emergency wards in both private and government hospitals are open 24 hrs. **Ram Manohar Lohia**, Willingdon Crescent, T011-2336 5525, 24-hr A&E. **Bara Hindu Rao**, Sabzi Mandi, T011-2391 9476. **JP Narayan**, J Nehru Marg, Delhi Gate, T011-2323 2400. **Safdarjang General**, Sri Aurobindo Marg, T011-2616 5060. **S Kripalani**, Panchkuin Rd, T011-2336 3728. **Chemists:** Many hospitals have 24-hr services: **Hindu Rao Hospital**, Sabzi Mandi; **Ram Manohar Lohia Hospital**, Willingdon Crescent; **S Kripalani Hospital**, Panchkuin Rd. In Connaught Pl: **Nath Brothers**, G-2, off Marina Arcade; **Chemico**, H-45. **Useful contacts** Fire: T101. **Foreigners' Registration Office:** East Block-VIII, Level 2, Sector 1, RK Puram, T011-2671 1443. **Police:** T100.

Contents

Footprint features

Delhi to Kolkata

Agra and around

The romance of what is arguably the world's most famous building still astonishes in its power. In addition to the Taj Mahal, Agra also houses the great monuments of the Red Fort and the I'timad-ud-Daulah, but to experience their beauty you have to endure the less attractive sides of one of India's least prepossessing towns. A big industrial city, the monuments are often covered in a haze of polluted air, while visitors may be subjected to a barrage of high-power selling. Despite it all, the experience is unmissable. The city is also the convenient gateway to the wonderful, abandoned capital of Fatehpur Sikri, the beautifully serene Akbar's Mauseuleum and some of Hinduism's most holy sites.

Arriving in Agra

Getting there
By far the best way to arrive is on the *Shatabdi Express* train from Delhi, which is much faster than travelling by car and infinitely more comfortable than the frequent 'express' buses, which can take five tiring hours.

Getting around
Buses run a regular service between the station, bus stands and the main sites. See Entrances, page 67. Cycle-rickshaws, autos and taxis can be hired to venture further afield, or hire a bike if it's not too hot. ▸▸ *See Transport, page 80.*

Tourist information
Government of India tourist office ① *191 The Mall, T0562-222 6378, guides available (Rs 100)*, helpful and friendly. **UPTDC** ① *64 Taj Rd, T0562-236 3377, also at Agra Cantt, T0562-242 1204,* and **Tourist Bungalow** ① *Raja-ki-Mandi, T0562-285 0120.* **UP Tours** ① *Taj Khema, Taj East Gate, T0562-233 0140.*

Note that there is an **Agra Development Authority Tax** of Rs 500 levied on each day you visit the Taj Mahal, which includes the Red Fort, Fatehpur Sikri and other attractions. This is in addition to the individual entry fees to the monuments.

The best time to visit is between November and March.

Background

With minor interruptions Agra alternated with Delhi as the capital of the Mughal Empire. **Sikander Lodi** seized it from a rebellious governor and made it his capital in 1501. He died in Agra but is buried in Delhi (see page 43). Agra was Babur's capital. He is believed to have laid out a pleasure garden on the east bank of the River Yamuna and his son Humayun built a mosque here in 1530. **Akbar** lived in Agra in the early years of his reign. Ralph Fitch, the English Elizabethan traveller, described a "magnificent city, with broad streets and tall buildings". He also saw Akbar's new capital at Fatehpur Sikri, 40 km west, describing a route lined all the way with stalls and markets. Akbar moved his capital again to Lahore, before returning to Agra in 1599, where he spent the last six years of his life. **Jahangir** left Agra for Kashmir in 1618 and never returned. Despite modifying the Red Fort and building the Taj Mahal, **Shah Jahan** also moved away in 1638 to his new city Shah Jahanabad in Delhi, though he returned in 1650, taken prisoner by his son Aurangzeb and left to spend his last days in the Red Fort. It was **Aurangzeb**, the last of the Great Mughals, who moved the seat of government permanently to Delhi. In the 18th century Agra suffered at the hands of the Jats, was taken, lost and retaken by the Marathas who, in turn, were ousted by the British in 1803. It was the centre of much fighting in the 'Uprising' and was the administrative centre of the Northwest Provinces and Oudh until that too was transferred to Allahabad in 1877.

Taj Mahal → *For listings, see pages 78-80.*

① *Sat-Thu sunrise to sunset (last entry 1700), foreigners Rs 750 (including Development Tax), Indians Rs 20, cash only, includes still camera, video cameras, tripods, other electronic items eg mobile phones not allowed, lockers at East and West Gates Rs 1. No photos inside the tomb (instant fines). Allow at least 1 hr. Full moon viewing 2 nights either side of full moon (see www.stardate.org/nightsky/moon for full moon dates), 2030-0030, separate entry fee of foreigners Rs 750, Indians Rs 510, book tickets day before at Architectural Survey of India, 22 The Mall, T0562-222 7261. The Archaeological Survey of India explicitly asks visitors not to make donations to anyone including custodians in the tomb.*

Of all the world's great monuments, the Taj Mahal is one of the most written about, photographed, televized and talked about. To India's Nobel Laureate poet, Tagore, the Taj was a "tear drop on the face of humanity", a building to echo the cry "I have not forgotten, I have not forgotten, O beloved" and its mesmerizing power is such that despite the hype, no one comes away disappointed.

Shah Jahan, the fifth of the Great Mughals, was so devoted to his favourite wife, Mumtaz Mahal (Jewel of the Palace) that he could not bear to be parted from her and insisted that she always travel with him, in all states of health. While accompanying him on a military campaign, she died at the age of 39 giving birth to her 14th child. On her deathbed, it is said, she asked the emperor to show the world how much they loved one another.

The grief-stricken emperor went into mourning for two years. He turned away from the business of running the empire and dedicated himself to architecture, resolving to build his wife the most magnificent memorial on earth. On the right bank of the River Yamuna in full view of his fortress palace, it was to be known as the Taj-i-Mahal (Crown of the Palace).

According to the French traveller Tavnier, work on the Taj commenced in 1632 and took 22 years to complete, employing a workforce of 20,000. The red sandstone was available locally but the white marble was quarried at Makrana in Rajasthan and transported 300 km by a fleet of 1000 elephants. Semi-precious stones for the inlay came from far and wide: red carnelian from Baghdad; red, yellow and brown jasper from the Punjab; green jade and crystal from China; blue lapis lazuli from Ceylon and Afghanistan; turquoise from Tibet; chrysolite from Egypt; amethyst from Persia; agates from the Yemen; dark green malachite from Russia; diamonds from Central India and mother-of-pearl from the Indian Ocean. A 3-km ramp was used to lift material up to the dome and, because of the sheer weight of the building; boreholes were filled with metal coins and fragments to provide

Agra

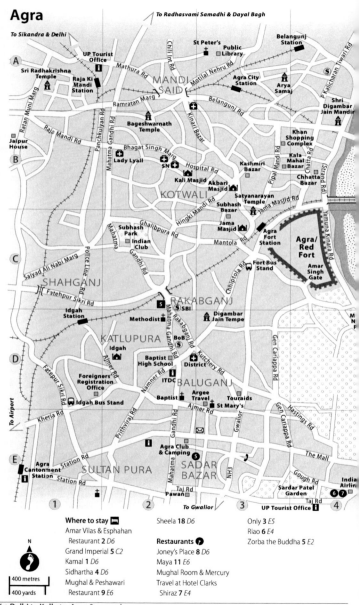

Where to stay 🛏
Amar Vilas & Esphahan
  Restaurant 2 *D6*
Grand Imperial 5 *C2*
Kamal 1 *D6*
Sidhartha 4 *D6*
Mughal & Peshawari
  Restaurant 9 *E6*

Sheela 18 *D6*

Restaurants 🍴
Joney's Place 8 *D6*
Maya 11 *E6*
Mughal Room & Mercury
  Travel at Hotel Clarks
  Shiraz 7 *E4*

Only 3 *E5*
Riao 6 *E4*
Zorba the Buddha 5 *E2*

N

400 metres
400 yards

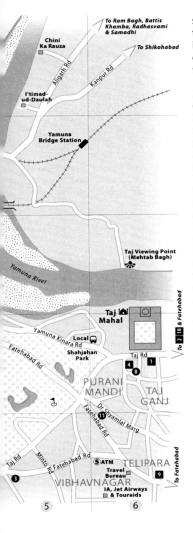

To Ram Bagh, Battis
Khamba, Radhasvami
& Samadhi

Chini
Ka Rauza

To Shikohabad

Aligarh Rd
Kanpur Rd

I'timad-
ud-Daulah

Yamuna
Bridge Station

Yamuna River

Taj Viewing Point
(Mehtab Bagh)

Taj Mahal

To 2, 18 & Fatehabad

Yamuna Kinara Rd   Local
Shahjahan   Taj Rd
Fatehabad Rd   Park

PURANI
MANDI   TAJ
GANJ

Dr Shyamlal Marg

Fatehabad Rd

ATM   TELIPARA
Travel
Bureau
VIBHAVNAGAR
IA, Jet Airways
& Touraids

To Fatehabad

Taj Rd
Minto Rd Fatehabad Rd

5   6

suitable foundations. The resemblance of the exquisite double dome to a huge pearl is not coincidental; a saying of the Prophet describes the throne of God as a dome of white pearl supported by white pillars.

Myths and controversy surround the Taj Mahal. On its completion it is said that the emperor ordered the chief mason's right hand to be cut off to prevent him from repeating his masterpiece. Another legend suggests that Shah Jahan intended to build a replica for himself in black marble on the other side of the river, connected to the Taj Mahal by a bridge built with alternate blocks of black and white marble. Some have asserted that architects responsible for designing this mausoleum must have come from Turkey, Persia or even Europe (because of the pietra dura work on the tomb). In fact, no one knows who drew the plans. What is certain is that in the Taj Mahal, the traditions of Indian Hindu and Persian Muslim architecture were fused together into a completely distinct and perfect art form.

Viewing

The white marble of the Taj is extraordinarily luminescent and even on dull days seems bright. The whole building appears to change its hue according to the light in the sky. In winter (December to February), it is worth being there at sunrise. Then the mists that often lie over the River Yamuna lift as the sun rises and casts its golden rays over the pearl-white tomb. Beautifully lit in the soft light, the Taj appears to float on air. At sunset, the view from across the river is equally wonderful.

Entrances

To reduce damage to the marble by the polluted atmosphere, local industries now have to comply with strict rules, and vehicles emitting noxious fumes are not allowed within 2 km of the monument. Visitors are increasingly using horse-drawn carriages or walking. You can approach the Taj from three directions. The western entrance is usually used by those arriving from the fort and is an easy 10-minute walk along a pleasant garden road. At the eastern entrance, rickshaws and camel drivers offer to take visitors to the gate for up to Rs 100 each; however, an official battery bus ferries visitors from the car park to the gate for a small fee.

The approach
In the unique beauty of the Taj, subtlety is blended with grandeur and a massive overall design is matched with immaculately intricate execution. You will already have seen the dome of the tomb in the distance, looking almost like a miniature, but as you go into the open square, the Taj itself is so well hidden that you almost wonder where it can be. The glorious surprise is kept until the last moment, for wholly concealing it is the massive red sandstone gateway of the entrance, symbolizing the divide between the secular world and paradise.

The gateway was completed in 1648, though the huge brass door is recent. The original doors (plundered by the Jats) were solid silver and decorated with 1100 nails whose heads were contemporary silver coins. Although the gateway is remarkable in itself, one of its functions is to prevent you getting any glimpse of the tomb inside until you are right in the doorway itself. From here only the tomb is visible, stunning in its nearness, but as you move forward the minarets come into view.

The garden
The Taj garden, well kept though it is, is nothing compared with its former glory. The guiding principle is one of symmetry. The *char bagh*, separated by the watercourses (rivers of heaven) originating from the central, raised pool, were divided into 16 flower beds, making a total of 64. The trees, all carefully planted to maintain the symmetry, were either cypress (signifying death) or fruit trees (life). The channels were stocked with colourful fish and the gardens with beautiful birds. It is well worth wandering along the side avenues for not only is it much more peaceful but also good for framing photos of the tomb with foliage. You may see bullocks pulling the lawnmowers around.

The mosque and its jawab
On the east and west sides of the tomb are identical red sandstone buildings. On the west (left-hand side) is a mosque. It is common in Islam to build one next to a tomb. It sanctifies the area and provides a place for worship. The replica on the other side is known as the **Jawab** (answer). This can't be used for prayer as it faces away from Mecca.

The tomb
There is only one point of access to the **plinth** and tomb, where shoes must be removed (socks can be kept on; remember the white marble gets very hot) or cloth overshoes worn (Rs 2, though strictly free).

The **tomb** is square with bevelled corners. At each corner smaller domes rise while in the centre is the main dome topped by a brass finial. The dome is actually a double dome and this device, Central Asian in origin, was used to gain height. The resemblance of the dome to a huge pearl is not coincidental. The exterior ornamentation is calligraphy (verses of the Koran), beautifully carved panels in bas relief and superb inlay work.

The **interior** of the mausoleum comprises a lofty central chamber, a *maqbara* (crypt) immediately below this, and four octagonal corner rooms. The central chamber contains replica tombs, the real ones being in the crypt. The public tomb was originally surrounded by a jewel-encrusted silver screen. Aurangzeb removed this, fearing it might be stolen, and replaced it with an octagonal screen of marble carved from one block of marble and inlaid with precious stones. It is an incredible piece of workmanship. This chamber is open at sunrise, but may close during the day.

Above the tombs is a **Cairene lamp** whose flame is supposed never to go out. This one was given by Lord Curzon, Governor General of India (1899-1905), to replace the original which was stolen by Jats. The tomb of Mumtaz with the 'female' slate, rests immediately beneath the dome. If you look from behind it, you can see how it lines up centrally with the main entrance. Shah Jahan's tomb is larger and to the side, marked by a 'male' pen-box, the sign of a cultured or noble person. Not originally intended to be placed there but squeezed in by Aurangzeb, this flaws the otherwise perfect symmetry of the whole complex. Finally, the acoustics of the building are superb, the domed ceiling being designed to echo chants from the Koran and musicians' melodies.

The **museum** ⓘ *above the entrance, Sat-Thu 1000-1700*, has a small collection of Mughal memorabilia, photographs and miniatures of the Taj through the ages but has no textual information. Sadly, the lights do not always work.

Agra Fort (Red Fort) → *For listings, see pages 78-80.*

ⓘ *0600-1800, foreigners Rs 300 (Rs 250 if you've been to the Taj on the same day), Indians Rs 15, video Rs 25; allow a minimum of 1½ hours for a visit. The best route round is to start with the building on your right before going through the gate at the top of the broad 100 m ramp; the gentle incline made it suitable for elephants.*

On the west bank of the River Yamuna, Akbar's magnificent fort dominates the centre of the city. Akbar erected the walls and gates and the first buildings inside. **Shah Jahan** built the impressive imperial quarters and mosque, while Aurangzeb added the outer ramparts. The outer walls, just over 20 m high and faced with red sandstone, tower above the outer moat. The fort is crescent-shaped with a long, nearly straight wall facing the river, punctuated at regular intervals by bastions. The main entrance used to be in the centre of the west wall, the **Delhi Gate**, facing the bazar. It led to the Jami Masjid in the city but is now permanently closed. You can only enter now from the **Amar Singh Gate** in the south. Although only the southern third of the fort is open to the public, this includes nearly all the buildings of interest. At the gate you will have to contend with vendors of cheap soapstone boxes and knick-knacks. If you want to buy something, bargain hard. Guides will offer their services – most are not particularly good.

Fortifications
The fortifications tower above the 9-m-wide, 10-m-deep moat (still evident but containing stagnant water) formerly filled with water from the Yamuna River. There is an outer wall on the riverside and an imposing 22-m-high inner main wall, giving a feeling of great defensive power. Although it served as a model for Shah Jahan's Red Fort in Delhi, its own model was the Rajput Fort built by Raja Man Singh Tomar of Gwalior in 1500. If an aggressor managed to get through the outer gate they would have to make a right-hand turn and thereby expose their flank to the defenders on the inner wall. The inner gate is solidly powerful but has been attractively decorated with tiles. The similarities with Islamic patterns of the tilework are obvious, though the Persian blue was also used in the Gwalior Fort and may well have been imitated from that example. The incline up to this point and beyond was suitable for elephants and as you walk past the last gate and up the broad brick-lined ramp with ridged slabs, it is easy to imagine arriving on elephant back. At the top of this 100-m ramp is a gate with a map and description board on your left.

Jahangiri Mahal Despite its name, this was built by Akbar (circa 1570) as women's quarters. It is all that survives of his original palace buildings. In front is a large **stone bowl**, with steps both inside and outside, which was probably filled with fragrant rose water for bathing. Almost 75 m sq, the palace has a simple stone exterior. Tillotson has pointed out that the blind arcade of pointed arches inlaid with white marble which decorate the façade is copied from 14th-century monuments of the Khaljis and Tughluqs in Delhi. He notes that they are complemented by some features derived from Hindu architecture, including the *jarokhas* (balconies) protruding from the central section, the sloping dripstone in place of *chajja* (eaves) along the top of the façade, and the domed *chhattris* at its ends. The presence of distinctively Hindu features does not indicate a synthesis of architectural styles at this early stage of Mughal architecture, as can be seen much more clearly from inside the Jahangiri Mahal. Here most of the features are straightforwardly Hindu; square-headed arches and extraordinarily carved capitals and brackets illustrate the vivid work of local Hindu craftsmen employed by Akbar without any attempt either to curb their enthusiasm for florid decoration and mythical animals nor to produce a fusion of Hindu and Islamic ideas. Tillotson argues that the central courtyard is essentially Hindu, in significant contrast with most earlier Indo-Islamic buildings. In these, an Islamic scheme was modified by Hindu touches. He suggests, therefore, that the Jahangiri Mahal marks the start of a more fundamental kind of Hinduization, typical of several projects during Akbar's middle period of rule, including the palace complex in Fatehpur Sikri. However, it did not represent a real fusion of ideas – something that only came under Shah Jahan – simply a juxtaposition of sharply contrasting styles.

Jodh Bai's Palace On the south side, this is named after one of Jahangir's wives. On the east the hall court leads onto a more open yard by the inner wall of the fort. In contrast to other palaces in the fort, this is quite simple. Through the slits in the wall you can see the Taj.

Shah Jahan's palace buildings
Turn left through to Shah Jahan's Khas Mahal (1636). The open tower allows you to view the walls and see to your left the decorated Mussaman Burj tower. The use of white marble transforms the atmosphere, contributing to the new sense of grace and light.

Anguri Bagh (Vine Garden) The formal, 85-m-sq, geometric gardens are on the left. In Shah Jahan's time the geometric patterns were enhanced by decorative flower beds. In the middle of the white marble platform wall in front is a decorative water slide. From the pool with its bays for seating and its fountains, water would drain off along channels decorated to mimic a stream. The surface was scalloped to produce a rippling waterfall, or inlaid to create a shimmering stream bed. Behind vertical water drops, there are little cusped arch niches into which flowers would be placed during the day and lamps at night. The effect was magical.

Golden Pavilions The curved *chala* roofs of the small pavilions by the Khas Mahal are based on the roof shape of Bengali village huts constructed out of curved bamboo, designed to keep off heavy rain. The shape was first expressed in stone by the Sultans of Bengal. Originally gilded, these were probably ladies' bedrooms, with hiding places for jewellery in the walls. These pavilions are traditionally associated with Shah Jahan's daughters, Roshanara and Jahanara.

Khas Mahal This was the model for the Diwan-i-Khas at the Red Fort in Delhi. Some of the original interior decoration has been restored (1895) and gives an impression of how splendid the painted ceiling must have been. The metal rings were probably used for *punkhas*. Underneath are cool rooms used to escape the summer heat. The Khas Mahal illustrates Shahs' original architectural contribution.

The buildings retain distinctively Islamic Persian features – the geometrical planning of the pavilions and the formal layout of the gardens, for example. Tillotson points out that here "Hindu motifs are treated in a new manner, which is less directly imitative of the Hindu antecedents. The temple columns and corbel capitals have been stripped of their rich carving and turned into simpler, smoother forms ... the *chhattris* have Islamic domes. Through these subtle changes the indigenous motifs have lost their specifically Hindu identity; they therefore contrast less strongly with the Islamic components, and are bound with them into a new style. The unity is assisted by the use of the cusped arch and the *Bangladar* roof". Seen in this light, the Khas Mahal achieves a true synthesis which eluded Akbar's designs.

Mussaman Burj On the left of the Khas Mahal is the Mussaman Burj (Octagonal Tower, though sometimes corrupted into Saman Burj, then translated as Jasmine Tower). It is a beautiful octagonal tower with an open pavilion. With its openness, elevation and the benefit of cooling evening breezes blowing in off the Yamuna River, this could well have been used as the emperor's bedroom. It has been suggested that this is where Shah Jahan lay on his deathbed, gazing at the Taj. Access to this tower is through a magnificently decorated and intimate apartment with a scalloped fountain in the centre. The inlay work here is exquisite, especially above the pillars. In front of the fountain is a sunken courtyard which could be filled by water carriers, to work the fountains in the pool.

Sheesh Mahal (Mirror Palace) Here are further examples of decorative water engineering in the *hammams*; the water here may have been warmed by lamps. The mirrors, which were more precious than marble, were set into the walls, often specially chiselled to accommodate their crooked shape. The defensive qualities of the site and the fortifications are obvious. In the area between the outer rampart and the inner wall gladiatorial battles were staged pitting man against tiger, or elephant against elephant. The tower was the emperor's grandstand seat.

Diwan-i-Khas (Hall of Private Audience, 1637) This is next to the Mussaman Burj, approached on this route by a staircase which brings you out at the side. The interior of the Diwan-i-Khas, a three-sided pavilion with a terrace of fine proportions, would have been richly decorated with tapestries and carpets. The double columns in marble inlaid with semi-precious stones in delightful floral patterns in pietra dura have finely carved capitals.

Terrace and Machhi Bhavan

In front of the Diwan-i-Khas are two throne 'platforms' on a **terrace**. Gascoigne recounts how Shah Jahan tried to trick a haughty Persian ambassador into bowing low as he approached the throne by erecting a fence with a small wicket gate so that his visitor would have to enter on hands and knees. The ambassador did so, but entered backwards, thus presenting his bottom first to the Emperor. The **black marble throne** at the rear of the terrace was used by Jahangir when claiming to be Emperor at Allahabad. The emperor sat on the white marble platform facing the **Machhi Bhavan** (Fish Enclosure), which once contained pools and fountains, waiting to meet visiting dignitaries.

Diwan-i-Am Go down an internal staircase and you enter the Diwan-i-Am from the side. The clever positioning of the pillars gives the visitor arriving through the gates in the right- and left-hand walls of the courtyard an uninterrupted view of the throne. On the back wall of the pavilion are *jali* screens to enable the women of the court to watch without being seen. The open-sided, cusped arched hall built of plaster on red stone, is very impressive. The throne alcove of richly decorated white marble completed in 1634 after seven years' work used to house the Peacock Throne. Its decoration made it extraordinary: "the canopy was carved in enamel work and studded with individual gems, its interior was thickly encrusted with rubies, garnets and diamonds, and it was supported on 12 emerald covered columns" writes Tillotson. When Shah Jahan moved his capital to Delhi he took the throne with him to the Red Fort, only for it to be taken back to Persia as loot by Nadir Shah in 1739.

Nagina Masjid From the corner opposite the Diwan-i-Khas two doorways lead to a view over the small courtyards of the *zenana* (harem). Further round in the next corner is the Nagina Masjid. Shoes must be removed at the doorway. Built by Shah Jahan, this was the private mosque of the ladies of the court. Beneath it was a *mina* bazar for the ladies to make purchases from the marble balcony above. Looking out of the Diwan-i-Am you can see the domes of the **Moti Masjid** (Pearl Mosque, 1646-1653), an extremely fine building closed to visitors because of structural problems. Opposite the Diwan-i-Am are the barracks and **Mina Bazar**, also closed to the public. In the paved area in front of the Diwan-i-Am is a large well and the **tomb of Mr John Russell Colvin**, the Lieutenant Governor of the Northwest Provinces who died here during the 1857 'Uprising'. Stylistically it is sadly out of place. The yellow buildings date from the British period.

Jama Masjid

The mosque built in 1648, near the fort railway, no longer connected to the fort, is attributed to Shah Jahan's dutiful elder daughter Jahanara. In need of repair and not comparable to buildings within the fort, its symmetry has suffered since a small minaret fell in the 1980s. The fine marble steps and bold geometric patterns on the domes are quite striking.

I'timad-ud-Daulah and Sikandra → *For listings, see pages 78-80.*

I'timad-ud-Daulah

ⓘ *Sunrise-sunset, foreigners Rs 100 plus Rs 10 tax, Indians Rs 10, video Rs 25.*

The tomb of I'timad-ud-Daulah (or 'Baby Taj'), set a startling precedent as the first Mughal building to be faced with white marble inlaid with contrasting stones. Unlike the Taj it is small, intimate and has a gentle serenity, but is just as ornate. The tomb was built for **Ghiyas Beg**, a Persian who had obtained service in Akbar's court, and his wife. On Jahangir's succession in 1605 he became *Wazir* (chief minister). Jahangir fell in love with his daughter, **Mehrunissa**, who at the time was married to a Persian. When her husband died in 1607, she entered Jahangir's court as a lady-in-waiting. Four years later Jahangir married her. Thereafter she was known first as **Nur Mahal** (Light of the Palace), later being promoted to **Nur Jahan** (Light of the World). Her niece Mumtaz married Shah Jahan.

Nur Jahan built the tomb for her father in the *char bagh* that he himself had laid out. It is beautifully conceived in white marble, mosaic and lattice. There is a good view from the roof of the entrance. Marble screens of geometric lattice work permit soft lighting of the inner chamber. The yellow marble caskets appear to have been carved out of wood. On the engraved walls of the chamber is the recurring theme of a wine flask with snakes as handles – perhaps a reference by Nur Jahan, the tomb's creator, to her husband Jahangir's excessive drinking. Stylistically, the tomb marks a change from the sturdy and masculine buildings of Akbar's reign to softer, more feminine lines. The main chamber, richly decorated in pietra dura with mosaics and semi-precious stones inlaid in the white marble, contains the tomb of I'timad-ud-Daulah (Pillar of the Goverment) and his wife. Some have argued that the concept and skill must have travelled from its European home of 16th-century Florence to India. However, Florentine pietra dura is figurative whereas the Indian version is essentially decorative and can be seen as a refinement of its Indian predecessor, the patterned mosaic.

Sikandra (Akbar's Mausoleum)

① *Sunrise-sunset, foreigners Rs 100, Indians Rs 10, includes camera, video Rs 25. Morning is the quietest time to visit.*

Following the Timurid tradition, Akbar (ruled 1556-1605) had started to build his own tomb at Sikandra. He died during its construction and his son **Jahangir** completed it in 1613. The result is an impressive, large but architecturally confused tomb. A huge gateway, the **Buland Darwaza**, leads to the great garden enclosure, where spotted deer run free on the immaculate lawns. The decoration on the gateway is strikingly bold, with its large mosaic patterns, a forerunner of the pietra dura technique. The white minarets atop the entrance were an innovation which reappear, almost unchanged, at the Taj Mahal. The walled garden enclosure is laid out in the *char bagh* style, with the mausoleum at the centre.

A broad paved path leads to the 22.5-m-high tomb with four storeys. The lowest storey, nearly 100 m sq and 9 m high, contains massive cloisters. The entrance on the south side leads to the tomb chamber. Shoes must be removed or cloth overshoes worn (hire Rs 2). In a niche opposite the entrance is an alabaster tablet inscribed with the 99 divine names of Allah. The sepulchre is in the centre of the room, whose velvety darkness is pierced by a single slanting shaft of light from a high window. The custodian, in expectation of a donation, makes "Akbaaarrrr" echo around the chamber.

Some 4 km south of Sikandra, near the high gateway of the ancient **Kach ki Sarai** building, is a sculptured horse, believed to mark the spot where Akbar's favourite horse died. There are also *kos minars* (marking a *kos*, about 4 km) and several other tombs on the way.

Fatehpur Sikri → For listings, see pages 78-80.

The red sandstone capital of Emperor Akbar, one of his architectural achievements, spreads along a ridge. The great mosque and palace buildings, deserted after only 14 years are still a vivid reminder of his power and vision. Perfectly preserved, it conjures up the lifestyle of the Mughals at the height of their glory.

Background

The first two Great Mughals, Babur (ruled 1526-1530) and his son Humayun (ruled 1530-1540, 1555-1556) both won (in Humayun's case, won back) Hindustan at the end of their lives, and they left an essentially alien rule. Akbar, the third and greatest of the Mughals, changed that. By marrying a Hindu princess, forging alliances with the Rajput leaders and making the administration of India a partnership with Hindu nobles and princes rather than armed foreign minority rule, Akbar consolidated his ancestors' gains, and won widespread loyalty and respect. Akbar had enormous magnetism. Though illiterate, he had great wisdom and learning as well as undoubted administrative and military skills. Fatehpur Sikri is testimony to this remarkable character.

Although he had many wives, the 26-year-old Akbar had no living heir; the children born to him had all died in infancy. He visited holy men to enlist their prayers for a son and heir. **Sheikh Salim Chishti**, living at Sikri, a village 37 km southwest of Agra, told the emperor that he would have three sons. Soon after, one of his wives, the daughter of the Raja of Amber, became pregnant, so Akbar sent her to live near the sage. A son Salim was born, later to be known as **Jahangir**. The prophecy was fulfilled when in 1570 another wife gave birth to Murad, and in 1572 to Daniyal. Salim Chishti's tomb is here.

Akbar, so impressed by this sequence of events, resolved to build an entirely new capital at Sikri in honour of the saint. The holy man had set up his hermitage on a low hill of hard reddish sandstone, an ideal building material, easy to work and yet very durable. The building techniques used imitated carvings in wood, as well as canvas from the Mughal camp (eg awnings). During the next 14 years a new city appeared on this hill – 'Fatehpur' (town of victory) added to the name of the old village, 'Sikri'. Later additions and alterations were made and debate continues over the function and dates of the various buildings. It is over 400 years old and yet perfectly preserved, thanks to careful conservation work carried out by the Archaeological Survey of India at the turn of the century. There are three sections to the city: the 'Royal Palace', 'Outside the Royal Palace' and the 'Jami Masjid'.

When Akbar left, it was slowly abandoned to become ruined and deserted by the early 1600s. Some believe the emperor's decision was precipitated by the failure of the water supply, whilst local folklore claims the decision was due to the loss of the court singer Tansen, one of the 'nine gems' of Akbar's court. However, there may well have been political and strategic motives. Akbar's change in attitude towards orthodox Islam and his earlier veneration of the Chishti saints supplanted by a new imperial ideology, may have influenced his decision. In 1585 he moved his court to Lahore and when he returned south again, it was to Agra. But it was at Fatehpur Sikri that Akbar spent the richest and most productive years of his 49-year reign.

The entrance
① *Sunrise to sunset, foreigners Rs 250, Indians Rs 5. It is best to visit early, before the crowds. Official guides are good (about Rs 100; Rs 30 off season) but avoid others. Avoid the main entrance (lots of hawkers); instead, take the right-hand fork after passing through Agra gate to the hassle-free 2nd entrance. Allow 3 hrs and carry plenty of drinking water.*

Entry to Fatehpur Sikri is through the **Agra Gate**. The straight road from Agra was laid out in Akbar's time. If approaching from Bharatpur you will pass the site of a large lake, which provided one defensive barrier. On the other sides was a massive defensive wall with nine gates (clockwise): Delhi, Lal, Agra, Bir or Suraj (Sun), Chandar (Moon), Gwaliori, Tehra (Crooked), Chor (Thief's) and Ajmeri. Sadly there are men with 'performing' bears along the road from Agra – they should be discouraged – avoid stopping to photograph or tip.

From the Agra Gate you pass the sandstone **Tansen's Baradari** on your right and go through the triple-arched **Chahar Suq** with a gallery with two *chhattris* above which may have been a **Nakkar khana** (Drum House). The road inside the main city wall leading to the entrance would have been lined with bazars. Next on your right is the square, shallow-domed **Mint** with artisans' workshops or animal shelters, around a courtyard. Workmen still chip away at blocks of stone in the dimly lit interior.

Royal Palace

The **Diwan-i-Am** (Hall of Public Audience) was also used for celebrations and public prayers. It has cloisters on three sides of a rectangular courtyard and to the west, a pavilion with the emperor's throne, with *jali* screens on either side separating the court ladies. Some scholars suggest that the west orientation may have had the added significance of Akbar's vision of himself playing a semi-divine role.

This backed onto the private palace. In the centre of the courtyard behind the throne is the **Pachisi Board** or Chaupar. It is said that Akbar had slave girls dressed in yellow, blue and red, moved around as 'pieces'!

The **Diwan-i-Khas** (Hall of Private Audience) to your right, is a two-storey building with corner kiosks. It is a single room with a unique circular throne platform. Here Akbar would spend long hours in discussion with Christians, Jains, Buddhists, Hindus and Parsis. They would sit along the walls of the balcony connected to the **Throne Pillar** by screened 'bridges', while courtiers could listen to the discussions from the ground floor. Decorative techniques and metaphysical labels are incorporated here – the pillar is lotus shaped (a Hindu and Buddhist motif), the Royal Umbrella (*chhattri*) is Hindu, and the Tree of Life, Islamic. The bottom of the pillar is carved in four tiers: Muslim, Hindu, Christian and Buddhist designs. The Throne Pillar can be approached by steps from the outside although there is no access to the upper floor. The design of the hall deliberately followed the archaic universal pattern of establishing a hallowed spot from which spiritual influence could radiate. In his later years, Akbar developed a mystical cult around himself that saw him as being semi-divine.

An Archaeological Survey of India team recently discovered an 'air-conditioned palace' built for Akbar, while digging up steps leading down to a water tank set in the middle of the main palace complex. The subterranean chambers were found under the small quadrangle in sandstone, set in the middle of a water tank and connected on all four sides by narrow corridors. It's not yet open to the public.

In the **Treasury** in the northwest corner of the courtyard is the **Ankh Michauli** (Blind Man's Buff), possibly used for playing the game, comprising three rooms each protected by a narrow corridor with guards. The *makaras* on brackets are mythical sea creatures who guard the treasures under the sea. Just in front of the Treasury is the **Astrologer's Seat**, a small kiosk with elaborate carvings on the Gujarati 'caterpillar' struts which may have been used by the court astrologer or treasurer.

The **Turkish Sultana's House** or Anup Talao Pavilion is directly opposite, beyond the Pachisi Board. Sultana Ruqayya Begum was Akbar's favourite and her 'house', with a balcony on each side, is exquisitely carved with Islamic decorations. Scholars suggest this may have been a pleasure pavilion. The geometrical pattern on the ceiling is reminiscent of Central Asian carvings in wood while the walls may have been set originally with reflecting glass to create a Sheesh Mahal (Mirror Palace). In the centre of this smaller south courtyard is the **Anup Talao** where the Emperor may have sat on the platform, surrounded by perfumed water. The *Akbarnama* mentions the emperor's show of charity when he filled the Talao with copper, silver and gold coins and distributed them over three years.

Dawlatkhana-i-Khas, the emperor's private chambers, are next to the rose-water fountain in the corner. There are two main rooms on the ground floor. One housed his library – the recesses in the walls were for manuscripts. Although unable to read or write himself, Akbar enjoyed having books read to him. Wherever he went, his library of 50,000 manuscripts accompanied him. The larger room behind was his resting area. On the first floor is the **Khwabgah** (Palace of Dreams) which would have had rich carpets, hangings and cushions. This too was decorated with gold and ultramarine paintings. The southern window (Jharokha Darshan) was where the emperor showed himself to his people every morning.

Leaving the Dawlatkhana-i-Khas you enter another courtyard which contained the **Ladies' Garden** for the *zenana*, and the **Sunahra Makan** or the Christian wife **Maryam's** House, a two-storeyed affair for the emperor's mother, which was embellished with golden murals in the Persian style. The inscriptions on the beams are verses by **Fazl**, Akbar's poet laureate, one of the '*Navaratna*' (Nine Jewels) of the Court. Toilets in the corner of the garden are quite clean.

The **Panch Mahal** is an elegant, airy five-storeyed pavilion just north of this, each floor smaller than the one below, rising to a single domed kiosk on top. The horizontal line of this terraced building is emphasized by wide overhanging eaves (for providing shade), parapets broken by the supporting pillars of which there are 84 on the ground floor (the magic number of seven planets multiplied by 12 signs of the zodiac). The 56 carved columns on the second floor are all different and show Hindu influence. Originally dampened scented *khuss* (grass screens) which were hung in the open spaces, provided protection from the heat and sun, as well as privacy for the women who used the pavilion.

Jodh Bai, the daughter of the Maharaja of Amber, lived in Raniwas. The spacious **palace** in the centre, assured of privacy and security by high walls and a 9-m-high guarded gate to the east. Outside the north wall is the 'hanging' **Hawa Mahal** (Palace of Winds) with beautiful *jali* screens facing the *zenana* garden which was once enclosed, and the bridge (a later addition) led to the Hathipol. Through the arch is the small **Nagina Masjid**, the mosque for the ladies of the court. The *hammams* (baths) are to the south of the palace. The centre of the building is a quadrangle around which were the harem quarters, each section self-contained with roof terraces. The style, a blend of Hindu and Muslim (the lotus, chain and bell designs being Hindu, the black domes Muslim), is strongly reminiscent of Gujarati temples, possibly owing to the craftsmen brought in (see *jarokha* windows, niches, pillars and brackets). The upper pavilions north and south have interesting ceiling structure (imitating the bamboo and thatch roof of huts), here covered with blue glazed tiles, adding colour to the buildings of red sandstone favoured by Akbar. Jodh Bai's vegetarian kitchen opposite the palace has attractive chevron patterns.

Raja Birbal's Palace is a highly ornamented house to the northwest of Jodh Bai's Palace. It has two storeys – four rooms and two porches with pyramidal roofs below, and two rooms with cupolas and screened terraces above. Birbal, Akbar's Hindu prime minister, was the brightest of Akbar's 'Nine Jewels'. Again the building combines Hindu and Islamic elements (note the brackets, eaves, *jarokhas*). Of particular interest is the insulating effect of the double-domed structure of the roofs and cupolas which kept the rooms cool, and the diagonal positioning of the upper rooms which ensured a shady terrace. Some scholars believe that this building, *Mahal-i-Ilahi*, was not for Birbal, but for Akbar's senior queens.

South of the Raja's house are the **stables**, a long courtyard surrounded by cells which probably housed zenana servants rather than the emperor's camels and horses, though the rings suggest animals may have been tied there.

Jami Masjid

Leaving the Royal Palace you proceed across a car park to the Jami Masjid and the sacred section of Fatehpur Sikri. The oldest place of worship here was the **Stone Cutters' Mosque** (circa 1565) to the west of the Jami Masjid. It was built near Sheikh Salim Chishti's cell which was later incorporated into it by stonecutters who settled on the ridge when quarrying for the Agra Fort began. It has carved monolithic 'S' brackets to support the wide sloping eaves.

The **Badshahi Darwaza** (King's Gate) is the entrance Akbar used. Shoes must be left at the gate but there are strips of carpet cross the courtyard to save burning your feet. The porch is packed with aggressive salesmen. The two other gates on the south and north walls were altered by subsequent additions. Built in 1571-1572, this is one of the largest mosques in India. Inside is the congregational courtyard (132 m by 111 m). To your right in the corner is the **Jamaat Khana Hall** and next to this the **Tomb of the Royal Ladies** on the north wall. The square nave carries the principal dome painted in the Persian style, with pillared aisles leading to side chapels carrying subsidiary domes. The **mihrab** in the centre of the west wall orientates worshippers towards Mecca. The sanctuary is adorned with carving, inlay work and painting.

The **Tomb of Sheikh Salim Chishti**, a masterpiece in brilliant white marble, dominates the northern half of the courtyard. The Gujarati-style serpentine 'S' struts, infilled with *jali*, are highly decorative while the carved pillar bases and lattice screens are stunning pieces of craftsmanship. The canopy over the tomb is inlaid with mother of pearl. On the cenotaph is the date of the saint's death (1571) and the date of the building's completion (1580); the superb marble screens enclosing the veranda were added by Jahangir's foster brother in 1606. Around the entrance are inscribed the names of God, the Prophet and the four Caliphs of Islam. The shrine inside, on the spot of the saint's hermitage, originally had a red sandstone dome, which was marble veneered around 1806. Both Hindu and Muslim women pray at the shrine, tying cotton threads, hoping for the miracle of parenthood that Akbar was blessed with.

Next to it, in the courtyard, is the larger, red, sandstone tomb of **Nawab Islam Khan**, Sheikh Salim's grandson, and other members of the family.

Buland Darwaza (Triumphal Gate) dominates the south wall but it is a bit out of place. Built to celebrate Akbar's brilliant conquest of Gujarat (circa 1576), it sets the style for later gateways. The high gate is approached from the outside by a flight of steps which adds to its grandeur. The decoration shows Hindu influence, but is severe and restrained, emphasizing the lines of its arches with plain surfaces. You see an inscription on the right of a verse from the Qur'an:

> Said Jesus Son of Mary (on whom be peace):
> The world is but a bridge; pass over it but build no houses on it.
> He who hopes for an hour, hopes for Eternity.
> The world is an hour. Spend it in prayer, for the rest is unseen.

Outside the Royal Palace

Between the Royal Palace and the Jami Masjid, a paved pathway to the northwest leads to the **Hathipol** (Elephant Gate). This was the ceremonial entrance to the palace quarters, guarded by stone elephants, with its *nakkar khana* and bazar alongside. Nearby are the **waterworks**, with a deep well which had an ingenious mechanism for raising water to the aqueducts above ridge height. The **caravanserai** around a large courtyard fits on the ridge side, and was probably one of a series built to accommodate travellers, tradesmen and guards. Down a ramp immediately beyond is the **Hiran Minar**, an unusual tower studded with stone tusks, thought to commemorate Akbar's favourite elephant, Hiran. However, it was probably an *Akash Diya* (lamp to light the sky) or the 'zero point' for marking road distances in *kos*. You can climb up the spiral staircase inside it but take care as the top has no rail. This part of Fatehpur Sikri is off the main tourist track, and though less well preserved it is worth the detour to get the 'lost city' feeling, away from the crowds.

Agra and around listings

For hotel and restaurant price codes and other relevant information, see pages 12-15.

🛏 Where to stay

Agra *p64, map p66*

It's a mixed bag in Agra. Some of the cheap hotels have great rooftop views in **Taj Ganj** but little else going for them. Unless you are staying at **Amar Vilas** (Oberoi) you are not likely to be blessed with a view. Most of the upscale hotels are along **Fatehabad Rd**, a rather charmless strip of pricey restaurants, international fast-food outlets and handicrafts emporia.

$$$$ Amar Vilas, near Taj East Gate, T0562-223 1515, www.amarvilas.com. 102 rooms, all Taj-facing – the only place in Agra with such superlative views – designed in strict adherence to the Mughal style. Beautiful rooms, the best feature being the view. Stunning swimming pool, lovely gardens, extraordinary ambience. Guests are entertained at sunset with traditional dancing and musicians. If you can splash out on your trip, this is the place to do it. A magical experience.

$$$$ Grand Imperial, Mahatma Gandhi Rd, T0562-225 1190, www.hotelgrandimperial. com. Agra's first bid at a genuine heritage hotel, with 30 opulent rooms, some still displaying their original red brickwork, arcaded around a pleasant lawn in a 100-year-old neoclassical mansion, all modern facilities, smart international restaurant with live classical Indian music at dinner. Swimming pool and small spa. Charming staff. The only drawback is the distance from the Taj and the proximity to a loud main road. Recommended.

$$$$ The Mughal, Fatehabad Rd, T0562-233 1701, www.itchotels.in. Stunning suites, beautiful gardens, lovely pool. The new wing is particularly lovely. They have the award-winning **Kaya Kalp** spa. Low-rise construction means only rooftop observatory offers good views of the Taj. Excellent restaurant.

$$-$ Hotel Kamal, South Gate, near Taj Ganj police station, T0562-233 0126, www. hotelkamal.com. Good option in this area – variety of rooms, some with more mod cons and a/c. Great view from the rooftop restaurant although food fairly mediocre.

$ Sidhartha, Western Gate, T(0)9719-456998, www.hotelsidharta.com. One of the best in this **Taj Ganj** area. Clean and basic rooms and close proximity to the Taj Mahal.

$ Sheela, East Gate, 2 mins' walk from the Taj, T0562-329 3437, www.hotelsheelaagra. com. Popular although fairly basic rooms. Friendly place – good for meeting other travellers. Pleasant garden, good restaurant. Very helpful manager. Good location in low pollution area.

🍴 Restaurants

Agra *p64, map p66*

$$$ Esphahan, Amar Vilas (see Where to stay). Outstanding, rich Avadhi food in high-class setting, but non-residents will find it hard to get a table.

$$$ Mughal Room, Hotel Clarks Shiraz, 54 Taj Rd. Standard 5-star fare, rich and meaty, mainly distinguished by glassed-in rooftop setting with great views over the city.

$$$ Peshawari, The Mughal (see Where to stay, left). Regarded as the city's best, refined North Indian cuisine, smart surroundings, vegetarian offerings less inspired.

$$ Only, 45 Taj Rd, T0562-236 4333. Interesting menu, attractive outside seating, popular with tour groups, live entertainment.

$$ Riao, next to Clarks Shiraz, 44 Taj Rd, T(0)9412-154311. Good North Indian food, puppet shows and live music, great garden and atmosphere.

$ Joney's Place, near South Gate, Taj Ganj. The original and, despite numerous similarly named imitators, still the best. Tiny place but the food is consistently good. Can produce Israeli and Korean specialities. Recommended.

$ Maya, 18 Purani Mandi Circle, Fatehabad Rd. Varied menu, good Punjabi *thalis*, pasta, 'special tea', friendly, prompt service, hygienic, tasty, Moroccan-style decor. Recommended.

$ Zorba the Buddha, E-19 Sadar Bazaar, T0562-222 6091, zorbaevergreen@yahoo. com. Open 1200-1500, 1800-2100. Run by disciples of Osho, one of India's more popular, and most libidinous, gurus. Unusual menu (in a good way), naan breads a speciality, very clean, undersize furniture gives doll's house feel, an enjoyably quirky experience.

❀ Festivals

Agra *p64, map p66*
18-27 Feb Taj Mahotsav, a celebration of the region's arts, crafts, culture and cuisine.
Aug/Sep A fair at Kailash (14 km away). A temple marks the spot where Siva is believed to have appeared in the form of a stone lingam.

O Shopping

Agra *p64, map p66*
Agra specializes in jewellery, inlaid and carved marble, carpets and clothes. The main shopping areas are Sadar Bazar (closed Tue), Kinari Bazar, Gwalior Rd, Mahatma Gandhi Rd and Pratap Pura. Beware, you may order a carpet or an inlaid marble piece and have it sent later but it may not be what you ordered. Never agree to any export 'deals' and take great care with credit card slips (scams reported). Many rickshaws, taxi drivers and guides earn up to 40% commission by taking tourists to shops. Insist on not being rushed away from sights and shop independently. To get a good price you have to bargain hard anyway.

Carpets
Silk/cotton/wool mix hand-knotted carpets and woven *dhurries* are all made in Agra. High quality and cheaper than in Delhi.

Kanu Carpet Factory, Purani Mandi, Fetehabad Rd, T0562-233 0167. A reliable source.
Mughal Arts Emporium, Shamshabad Rd. Also has marble. Artificial silk is sometimes passed off as pure silk.

Marble
Delicately inlaid marble work is a speciality. Sometimes cheaper alabaster and soapstone is used and quality varies.
Akbar International, Fatehabad Rd. Good selection, inlay demonstration, fair prices.
Handicrafts Inn, 3 Garg Niketan, Fatehabad Rd, Taj Ganj.
Krafts Palace, 506 The Mall. Watch craftsmen working here.
UP Handicrafts Palace, 49 Bansal Nagar. Wide selection from table tops to coasters, high quality and good value.

◑ What to do

Agra *p64, map p66*
Tour operators
Mercury, Hotel Clarks Shiraz, 54 Taj Rd, T0562-222 6531. Helpful and reliable.
Travel Bureau, near Taj View Hotel, T0562-233 0245, www.travelbureauagra.com. Long-established local company, highly experienced (handle ground arrangements for most foreign travel agents), helpful, can arrange anything. Recommended.
UP Tours, Taj Khema (5 mins' walk from Taj East Gate), T0562-233 0140, tajkhema@ up-tourism.com. Coach tours: Fatehpur Sikri-Taj Mahal–Agra Fort (full day) 1030-1830, Rs 1700 (Indian Rs 400) including guide and entry fees; half-day Fatehpur Sikri tour ends at 1300 which only gives 45 mins at the site, not worthwhile, better take a taxi if you can afford it. Sikandra–Fatehpur Sikri (half day) 0930-1400, Rs 100 (excludes entry fees); Sikandra–Fatehpur Sikri–Taj Mahal–Agra Fort (full day), 1030-1830. Tours start and finish at Agra Cantt Railway Station and tie in with arrival/departure of *Taj Express* (see Transport); check times. Pick-up also possible from India Tourism office on The Mall.

World Ways, Taj East Gate, T(0)9358-499616, worldways@mail.com. Arrangements for budget travellers.

⊖ Transport

Agra *p64, map p66*
Air Kheria Airport is 7 km from city centre. Only charter flights and in theory it's quicker by train anyway.

Auto rickshaw Pre-paid stand at Agra Cantt Station has prices clearly listed for point-to-point rates and sightseeing. Expect to pay Rs 80-100 to Fatehabad Rd or Taj Ganj.

Cycle rickshaw Negotiate (pay more to avoid visiting shops); Taj Ganj to Fort Rs 5; Rs 80-200 for visiting sights.

Local bus City Bus Service covers most areas and main sights. Plenty leave from the Taj Mahal area and the Fort Bus Stand.

Long-distance bus Most long-distance services leave from the Idgah Bus Stand, T0562-242 0324, including to: **Delhi** (4-5 hrs) via **Mathura** (1 hr); **Fatehpur Sikri** (40 km, 1 hr); **Bharatpur** (2 hrs); **Khajuraho** (10 hrs). Agra Fort Stand, T0562-236 4557, has additional buses to **Delhi**. Deluxe buses for **Jaipur** arrive and depart from a stop near Hotel Sakura: closer to most hotels and where there is less hassle from touts. **Delhi** from tourist office, 0700, 1445, deluxe, 4 hrs.

Taxi/car hire Tourist taxis from travel agents, remarkably good value for visiting nearby sights. Full day Rs 1500 (100 km), half day Rs 950 (45 km); a/c rates and more luxury cars are pricier; to Fatehpur Sikri Rs 2300 again can be pricier depending on car). **Travel Bureau**, T0562-233 0230; **UP Tours**, T0562-233 0140.

Train To/from **Delhi** train is the quickest and most reliable way. Most trains use **Agra Cantonment Railway Station**, 5 km west of Taj Mahal, enquiries T131, reservations T0562-242 1039, open 0800-2000. Foreigners' queue at Window 1. Pre-paid taxi/auto-rickshaw kiosk outside the station. Some trains to Rajasthan from quieter **Agra Fort Station**, T132, T0562-236 9590. Trains mentioned arrive and depart from **Agra Cantt** unless specified. To **Delhi**: *Shatabdi Exp 12001* (**ND**), 2040, 2½ hrs; *Taj Exp 12279*, (**HN**), 1855, 3¼ hrs (CC/II); *Intercity Exp 11103*, (**HN**), 0600, 3½ hrs (2nd class only). To **Jaipur**: *Intercity Exp 12307*, 1645, 6 hrs (from Agra Fort); *Marudhar Exp 14853/63*, 0715, 6¾ hrs. **Jhansi** (via Gwalior): *Taj Express 12280*, 1015, 3 hrs (Gwalior 1¾ hrs), **Sawai Madhopur** (for Ranthambore) at 0600, 0900, 1800.

Fatehpur Sikri *p73*
Bus Frequent buses from Agra Idgah Bus Stand (1 hr) Rs 17.

Taxi Taxis from Agra include the trip in a day's sightseeing (expect to pay around 2300 return depending on car).

⊙ Directory

Agra *p64, map p66*
Medical services Ambulance: T102. District Hospital, Chhipitola Rd/Mahatma Gandhi Rd, T0562-236 2043. Dr VN, Kaushal, opposite Imperial Cinema, T0562-236 3550. Recommended. **Police** T100. **Post** GPO opposite India Tourist Office.

Madhya Pradesh

From the proud forts of Gwalior and Orchha to the sacred temples of Khajuraho and the jungles of Bandhavgarh, these are some of the key sites in the state of Madhya Pradesh which contains many of the tribal groups least touched by modernization and most of India's remaining genuine forest. The magnificent palaces of Orchha and temples of Khajuraho testify to the power of Rajput dynasties for over a thousand years.

Background

The land
Geography Madhya Pradesh has some magnificent scenery. The dominating **Vindhyan mountains** run diagonally across the heart of Madhya Pradesh while the Kaimur range runs to the north and east, overlooking the Gangetic plain around Varanasi and Allahabad. Both rise to 600 m but are frequently cut by deep forest-clad ravines. Behind the Kaimur range is the **Baghelkhand plateau** while the Hazaribagh range juts into the state in the east. The **Narmada** rising in the east, flows west to the Arabian Sea, along with the Tapti to its south. Black volcanic soils are often visible across the state, but in some places the land is stony and inhospitable. Between Gwalior and Jhansi the Chambal River has dug deep gorges, creating a *badlands* area which **dacoits** have enjoyed as hideouts. Wildlife wise, things seem to be looking up for the tigers of Madhya Pradesh. In the 2010 Tiger Census, the tiger population of this state was up by 43 to 257. Some say that the improved numbers nationwide (1706 tigers, up 295 since the last count) is due to improved counting, but the results are still good.

History
Rock paintings and stone artefacts prove the existence of Stone Age cultures. Although the region was incorporated into successive states from the empire of Asoka to that of the Mughals, it was rarely the centre of a major power.

In the 10th century a number of dynasties controlled different parts of the region, most notably the Chandelas at Khajuraho. Gwalior was conquered in the 11th century by the Muslims, whose influence spread southeast under the Khaljis into Malwa during the 13th century. Akbar annexed this into his empire in the mid-16th century. The Scindia and Holkar dynasties of Marathas ruled independently at Gwalior and Indore respectively during the 18th century.

Under the British the region became known as the Central Provinces and under the state re-organization after Independence the modern state of Madhya Pradesh was created.

Culture
Even though the majority of the former state of Madhya Pradesh's tribal people now have their own state of Chhattisgarh, Madhya Pradesh remains the home of many tribals, including Bhils, Gonds and Baigas. Many have been painfully absorbed into the mainstream of Indian life. Hindi is the most widely spoken language. On each of the

borders the languages of neighbouring states – particularly Marathi and Gujarati in the west – are quite commonly used. The Bhils speak **Bhili** and the Gonds **Gondi**, independent in origin to the Indo-European and Dravidian language groups.

Textiles are important but Madhya Pradesh also has a strong traditional village handicraft industry. Handloom *Chanderi* and *Maheshwar* silks are especially sought after. The tribal people produce attractive handicrafts.

The boulder-strewn, thinly wooded Vindhya hills stretch across the north of the state, connecting some of the most fascinating historic monuments in central India. Foremost among them are the fascinating Tantric temples of Khajuraho, the sole raison d'être of a touristy village rendered slightly seedy by a cadre of boys who assume that anyone willing to endure the bus odyssey required to get here must be desperate for something. Further west, the riverside village of Orchha has all the ingredients for a relaxing break from the road, with palaces and lots of ruined mausoleums to explore, while Gwalior, a couple of hours by train from Agra, has one of the most awesome palace forts in the state.

Gwalior → *For listings, see pages 98-103.*

Surrounded by attractive open plateau country immediately to the north of the Vindhyas, Gwalior is set in one of the state's driest regions. The majestic hill fort, formerly the key to control of the Central Provinces, dominates a ridge overlooking the town spread out below. It contains awe-inspiring Jain sculptures, Jain and Hindu temples and the charming sandstone palace. The Jai Vilas Palace, within its walls, bears testimony to the idiosyncratic

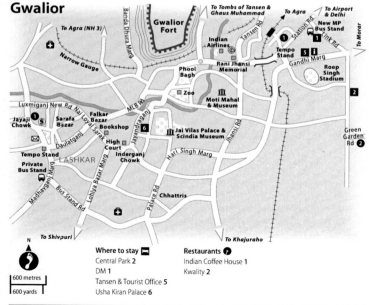

Gwalior

Where to stay 🛏
Central Park 2
DM 1
Tansen & Tourist Office 5
Usha Kiran Palace 6

Restaurants 🍴
Indian Coffee House 1
Kwality 2

tastes of the Scindia Maharajas. Much of the town, which sees few tourists, is very busy, noisy and crowded.

Arriving in Gwalior

Getting there There are daily flights from Delhi and Indore, but the *Shatabdi Express* gives Gwalior excellent train connections with Agra and Delhi to the north and Jhansi and Bhopal to the south. The railway station and Madhya Pradesh State Bus Stand are southeast of the fort. From there, it is 6 km along the dusty MLB Road to the Jayaji Chowk area of Lashkar, the New Town. ➤➤ *See Transport, page 102.*

Getting around In addition to a *tempo* stand near the station, there are unmetered autos and taxis. Gwalior is quite spread out and the fort is a stiff climb.

Tourist information Tourist office ⓘ *Platform 1, railway station, T0751-504 0777, and at MPTC hotel Tansen Residency, T0751-234 0370.*

History

In legend, Gwalior's history goes back to AD 8 when the chieftain **Suraj Sen** was cured of leprosy by a hermit saint, Gwalipa. In gratitude he founded and named the city after him. An inscription in the fort records that during the fifth-century reign of Mihiragula the Hun, a temple of the sun was erected here. Later, Rajput clans took and held the fort. Muslim invaders like **Qutb-ud-din-Aibak** (12th century) ruled Gwalior before it passed through a succession of Tomar Rajput, Mughal, Afghan and Maratha hands. During the 1857 **Mutiny**, the Maharaja remained loyal to the British but 6500 of his troops mutinied on 14 June. The next year, there was fierce fighting round Gwalior, the rebels being led by Tantia Topi and the **Rani of Jhansi**. When the fort was taken by the British, the Rani was found, dressed in men's clothes, among the slain.

The fort

ⓘ *Sunrise-sunset, Foreigners Rs 100, Indians Rs 5 allow at least 2-3 hrs. Palaces open 0930-1700. English-speaking guides here expect Rs 200 (hotel guides charge more).*
The fort stands on a sandstone precipice 91 m above the surrounding plain, 2.8 km long and 200-850 m wide. In places the cliff overhangs, elsewhere it has been steepened to make it unscaleable. The main entrance to the north comprised a twisting, easily defended approach. On the west is the **Urwahi Gorge** and another well-guarded entrance. The fort's size is impressive but the eye cannot capture all of it at once. Apart from its natural defences, Gwalior had the advantage of an unlimited water supply with many tanks on the plateau.

Approach The fort is a long walk from the town. You may enter from the northeast by the Gwalior or Alamgiri Gate but it is quite a steep climb. Mineral water is sold at the ticket counter; decline the booklet. Alternatively, take a taxi or an auto-rickshaw and enter from the west by the Urwahi Gate, where there are interesting Jain sculptures. After visiting the temples and palaces, you can descend to the Gujari Mahal in the northeast and pick up an auto from the Gwalior Gate. Visitors to the fort, particularly young women, should be prepared and aware that they may receive some unwanted attention from bored local teenage boys who often hang around inside the fort. Dressing modestly is definitely recommended.

Western entrance Above the **Urwahi Gate** there are 21 Jain sculptures dating from the seventh to 15th centuries, some up to 20 m tall. An offended Babur ordered their faces and genitalia to be destroyed. Modern restorers have only repaired the faces. There is a paved terrace along one side (ask to be dropped near the steps to view the sculptures since vehicles may not park along the road).

Northeast entrance A 1-km steep, rough ramp, with good views, leads to the main palace buildings. You pass through the **Gwalior Gate** (1660), the first of several gates, mostly built between 1486 and 1516. Next is the Badalgarh or **Hindola Gate**, named because of the swing which was once here. It is (unusually) a true structural arch, flanked by two circular towers. Note the use of material from older buildings.

At the base of the ramp the **Gujari Mahal Palace** (circa 1510) containing the **Gujari Mahal Archaeological Museum** ⓘ *Tue-Sun 1000-1700, Rs 30*. The pretty palace has an interesting collection including sculptures and archaeological pieces (second and first century BC), terracottas (Vidisha, Ujjain), coins and paintings and copies of frescoes from the Bagh caves. Ask the curator to show you the beautiful 10th-century Shalbhanjika (Tree Goddess) miniature. Some museums and palaces are closed on Monday. Some distance from the fort above, this palace was built by Raja Man Singh for his Gujar queen Mrignayani. The exterior is well preserved. The 'Bhairon' Gate no longer exists and the fourth is the simple **Ganesh Gate** with a *kabutar khana* (pigeon house) and a small tank nearby. The mosque beyond stands on the site of an old shrine to the hermit Gwalipa, the present temple having been built later with some of the original material. Before the **Lakshman Gate** (circa 14th century) is the ninth-century Vishnu **Chaturbhuja Temple**, with later additions, in a deep gap. A Muslim tomb and the northeast group of Jain sculptures are nearby. **Hathia Paur** (Elephant Gate, 1516), the last, is the entrance to the main Man Mandir palace which also had a Hawa gate, now demolished.

Man Mandir Palace (1486-1516) Built by Raja Man Singh, this is the most impressive building in the fort. The 30-m-high eastern retaining wall is a vast rock face on the cliff-side interrupted by large rounded bastions. The palace had ornamental parapets and cupolas, once brightly gilded, while blue, green and yellow tile-work with patterns of elephants, human figures, ducks, parrots, banana plants and flowers covered the exterior walls. The remarkable tiles, and the style of their inlay, are probably derived from Chanderi (200 km south) or Mandu. The beautifully decorated little rooms arranged round two inner courts have small entrances, suggesting they were built for the royal ladies. The iron rings here were used for swings and decorative wall hangings.

Interestingly, in addition to the two storeys above ground there are two underground floors which provided refuge from hot weather and acted as circular dungeons when required; these should not be missed. Guru Har Gobind who was once detained here was freed at the behest of Nur Jahan – he was permitted to take out any others who could touch his shawl so he attached eight tassels which enabled 56 prisoners to be freed with him. On 24 June 1658 Emperor Aurangzeb took his elder brother Murad captive en route to Delhi and then transferred him to Gwalior fort to be imprisoned. In December of the same year Aurangzeb ordered his execution.

Angled ventilation ducts allowed in fresh air while pipes in the walls were used as 'speaking tubes'. You will find an octagonal bath which would have been filled with perfumed water – the water welled up through inlet holes in the floor which have now been blocked. The south wall which incorporates the arched Hathia Paur with its guardroom above is particularly ornate with moulded and colourfully tiled friezes. A small **museum** ① *Sat-Sun 0800-1800, guides available, worthwhile for the underground floors if you don't have a torch; give a small tip,* opposite the façade, has interesting archaeological pieces of Hindu deities. **Note** A torch is essential to explore the lower floors: there are holes in the floor, some of which are quite deep. Underground levels are infested with bats (easily disturbed) and so there is a revolting smell.

The nightly **Son et Lumière** ① *Hindi at 1830, English at 1930 (1 hr later in summer), 45 mins, foreigners Rs 150, Indians Rs 40,* is well worth attending for stunning illumination of Man Mandir. The colourful spectacle traces the history of Gwalior fort through interesting anecdotes. Winter evenings can be chilly, so bring warm clothes; a torch is useful at any time of year. There is unlikely to be any transport available at the end of the show, so hire a taxi (Rs 250-300 return including wait), or make the fort your last stop when hiring a car for the day in the summer (day hire covers only a single fort visit).

Vikramaditya Palace (1516) ① *Tue-Sun 0800-1700 (1 Apr-30 Sep, 0700-1000, 1500-1800), free.* Located between Man Mandir and Karan Mandir, the palace is connected with them by narrow galleries. Inside is a *baradari* (open hall) with a domed roof. Opposite the Dhonda Gate is the **Karan Mandir** (1454-1479), more properly called the Kirtti Mandir after its builder Raja Kirtti Singh. It is a long, two-storeyed building with a large, pillared hall and fine plaster moulding on ceilings of adjacent rooms. Just northwest is the **Jauhar Tank** where the Rajput women performed *jauhar* (mass suicide) just before the fort was taken by Iltutmish in 1232, and also at Chittaurgarh. The two unremarkable Muslim palaces, Jahangiri and Shah Jahan Mahals are further north. Moving south from Hathia Paur, towards the east wall, are the **Sas Bahu Mandirs**. Dedicated to Vishnu, the 11th-century 'Mother and Daughter-in-law' pair of temples built by Mahipala Kachhawaha (1093) still preserve fine carvings in places. The larger 12-sided temple is more interesting although only the *Mahamandapa* (Assembly Hall) remains. The smaller temple has an ornately carved base with a frieze of elephants, and a vaulted ceiling under the pyramidal roof. The wide ridged stone 'awning' is well preserved. An impressive modern marble **gurudwara** (1970) in memory of Sikh Guru Har Gobind (1595-1644), who had been imprisoned in the fort, is to its south, providing a haven of cool respite for visitors; the Guru Granth Sahib is read throughout the day. West of the *gurudwara* is **Suraj Kund**, a large tank, first referred to in the fifth century, where Suraj Sen's leprosy was cured. The water is now green and stagnant.

Teli-ka Mandir Teli-ka Mandir probably means 'oil man's temple'. It is the earliest temple in Gwalior, and architecturally has more in common with some early Orissan temples than those in the south (though sometimes guides suggest a link with Telangana in modern Andhra Pradesh indicating the fusion of Dravidian and North Indian architectural styles). This unique 25-m-high Pratihara (mid-eighth century) Vishnu Temple is essentially a sanctuary with a *Garuda* at the entrance. The oblong vaulted roof rather resembles a Buddhist *chaitya* and the Vaital Deul (Bhubaneswar). Tillotson records how after the 'Mutiny' "this great medieval temple, for example, was put to service as a soda-water factory and coffee shop. By such acts of desecration the British showed Indian rulers how the ancient Hindu heritage was then regarded by those who laid claim to power and authority". It was reconstructed in 1881-1883. The Katora Tal behind was excavated when the fort was built, like many others here. The Ek-khamba Tal has a single stone column standing in it.

Rani Tal, further south, was supposedly intended for the royal ladies; it is connected underground to the neighbouring **Chedi Tal**. Jain sculptures in the southeast corner can be seen from a path below the wall.

The town

After Daulat Rao Scindia acquired Gwalior in 1809 he pitched camp to the south of the fort. The new city that arose was **Lashkar** (The Camp) with palaces, King George Park (now Gandhi Park) and the *chhattris* of the Maharajas. **Jayaji Chowk**, once an elegant square, dominated by late 19th- and early 20th-century buildings, notably the Regal Cinema, and the Chowk Bazar can still be a pleasant place to watch people going about their business from one of the good little restaurants.

Jai Vilas Palace (1872-1874) ① *Tue-Sun 1000-1730, tickets at gate: foreigners Rs 300, Indians Rs 40, guided tours (1 hr) sometimes compulsory*, designed by Lieutenant-Colonel Sir Michael Filose, resembles an Italian palazzo in places, using painted sandstone to imitate marble. Part of the palace is the present maharaja's residence but 35 rooms house the **Scindia Museum**, an idiosyncratic collection of royal possessions, curiosities (eg 3-D mirror portraits), carpets (note the Persian rug with royal portraits) and interesting memorabilia.

In a separate building opposite (show ticket) is the extraordinary **Durbar Hall**. It is approached by a crystal staircase, gilded in 56 kg of gold, and in it hang two of the world's largest chandeliers each weighing 3.5 tonnes; before they were hung the ceiling was tested by getting 10 elephants to climb on to it via a 2-km ramp. Underneath is the dining room. The battery-operated silver train set transported cigars, dry fruit and drinks round the table, after dinner. The lifting of a container or bottle would automatically reduce pressure on the track, and so stop the train. Southeast of the fort is the spot where **Rani Lakshmi Bai** of Jhansi was cremated, marked by a stirring statue.

The **Royal Chhattris**, south of town, are each dedicated to a Gwalior Maharaja. These ghostly pavilions are in various stages of neglect. The lighted images are still clothed and 'fed' daily. Be there at 1600 when they are shown again by the guardians after their afternoon nap.

In the crowded Hazira in the **Old Town**, northeast of the fort, is the **Tomb of Ghaus Muhammad**, a 16th-century Afghan prince who helped Babur to win the fort. It is in an early Mughal style with finely carved *jali* screens. Hindus and Muslims both make pilgrimage to the tomb. Nearby, in an attractive garden setting, is the **Tomb of Tansen**, the most famous musician of Akbar's court. It is the venue for the annual music festival (November/December). The present tamarind tree replaces the old one which was believed to have magical properties. Tansen was an exponent of the *dhrupad* style, and laid the foundations for what in the 19th century became the Gwalior *ghurana* style, noted for its stress on composition and forceful performance. One of the best-known contemporary exponents is Amjad Ali Khan, a renowned sarod player. A recently built **Sun Temple** similar in style to Konark is at Morar, a few kilometres east of the tombs.

Orchha → *For listings, see pages 98-103.*

Highly picturesque, in the middle of nowhere, abandoned and somewhat neglected, Orchha is an ideal stop between Gwalior and Khajuraho. Set on an island on a bend in the Betwa River, the fort palace from a bygone era is raised on a rocky promontory above the surrounding wooded countryside. This largely untouched island of peace and calm is approached from the congested, increasingly touristy village centre by a remarkable early 17th-century granite bridge built by Bir Singh Deo, while all around, the forest encroaches on the tombs and monuments.

Arriving in Orchha

Getting there Orchha is quite easily reached by road from Jhansi (major trains stop here). After travelling 9 km southeast along the Khajuraho Road, a minor road turns south for the remaining 7 km to Orchha. There are taxis, *tempos* or buses from Jhansi station, but it is best to travel during daylight hours, and book and enquire about onward buses well ahead.

Getting around The fort palace complex and the village are all easily seen on foot. The riverside is a 10-minute stroll away. If you are laden with luggage you can get a rickshaw from the village centre to your hotel. Women are advised not to wander around the site alone.

History

The Bundela chief **Raja Rudra Pratap** (1501-1531) chose an easily defended and beautiful site for his capital. In the 11th century, a Rajput prince is said to have offered himself as a sacrifice to the mountain goddess Vrindavasini; she prevented his death and named him 'Bundela' (one who offered blood). The dynasty ruled over the area between the Yamuna and Narmada rivers, having stepped into the vacuum left by the Tughlaqs and extended their power, moving their base to Orchha (meaning hidden). Raja Rudra Pratap threw a wall around the existing settlement and began work on the palace building (circa 1525-1531) and an arched bridge to it. This was completed by his successor Bharti Chand (1531-1554) who was installed in the Raj Mahal with great ceremony.

The continuing fortunes of the dynasty may have stemmed from the rulers' diplomatic skills. Though the third ruler, the religious **Madhukar Shah**, was defeated in battle by Akbar and was exiled in 1578 (died 1592), he nevertheless won the Mughal emperor's friendship. Later **Bir Singh Deo** (1605-1627), while opposing Akbar, aligned himself with Prince Salim (Jahangir), who later rewarded him with the throne of Orchha, thus ensuring its ongoing prosperity. The Jahangir Mahal was built to commemorate the emperor's visit to Orchha. However, Bir Singh's first son, Jhujan, ran foul of Shah Jahan and, ignoring orders, treacherously killed the neighbouring chief of Chauragarh. The imperial army routed Jhujan and Orchha was pillaged. In 1783 the Bundela capital was moved to Tikamgarh, leaving Orchha to the *dhak* forests, the Betwa River and its guardian eagles.

The site

ⓘ *Foreigners Rs 250, Indians Rs 5, camera (no flash) Rs 20, video Rs 50; ticket office at palace, 0800-1800. Allow 2 hrs. Audio tour from Sheesh Mahal hotel, Rs 50. Highly recommended. The buildings are in a bad state of repair. If you go to the top take extra care and carry a torch.*

Orchha is a wonderful example of a medieval fort palace. Within the turreted walls are gardens, gateways, pavilions and temples, near the Betwa and Jamni rivers. On a moonlit night, the view across the palaces with their *chhattris* and ornamented battlements is enchanting. A suggested route is to visit the Raj Mahal with its Hall of Private Audience then go through the doorway to the Hall of Public Audience. From here go down the ramp and follow the path to the Rai Praveen Mahal. Continue along the path to the Jahangir Mahal, arriving back at the courtyard of the Sheesh Mahal.

The **Raj Mahal**, to the right of the quadrangle, exemplifies Bundela Rajput architecture. There are two rectangular courtyards around which the floors rise in tiers (inspired by the Koshak Mahal in Chanderi, which was built a century earlier); typically there are cool chambers below ground and a fountain. Some of the original blue tile decoration remains on the upper outer walls. To the left of the first courtyard is the Hall of Private Audience which would have been covered with rich carpets and cushions (note floor-level windows). The Hall of the Public Audience has two quarter-size plaster elephants. Despite the neglected appearance of the royal chambers off the second courtyard, some have beautiful murals on the ceilings and walls. Representing both religious and secular themes, one series is devoted to the *Ramayana*, another to Vishnu's incarnations, others to scenes of court life – musicians, hunters, river excursions, fairground. Normally locked, but the caretaker will unlock some ground floor rooms. Don't miss Rooms 5 and 6 which have the best paintings but you will need a torch. There is a Sheesh Mahal upstairs as well as good views of other palaces and temples from the very top; watch your step though, especially in strong winds.

Rai Praveen Mahal was probably named after the musician-courtesan who was a favourite at the princely court of Indrajit, brother of Ram Shah (1592-1604). The low two-storey brick palace with cool underground chambers and beautifully carved stone niches is built to scale with surrounding trees and the Anand Mandal gardens. To get to the underground rooms, turn left down steps on exiting the main rooms.

The octagonal flowerbeds are ingeniously watered from two wells. A new path takes you via the **hamaam**, bypassing the **Royal Gate**, and past the **Camel Stables** to the most impressive of the three palaces.

Jahangir Mahal, built in the 17th century by Raja Bir Singh Deo to commemorate the Emperor's visit, synthesizes Hindu and Muslim styles as a tribute to his benefactor. The 70-m-sq palace, which is best entered from the east, the original main entrance flanked by elephants, can also be entered from the south. It has a large square interior courtyard, around which are the apartments in three storeys. The guided tour goes to the top of these up narrow and dark stairways. Each corner bastion and the projection in the middle of each side is topped by a dome. These contain apartments with intervening terraces – hanging balconies with balustrades and wide eaves create strong lines set off by attractive arches and brackets, decorative cobalt and turquoise blue tiles, *chhattris* and *jali* screens giving this huge palace a delicate and airy feel. There is a small **museum** ① *Sat-Thu 1000-1700*, with a run-down assortment of photos, sculptures and *sati* stones; labels are in Hindi.

A few minutes' walk south of the main palace complex is **Saaket** ① *1000-1700, Rs 40*, an excellent new museum displaying Ramayana paintings in traditional folk styles from Orissa, Bihar, Maharashtra, Andhra Pradesh and Bengal. The paintings, on palm leaves, silk and organically dyed cotton, are of the highest quality, and the stories behind them fascinating.

The village

Just south of the crossroads is the **Ram Raja Temple** ① *0800-1230, 1900-2130 (1 hr later on summer evenings), cameras and leather articles must be left outside*, which forms a focus for village life. The temple courtyard and the narrow lane leading to it have stalls selling souvenirs and the area occasionally swells with pilgrims and *sanyasis*. The pink and cream paint is not in keeping with the other temples. It is interesting to visit during *arati*; otherwise there is little to see inside. Following the appearance of Rama in a dream, the pious Madhukar Shah brought an image of the god from Ayodhya and placed it in this palace prior to its installation in a temple. However, when the temple was ready it proved impossible to shift the image and the king remembered, only too late, the divine instruction that the deity must remain in the place where it was first installed. It is the only palace-turned-temple in the country where Rama is worshipped as king.

Chaturbhuj Temple ① *usually open 0800-1700*, up the steps from the Ram Raja Temple courtyard, was built by King Madhukar Shah for his Queen Kunwari to house the image of Rama brought from Ayodhya. Laid out in the form of a cross, a symbolic representation of the four-armed god Krishna, there is a triple-arched gate with attractive *jharokas* on the exterior. The tallest *sikhara* is over the Garbagriha shrine, to the left of which you will see a Ganesh and a set of kettle drums. The high arches and ceilings with vaulting and lotus domes painted in a rich red in places, are particularly striking. You can climb up any of the corner staircases, which lead up, by stages, to the very top of the temple. The second level gives access to tiny decorated balconies which provided privileged seating. There are good views of the nine palaces from the top, reached by the mini labyrinth of narrow corridors and steps. On the roof are langurs, wild bee hives and vultures nesting in corner towers.

A 1-km paved path links the Ram Raja with Bir Singh Deo's early 17th-century **Lakshminarayan Temple** ① *0900-1700, 15-min walk*, on a low hill, which incorporates elements of fort architecture. The ticket attendant gives a 'tour', naming the characters illustrated; go up the tower, the steps are steep but there are very good views of the entire area. The typical village houses along the path are freshly whitewashed for **Diwali**. The diagonal plan enclosing the central square temple structure is most unusual. The excellent murals (religious and secular), on the interior walls and ceilings of the four cool galleries around the temple here, are well-preserved examples of the Bundela school. The paintings in red, black, yellow, grey and turquoise portray Hindu deities, scenes from the epics, historical events including the early British period (note the interesting details of Lakshmi Bai's battle against the British), as well as giving an insight into the domestic pleasures of royalty.

Phool Bagh is a formal garden and an eight-pillared pavilion which has a cool underground apartment. Well worth a visit.

Of the 15 **Royal Chhattris** to former rulers grouped by the Kanchana Ghat by the river, about half are neglected and overgrown but pleasant for walking around in the late afternoon. A few are well preserved; ask the watchman if you want to look inside. He will take you to the upper levels by some very narrow, dark stairs: good fun but take a torch and be careful. He will expect a small tip. The chhattris are best photographed from the opposite bank: take a stick as dogs can be a problem.

The small but busy **village bazar**, with some interesting temples nearby, is about 10 minutes walk from the riverside where a series of royal *chhattris* still stand as sentinels. The riverside is ideal for lazing under a shady tree. Cross the bridge and head upstream for better spots for swimming (watch out for currents).

Khajuraho → *For listings, see pages 98-103.*

Khajuraho, home to what are now perhaps the most famous of India's temples on account of their remarkable erotic sculptures, lies in a rich, well-watered plain. Set miles from the nearest town in an open forested and cultivated landscape with the striking Vindhyan ranges as a backdrop, it is listed as a World Heritage Site. Sadly, Khajuraho's drastically defined rich and lean seasons have bred a particular culture, and you may find yourself subjected to a barrage of sleazy salesmen, touts and junior con artists capable of sweet-talking you in three different languages. Nevertheless, the village away from the tourist areas maintains a pleasant laid-back feel, and early mornings even at the main temples can be wonderfully calm and peaceful. The best time to visit is between October and March. From April to June it becomes very hot, dry and dusty.

Arriving in Khajuraho
Getting there Daily flights connect Khajuraho with Delhi and Varanasi. The airport is only 5 km from most hotels, with cycle-rickshaws and taxis available for transfer. Buses

travel to Jhansi and Satna, both with good railway connections, but they become horrifically packed: if you can afford only one taxi ride in India, let it be here. We hope that MP Tourism and the local governments get around to doing something about the roads. There is a railway station around 7 km north of town, on the line to Mahoba and Varanasi with daily trains between Jhansi and Khajuraho. ▸▸ *See Transport, page 102.*

Getting around Khajuraho is still a small village though the temples are scattered over 8 sq km. Although some are within walking distance, hiring a bike is a good alternative to getting a cycle-rickshaw to visit the temples to the east and south.

Tourist information Government of India Tourist Office ① *T07686-274051, Mon-Fri 0930-1800.* **Madhya Pradesh Tourism** ① *at airport T07686-274648 and railway station T07686-288880.*

Background
Khajuraho was formerly the capital of the old kingdom of Jajhauti, the region now known as **Bundelkhand**. The name Khajuraho may be derived from *khajura* (date palm), which grows freely in the area and perhaps because there were two golden *khajura* trees on a carved gate here. The old name was Kharjuravahaka (scorpion bearer), the scorpion symbolizing poisonous lust.

Khajuraho's temples were built under later Chandela kings between AD 950 and 1050 in a truly inspired burst of creativity, but were 'lost' for centuries until they were accidentally 'discovered' by a British army engineer in 1839. Of the original 85 temples, the 20 surviving are among the finest in India.

Basham suggested that India's art came from secular craftsmen who, although they worked to instructions, loved the world they knew, their inspiration not so much a ceaseless quest for the absolute as a delight in the world as they saw it.

The gods and demi-gods in temples all over India are young and handsome, their bodies rounded, often richly jewelled. They are often smiling and sorrow is rarely portrayed. Temple sculpture makes full use of the female form as a decorative motif. Goddesses and female attendants are often shown naked from the waist up, with tiny waists and large, rounded breasts, posing languidly – a picture of well-being and relaxation.

Shakti worship and erotic sculptures Although each temple here is dedicated to a different deity, each expresses its own nature through the creative energy of Shakti. Tantric beliefs within Hinduism led to the development of Shakti cults which stressed that the male could be activated only by being united with the female in which sexual expression and spiritual desire were intermingled. Since this could not be suppressed it was given a priestly blessing and incorporated into the regular ritual. Romila Thapar traces its origin to the persisting worship of the Mother Goddess (from the Indus Valley civilization, third millennium BC), which has remained a feature of religion in India. Until last century, many temples kept *devadasis* (literally, servants of God), women whose duty included being the female partner in these rituals.

The presence of erotic temple sculptures, even though they account for less than 10% of the total carvings, have sometimes been viewed as the work of a degenerate society obsessed with sex. Some believe they illustrate the Kama Sutra, the sensuality outside the temple contrasting with the serenity within. Yet others argue that they illustrate ritual symbolism of sexual intercourse in **Tantric belief**. The Chandelas were followers of the

Tantric cult which believes that gratification of earthly desires is a step towards attaining the ultimate liberation or *moksha*.

Whatever the explanation, the sculptures are remarkable and show great sensitivity and warmth, reflecting society in an age free from inhibitions. They express the celebration of all human activity, displaying one aspect of the nature of Hinduism itself, a genuine love of life.

Chandela Rajputs The Chandela Rajputs claimed descent from the moon. **Hemwati**, the lovely young daughter of a Brahmin priest, was seduced by the Moon God while bathing in a forest pool. The child born of this union was **Chandravarman**, the founder of the dynasty. Brought up in the forests by his mother who sought refuge from a censorious society, Chandravarman, when established as ruler of the local area, had a dream visitation

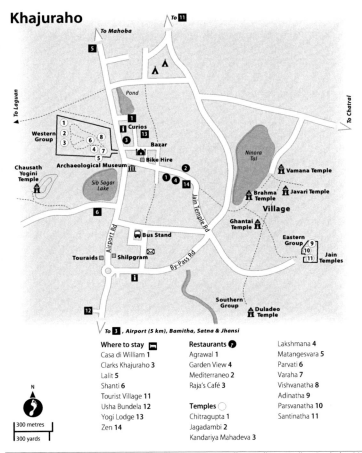

Khajuraho

Where to stay 🛏
Casa di William 1
Clarks Khajuraho 3
Lalit 5
Shanti 6
Tourist Village 11
Usha Bundela 12
Yogi Lodge 13
Zen 14

Restaurants 🍴
Agrawal 1
Garden View 4
Mediterraneo 2
Raja's Café 3

Temples ◯
Chitragupta 1
Jagadambi 2
Kandariya Mahadeva 3

Lakshmana 4
Matangesvara 5
Parvati 6
Varaha 7
Vishvanatha 8
Adinatha 9
Parsvanatha 10
Santinatha 11

from his mother. She implored him to build temples that would reveal human passions and in doing so bring about a realization of the emptiness of desire.

The Chandelas, whose symbol recalls the 16-year-old king who slayed a lion bare-handed, developed into a strong regional power in the early 10th century. Under their patronage Jajhauti became prosperous, and the rulers decorated their kingdom with forts, palaces, tanks and temples, mainly concentrated in their strongholds of Mahoba, Kalinjar, Ajaigarh and also Dudhai, Chandpur, Madanpur and Deogarh (Jhansi District).

With the fading of Chandela fortunes, the importance of Khajuraho waned but temple building continued, at a much reduced pace, until the 12th century. Far removed from the political centres of the kingdom, the location of Khajuraho minimized the danger of external attack and symbolized its role as a celestial refuge.

The temples

ⓘ *Sunrise to sunset. Foreigners Rs 250, camera Rs 25. Guides charge around Rs 400 for a small group (enquire at the India Tourism Office). Choose carefully as some push the new Cultural Centre, souvenir shop and puppet show (overpriced at Rs 250) and others can be a little leary around the sculptures. Audio tours Rs 50 plus Rs 500 deposit. Avoid the toilets. Son et lumière every evening at the Western group of temples, in English at 1900, Hindi at 2000, foreigners Rs 350, Indians Rs 120.*

The temples, built mostly of a fine sandstone from Panna and Ajaigarh – although granite was used in a few – can be conveniently divided into three groups: the **Western** (opposite bazar), **Eastern** (30 minutes away on foot) and **Southern**. The Western Group, which dominates the village, is the most impressive and the gardens the best kept. The temples in the other two groups are remarkable and pleasing in their own right but if you feel that temple fatigue is likely to set in, then the Western Group is the one to see, especially the Lakshmana Temple. Allow a day (minimum five hours) for sightseeing. Naturally early morning offers the best light – grab a chai in the square opposite the entrance and get in the temples before the crowds.

The temples here are compact and tall, raised on a high platform with an ambulatory path around, but with no enclosure wall. Each follows an east-west axis and has the essential *garbha-griha* (sanctum) containing the chief image, joined to the hall for *mandapa* (worshippers) by a *antarala* (vestibule). The hall is approached through an *ardha mandapa* (porch); both have pyramidal towers. Larger temples have lateral transepts and balconied windows, an internal ambulatory and subsidiary shrines. The sanctuary is surmounted by a tall *sikhara* (tower), while smaller towers rise from other parts of the temple, imitating mountain peaks culminating in the highest. The sanctum is usually *sapta-ratha* (seven projections in plan and elevation), while the cubical section below the *sikhara* repeats the number, having seven bands, *sapta-bada*. The whole, studded with sculptured statues with clear lines of projections and recesses, makes most effective use of light and shade. The sculptures themselves are in the round or in high or medium relief depicting cult images, deities, celestial nymphs, secular figures and animals or mythical beasts.

In India's medieval period of temple building, simple stonework techniques replaced previous wooden and brick work. Temples were heavily and ornately decorated. Heavy cornices, strong, broad pillars and the wide base of the *sikhara* (tower) give them the feeling of strength and solidity, only partly counteracted by the ornate friezes.

Western Group Varaha Temple (circa AD 900-925), a shrine dedicated to Vishnu in his third incarnation as Varaha, the boar. Vishnu, the preserver, is usually depicted resting on a bed of serpents, until summoned to save the world from disaster. The rat-demon Hiranyaksha stole the earth and dragged it down to his underwater home. The gods begged for Vishnu's help. The demon created 1000 replicas of himself to confuse any pursuer, but Vishnu incarnated himself as a boar and was able to dig deep and seek out the real demon. Thus, Hiranyaksha was destroyed and the world saved. The 2.6-m-long Varaha is of highly polished sandstone covered with 674 deities. He is the Lord of the Three Worlds – water, earth and heaven, and under him is the serpent *Sesha* and the feet of the broken figure of *Prithvi*, the earth goddess. The lotus ceiling shows superb relief carving.

Lakshmana Temple (circa AD 950) best preserves the architectural features that typify the larger temples here. The **platform** has friezes of hunting and battle scenes with soldiers, elephants and horses as well as scenes from daily life including the erotic. The **basement** again has bands of carvings – processional friezes showing animals, soldiers, acrobats, musicians, dancers, domestic scenes, festivities, ceremonies, loving couples and deities. The details differentiate between an **officer** (beard), **general** (beard and belly) and **priest** (beard, belly and stick). An ordinary soldier has none of these. You might spot the occasional error – a camel with legs jointed like a horse, for example. Note the beautifully carved elephants at shoulder height, each one different. On the **walls** are the major sculptures of gods and goddesses in two rows, with *sura-sundaris* or *apsaras* in attendance on the raised sections and loving couples discreetly placed in the recesses. All the figures are relaxed, resting their weight on one leg, thus accentuating their curves. The bands are broken by ornate balconied windows with carved pillars and overhanging eaves. The nymphs shown attending to their toilet, bearing offerings, dancing, playing musical instruments or as sensual lovers, are executed with great skill. They are graceful and fluid (note the taut muscle or creased skin), with expressive faces and gestures. The best examples are seen in the recesses below the main tower. The **façades** are covered in superb sculpture. On the south façade are a couple of minstrels, their faces expressing devotional ecstasy, a dancing Ganesh, ladies attending to their toilet, and groups of lovers. Moving to the southwest, a *sura-sundari* applies vermilion while another plays with a ball. In the northwest corner is a nymph after her bath in her wet clothes. The south face of the northwest shrine has a fine Ganesh panel. On the north face, returning towards the porch, there is a group of *apsaras* accomplished in art and music (one plays the flute, another paints, yet another writes a letter). The east face of the subsidiary shrine in the southeast corner has a master architect with his apprentices. Leave shoes at the entrance and enter the **interior** through a simple *makara-torana* flanked by gladiators. The circular ceiling of the porch (*ardha mandapa*) is a superbly carved open lotus blossom. In the hall (*mandapa*) is a raised platform possibly used for dancing and tantric rituals. At each corner of the platform are pillars with carved brackets with *apsaras* which are among the finest sculptures at Khajuraho. There are eight figures on each column, representing the eight sects of Tantra. The sanctum (*garba-griha*) doorway has a panel showing incarnations of Vishnu while the lintel has Lakshmi with Brahma and Siva on either side. A frieze above depicts the nine planets including *Rahu*, while Krishna legends and innumerable carvings of animals, birds and humans, appear on the wall. The *pancha-ratha* sanctum has a three-headed Vishnu as Vaikuntha, and around it are 10 incarnations and 14 forms of Vishnu.

Kandariya Mahadeva Temple (circa 1025-1050) is the most developed, the largest and tallest of the Khajuraho temples. Dedicated to Siva, the elaborately carved *makara torana* doorway leads to a porch with an ornate ceiling and a dark inner sanctum with a marble linga. The temple roof rises in a series of seven bands of peaks to the summit of the central, 31-m-high *sikhara*. There are 84 smaller, subsidiary towers which are replicas. The architectural and sculptural genius of Khajuraho reaches its peak in this temple where every element is richly endowed. The platform is unique in the way it projects to the sides and rear, reflecting the plan of the transepts. It also has the highest and most ornamental basement with intricately carved processional friezes. Leaving the temple, walk to the rear of the delightful gardens to the other two temples.

Along the same platform, to Kandariya's north is the **Jagadambi Temple** (early 11th century), which is similar in layout and predates the next temple, the Chitragupta. It has a standing Parvati image in the sanctum but was originally dedicated to Vishnu. The outer walls have no projecting balconies but the lavish decorations include some of the best carvings of deities – several of Vishnu, a particularly fine *Yama*, numerous nymphs and amorous couples. In between is the ruined **Mahadeva Shrine** (11th century). Little remains except a porch, under which Sardula, a mythical lion, towers over a half-kneeling woman.

Chitragupta Temple (early 11th century) is the only one here dedicated to Surya, the Sun God. Longer and lower than its companions, it has been much restored (platform, steps, entrance porch, northeast façade). Unlike the simple basement mouldings of the Jagadambi, here there are processional friezes; the *maha-mandapa* ceiling too has progressed from the simple square in the former to an ornate octagonal ceiling. The *garbha griha* has Surya driving his chariot of seven horses, while on the south façade is a statue of Vishnu with 11 heads signifying his 10 incarnations.

Vishvanatha Temple (1002) is dedicated to Siva. According to the longer inscription on the wall, it originally had an emerald linga in addition to the stone one present today. Built before the Kandariya Mahadeva, they are similar in design and plan. The high, moulded basement has fine scrollwork and carvings of processions of men and animals as well as loving couples. On the nine principal basement niches of both are the *Sapta-matrikas* (seven 'Mothers') with Ganesha and Virabhadra. The excellent carvings include a fine musician with a flute and amorous couples inside the temple, and divinities attended by enchanting nymphs in innumerable poses (one removing a thorn from her foot), on the south façade. Only two subsidiary shrines of the original four remain. Sharing the same raised platform and facing the temple is the **Nandi Pavilion** with a fine elephant frieze on the basement. It houses a 2.2-m polished sandstone Nandi bull (Siva's vehicle). Before coming down the steps note the sleeping *mahout* on an elephant!

Outside this garden complex of temples and next to the Lakshmana temple is the **Matangesvara Temple** (AD 900-925), simpler in form and decoration than its neighbour and unlike all the others, still in everyday use. It has an interesting circular interior which contains a large Siva linga dating back 1000 years. You do not need to pay to get into this temple and morning or evening *puja* is very beautiful and very welcoming.

Chausath Yogini (late ninth century) is a ruined Jain temple in coarse granite on a platform. It stands apart from the rest of the Western Group beyond the tank. Only 35 of the original *chausath* (64) shrines to the *yoginis* (attendants of Kali), of the 'open-air' temple, remain.

Eastern Group South of the village is the ruined **'Ghantai' Temple** (late 10th century). The fine carvings of *ghanta* (chains-and-bells) on the pillars, the richly ornamented doorway and ceiling of the entrance porch can only be seen from the road. Walk through Khajuraho village to the small **Javari Temple** (late 11th century), with its tall, slender *sikhara*. It has a highly decorative doorway and finely sculpted figures on the walls. About 200 m north is the **Vamana Temple** (late 11th century), with a four-armed Vamana incarnation of Vishnu in the sanctum. This is in the fully developed Chandela style and has a single tower and no ambulatory. The walls are adorned with sensuous *sura-sundaris*. Returning to the modern part of Khajuraho, you pass the early 10th-century so-called **Brahma Temple** on the bank of Ninora-tal. A Vishnu temple, wrongly attributed to Brahma, it has a sandstone *sikhara* on a granite structure.

Three Jain temples stand within an enclosure about 500 m southeast of the Ghantai Temple; others are scattered around the village. The **Parsvanatha Temple** (mid-10th century), is the largest and one of the finest. The curvilinear tower dominates the structure and is beautifully carved. There are no balconies but light enters through fretted windows. Although a Jain temple, there are numerous Vaishnav deities, many of them excellently carved on the three wall panels. Some of the best known non-erotic sculptures too are found here, particularly the graceful *sura-sundaris* (one applying kohl and another removing a thorn, on the south façade; one tying ankle-bells on the north façade), as well as the fine *Dikpalas* in the corners. The interior is richly carved with elephants, lions, sea goddesses and Jain figures. The temple was originally dedicated to Adinatha, but the modern black marble image of Parsvanatha was placed in the sanctum in 1860. Next, is the smaller and simpler **Adinatha Temple** (late 11th century), where only the sanctum (containing a modern image) and vestibule have survived – the porch is modern. The sculptures on three bands again depict attractive *sura-sundaris*, the niches have *yakshis*, the corners, *Dikpalas*. **Santinatha Temple** with its 4.5-m statue of Adinatha is the main place of Jain worship. An inscription dating it at AD 1027-1028 is covered with plaster – the thoroughly renovated temple retains its ancient heart and medieval sculptures. The small sand-coloured structures around the temples are reconstructions around remains of old shrines. There is also a small Jain museum and picture gallery here.

Southern Group The two temples stand on open land. The setting, attractive at sunset, lacks the overall ambience of the Western Group but the backdrop of the Vindhyas is impressive. **Duladeo Temple**, 800 m southwest of the Jain temples down a path off the road, is the last the Chandelas built here, when temple building was already in decline. There are 20 *apsara* brackets but the figures are often repetitive and appear to lack the quality of carving found in earlier temples. The shrine door and *mandapa* ceiling have some fine carving while the linga has 11 rows of 100 lingas. **Chaturbhuja Temple** (circa 1100), 3 km south of the village, anticipates the Duladeo but lacks erotic sculptures. The sanctum contains an exceptional 2.7-m four-armed *Dakshina-murti* Vishnu image while outside there are some fine *Dikpalas*, nymphs and mythical beasts in niches.

Excursions from Khajuraho
At **Rajgarh**, 5 km south, is the imposing ruined 19th-century hilltop fort-palace of the Maharaja which the Oberoi Group will convert to a heritage hotel. It is particularly interesting when villagers congregate for the Tuesday Market. Get there by auto-rickshaw or car. **Panna National Park** ① *Nov-May, and the entrance fee is Rs 2000 for foreigners, Rs 1000 for Indians and elephant safari is Rs 1500 for foreigners and Rs500 for Indians*. Panna, is accessed along the Satna Road with attractive waterfalls (Rs 100) on the way. Ken River, parts of which have been declared a sanctuary for fish eating gharials, flows across the Panna National Park, which is a Project Tiger Reserve. The park, rich in biodiversity, covers dense forest, open meadows, plateaus and gorge with waterfalls, and supports chinkara, sambar, nilgai and the big cats. Although tiger sightings are rare, it is pleasant to visit in

winter. There is little wildlife to be seen in the dry season (when the gharials are removed for their own protection).There are some beautiful places to stay. Access is easiest from Madla, 27 km from Khajuraho. Jeep or motorbike hire from Khajuraho, or bus; tour of park can be arranged in Madla.

Kanha National Park → *For listings, see pages 98-103.*

This is the country about which Kipling wrote so vividly in his *Jungle Book*. The area was famed as a hunter's paradise but now the valley has been well developed as a national park. It is worth spending a couple of days here. Lying in the Maikal hills in the eastern part of the Satpura Range, 40 km from Mandla, the park has deciduous hardwoods, rolling grasslands and meandering streams of the Banjar River. The park forms the core of the Kanha Tiger Reserve. It was created in 1974 and also protects the rare hardground-adapted *barasingha* (swamp deer). George Schaller, the zoologist, conducted the first ever scientific study of the tiger here and research is also being done on deer and langur habitat.

Arriving in Kanha National Park
Getting there The journey by car takes about five hours from Jabalpur on a poor road. The main gates are at Kisli and Mukki. If arriving in the evening, stop overnight at Khatia or Kisli as vehicles are not allowed into the park after dark. From Nagpur or Raipur enter via Mukki Gate. Diesel vehicles, motorcycles and bicycles are not allowed in the park.
→ *See Transport, page 103.*

Getting around Visitors may not walk around inside the park, but you can walk in the peaceful forest between the gate at Kanha and the park itself.

Park information Area: 1945 sq km. Visitor centres at Khatia and Mukki gates and at Kanha (the largest). Open 0700-1030, 1600-1800. Informative displays, short films, audio-visual shows and books for sale. Recommended minimum stay two nights.

Climate It can get very cold on winter nights. Summer: maximum 43°C, minimum 11°C; winter: maximum 29°C, minimum 2°C. Annual rainfall: 1250 mm; monsoon July-September. The best time to visit is January to June. The park is closed 1 July-31 October.

Wildlife
Kanha has 22 species of mammal, the most easily spotted of which are the three-striped palm squirrel, common langur monkey, jackal, wild boar, cheetal, sambar, Branden barasingha and blackbuck. Less commonly seen are Indian hare, *dhole* (Indian wild dog) and gaur. Rarely seen are Indian fox, sloth bear, striped hyena, tiger (estimated at about 100), leopard, *nilgai* (blue bull), Indian porcupine, wolf (outside park proper) and the Indian pangolin (sometimes called a scaly anteater).

As for birds, Kanha has 230 species recorded. Good vantage points are in the hills where the mixed and bamboo forest harbours many species. Commonly seen species are: leaf warblers, minivets, black ibis, common peafowl, racket-tailed drongo, hawk eagle, red-wattled lapwing, various species of flycatcher, woodpecker, pigeon, dove, parakeet, babbler, mynah, Indian roller, white-breasted kingfisher and grey hornbill.

Viewing

Forest Department guides accompany visitors around the park on mapped-out circuits to see a cross-section of wildlife from a jeep; there are two viewing sessions a day, the first beginning 30 minutes before sunrise and the second ending 30 minutes after sunset; confirm locally for the exact times. Current rates are Foreigners Rs 3000 Indians Rs1500 for Kanha zone and Rs 2000 and Rs 1000 respectively for Mukki zone, but double check as these rates are prone to change However, one traveller comments that "vehicles chase each other round, their paths crossing and re-crossing and their noisy engines presumably driving the more timid wildlife way back from the tracks". It is better to stop the vehicle on the forest track and in front of the grasslands.

The *sal* forests do not normally allow good viewing. The best areas are the meadows around Kanha. **Bamni Dadar** (Sunset Point) affords a view of the dense jungle and animals typical of the mixed forest zone: sambar, barking deer and chausingha (four-horned antelope). Early morning and late afternoon are ideal times and binoculars are invaluable. *Machans* (viewing platforms/observation towers), are available for use during daylight; those above waterholes (eg **Sravantal**), are recommended.

Elephants, once used for tiger tracking, are now only available for 'joy rides' outside the park at Kisli. MP Tourism hires out Gypsy 4WDs and jeeps from the **Baghira Log Huts**, Kisli in the park (for maximum six), Rs 9 per kilometre. Book the previous day. Petrol is often not available at Kisli; nearest pumps at Mandla.

Bandhavgarh National Park → *For listings, see pages 98-103.*

The park is set in extremely rugged terrain with many hills. The marshes which used to be perennial now support a vast grassland savannah. Though it involves quite a journey you may be rewarded with sighting one of the few tigers; a three-day stay gives you a 90% chance of seeing one. There are also interesting cave shrines scattered around the park, with Brahmi inscriptions dating from the first century BC. You can visit the remains of a fort believed to be 2000 years old where you may spot crag martins and brown rock thrush.

Arriving in Bandhavgarh National Park

This compact park is in the Vindhya hills with a core area of 105 sq km and a buffer zone of 437 sq km. The main entrance and park office is at Tala to the north of the park. The park is open 1 October-30 June. Temperature range: 42-42°C. Rainfall: 1500 mm. For information, contact Field Director, Bandhavgarh Tiger Reserve, Umaria, T07653-222214. → *For Transport, see page 103.*

Wildlife

The park has a wide variety of game and has a longer 'season' than Kanha. Its main wild beasts are tiger, leopard, sloth bear, gaur, sambar, chital, muntjac, *nilgai*, chinkara and wild pigs. There are over 60 tigers, but they remain very elusive. The flowering and fruit trees attract woodland birds which include green pigeon, Jerdon's leaf bird, crested serpent eagle and variable hawk eagle.

Viewing

You need to plan a long way ahead. As a way of restricting visitors and conserving the wildlife, the daily quota of safaris is very limited, and in Tala zone (the best place to visit) game drives book out six months in advance. Unfortunately, at the time of writing the online booking system refuses payment from non-Indian credit cards, so the only way you can ensure your safari is to book it well in advance through your hotel. Annoyingly, park fees and regulations change regularly, again best to check with your hotel. Currently the fees are Game safari in Tala zone is Rs 6500 per trip for foreigners. Six people are allowed in one vehicle. Other zone are Rs 4500 per trip for foreigners. Forest Department elephants are a good way of seeing wildlife, but present challenges to the photographer; lodges sell vouchers entitling you to a place in the waiting list for 'tiger show', in which visitors are rushed by jeep to an elephant which has tracked a tiger. Some feel the constant traffic of elephants and jeeps is affecting wildlife – "a bit like a circus". Nevertheless, the forest authorities are making efforts to improve the experience for visitors, by encouraging a code of respect for wildlife and the environment and constructing new *machans* (viewing platforms/ observation towers). The watchtower at Bhadrashila is a good place to look for gaur.

Madhya Pradesh listings

For hotel and restaurant price codes and other relevant information, see pages 12-15.

● Where to stay

Gwalior *p82, map p82*
$$$$ Usha Kiran Palace, Jayendraganj Lashkar, T0751-244 4000, www.tajhotels.com. 40 unique and very atmospheric a/c rooms (some vast suites) in 120-year-old maharaja's palace. Beautiful spa (musicians play live behind jali screens) and gardens, swimming pool, good restaurant, billiards and bar.
$$$ Central Park, Madhav Rao Scindia Marg, City Centre, T0751-2232440, www.thecentralpark.net. Modern a/c rooms in Gwalior's top business hotel. Pool, health club, coffee shop, good restaurant and bar, currency exchange and breakfast included. Recommended.
$$$-$$ Tansen, 6A Gandhi Rd, T0751-234 0370, www.mptourism.com. 36 rooms, mostly a/c, good restaurant, bar, garden, car hire, tourist information, quiet location and handy for bus and train.
$ DM, Link Rd, near New Bus Stand, T0751-234 2083. Small and pretty shabby rooms with attached bath (hot water) and small garden at the back. Best of the budget options. Reasonably quiet and handy for bus stand.

Orchha *p86*
Hotels are best on the idyllic riverside.
$$$$ Amar Mahal, T07680-252102, www.amarmahal.com. Experience how a Maharaja palace would have looked back in its day in this modern day version built and decorated in traditional Bundelkhand architectural style. Well-maintained and tranquil gardens where local musicians play during the evening. Excellent buffet style restaurant with 24-carat gold-painted ceiling, Ayurvedic massage, gym and doctor on call. Recommended.
$$$$-$$ Betwa Retreat (MP Tourism), overlooking river, 10-min walk from bus stand, T07680-252618, betwa@mptourism. com. 15 clean and bright, typically dated government style cottages, some a/c, the best (**$$$$**) in beautiful high-ceilinged Maharaja Villa, plus 10 'luxury' tents, in serious need of mould fumigation. Spacious well-kept gardens, scattered ruins, nightly folk music and dance, average restaurant.
$$$$-$$ Sheesh Mahal (MP Tourism), in a breathtakingly stunning location inside the fort, T07680-252624 (book in advance). 8 beautiful ornate rooms and 2 majestic suites (**$$$$**) with terrace, antique fittings and furniture, huge marble tub, panoramic view from toilet. Full of character and atmospheric charm, restaurant has great views, friendly staff. Highly recommended.

$$-$ Ganpati, just north of main crossroads, T07680-252765, www.orchhahotelganpati palaceview.com. A wide range of clean rooms (even more were being built at time or writing). Best are the large, amusingly named 'sweet rooms' with a/c, murals and great views of the fort. Hot showers, small courtyard and gardens, great views of palace and very friendly owner. Recommended.

$ Orchha Homestay, Lakshmi Mandir Rd, Ganj Mohalla, T(0)9993-385405, www. orchha.org. This is a very special place to stay – you are welcomed with open arms into village life. Set up by **Friends of Orchha**, a non-profit organization run by an Indian/ Swiss couple to feed money and energy back into the community, to empower local women and create better education. Coming to stay here, you will find simple rooms, composting toilets, home-cooked food (and they promise to tone down the spice for you) and an insight into India. There are also possibilities to stay longer and volunteer perhaps on marketing ecotourism or helping to create an ecological waste management system. Highly recommended.

Khajuraho *p89, map p91*

$$$$ Clarks Khajuraho, Khajuraho Village, T07686-274038, www.hotelclarks.com. With a deceptively plain exterior, inside are 104 classically decorated, modern rooms with views of the pool and extensive well kept grounds, badminton and tennis courts, large restaurant, massage and gym.

$$$$ The Lalit, opposite Circuit House, T0786-272111, www.thelalit.com. Top-notch hotel with all the trimmings including sparkling new rooms and extravagant suites.

$$$ Usha Bundela, Airport Rd, T07686-272386, www.ushalexushotels.com. Full of character. Comfy rooms, well managed, restaurant, bar and good pool.

$$ Tourist Village, T07686-274062, www. mptourism.com. Veering away from the norm,13 well-equipped attractive 2-room 'ethnic' huts, bathroom and a/c, outdoor restaurant, bike useful, campsite nearby.

$$-$ Hotel Shanti, opposite Shiv Sagar Lake, T07686-274560, shanti.hotelkhajuraho@ yahoo.com. Great location by lake, spacious, clean and light rooms with bath, temple views and TV, restaurant. Good value.

$$-$ Zen, Jain Temple Rd, T07686-274228, www.hotelzenkhajuraho.co.in. Large, bright ramshackle rooms with clean attached bath, nice garden with water features, a good place to stay but strange atmosphere – beware of attempts to charge spurious 'luxury tax' on cheap rooms. Italian restaurant in the garden and owner now promises 10% discount for all Footprint readers!

$ Casa di William, opposite western group of temples, T07686-274244. Very conveniently located,15 pleasant and clean rooms with bath, some a/c. Absolutely stunning sunset views of temples from roof restaurant, massage, internet, bike rental. Very friendly and helpful staff, Italian management. Good value

$ Yogi Lodge, western temples, T07686-274158. Excellent budget option, spartan but clean rooms, rooftop café, internet, bike hire, yoga classes, well run, links to nearby ashram for a quiet retreat

---

Excursions from Khajuraho *p96*
Panna National Park

$$$$ Pashan Ghar, 12 km from park entrance, www.tajsafaris.com. Newly opened, this is at the supreme luxe end of the spectrum with beautifully decorated stone cottages with a nod to traditional style and a watchtower overlooking the water hole. This is the place for a romantic getaway with candlelit suppers in a palanquin or dinners delivered through the 'butler hatch' to your own private veranda.

$$$$-$$$ Ken River Lodge, Village Madla, T07732-275235, www.kenriverlodge.com. In a beautiful location with both cottages and 'Swiss' tents, tree-top restaurant, fishing, boating, swimming.

$$-$ Panna Tiger Resort, Village Mandla, T7732-275248, www.pannatigerresort.com. Basic rooms and tented accommodation but it's beauty is in how close to nature you are.

$ Rest Houses, ask at gate or park office, Panna National Park. Take provisions.

Kanha National Park *p96*

$$$$ Kanha Jungle Lodge, Balaghat–Raipur Rd, just south of Mukki, 12 km from Baihar and main road, T07637-216015, www.tiger-resorts.com. Beautifully decorated cottages with private patios overlooking the forest. Modern facilities, attached bathroom, hot water, comfortably furnished. Even a hot water bottle to keep you warm at night.

$$$$ Shergarh, Bahmni Village, T(0)9098-187346. Nov-May. Beautiful new camp run by Anglo-Indian couple, 6 tents surrounding picturesque lake, 2 safaris and all meals included, plus possibilities to birdwatch, visit local markets and even paint elephants. With a nod to eco-tourism using local knowledge and traditions. Highly recommended.

$$$ Wild Chalet Resort, Mocha Village, T07649-277203. Reservations **Indian Adventures**, T022-2640 8742 (Mumbai), www.indianadventures.com. Cottages with shower overlooking river, good food and park tours, helpful and efficient manager. Recommended.

Inside the park

Arrive by sunset as no entry after dark. Reservations can be made through **MP Tourism**, Bhopal, T0755-277 4340.

$$ Baghira Log Huts, Kisli, T07649-277227, www.mptourism.com. 16 rooms, restaurant, cheaper canteen, restaurant.

$ Tourist Hostel, Kisli, opposite bus stand, www.mptourism.com. 24 dorm beds (roof may leak), no nets (mosquito ridden), Uninspiring vegetarian meals in a grim canteen on offer.

Bandhavgarh National Park *p97*

$$$$ Samode Safari Lodge, www.samode.com. This stunning addition to the **Samode** chain in Rajasthan is the ultimate in luxury, while still leaving a light footprint on the earth. Designed to blend with the surroundings, no trees were cut down in this new build and there is a good nod to eco-tourism with rainwater harvesting, solar energy and villas made from local materials with local craftsmen.

$$$$ Treehouse Hideaway, Village Vijarhia, T(0)8800-637711, www.treehousehideaway.com. Worlds apart from anything you might have had as a kid, these are boutique treehouses made of regularized dark wood with beautiful decor and stunning views. They also have a hide overlooking the water hole. They have a 2-tiered restaurant in a large *mahua* tree. All meals are included in the price. Very special.

$$$ Skays Camp, T(0)9425-331209, www.skayscamp.in. This is a great value place with a beautiful garden and delicious food. What makes this place so special is the passion of the owners – both naturalists. Satyendra Tiwari is an acclaimed wildlife photographer and knowledgeable birder, guide and naturalist. His British wife Kay is a wildlife artist. Together they gather information on flora and fauna of the area as well as producing tourist guides to the butterflies, snakes and birds and creating tiger identification papers. Satyendra is working on a book on Tigers. Recommended.

$$$-$$ White Tiger Forest Lodge (MP Tourism), Tala, overlooking river, T07627-265366, www.mptourism.com. Reservations: **MP Tourism**, Bhopal, T0755-277 4340. Also **Forest Rest House**, www.mpforest.org. 26 rooms (8 a/c), restaurant (expensive, tiny portions, but good), bar, jeep hire (for residents), modest but good value, the best rooms are in detached cottages by the river, "in need of a good sweep".

$$-$ V Patel Resort, off Umaria Rd, T07653-265323. Clean rooms with hot water, meals in garden; 4 rooms, also complete packages.

$ Kum-kum, opposite White Tiger, T(0)9424-330200. Very basic, 4 large, clean rooms with fan, hot water, excellent vegetarian food, friendly, helpful, well-run, jeep driver Saleem is an expert tiger spotter. Recommended.

🍴 Restaurants

Gwalior *p82, map p82*
$$$ Usha Kiran Palace, International.
Good rich Mughlai meals and snacks,
live classical music, bar, attentive service,
pleasant ambience in ornate surroundings
looking out over attractive gardens.
$$ Kwality, Green garden road behind
SP Office. Pretty decent and tasty mainly
Indian and snacks. Clean but rather dark
helpful staff.
$ Indian Coffee House, India Hotel, just
off Jayaji Chowk. Great for South Indian
breakfasts, snacks and *thalis*.

Orchha *p86*
$$ Betwa Tarang, near fort bridge (upstairs).
Good food, pleasant roof terrace or indoor,
clean toilets. Also 'picnic' meals by the river.
$$ Sheesh Mahal (see Where to stay,
page 98). International, non-vegetarian
served in a large foyer in the fantastic and
atmospheric palace location. Great North
Indian, chilled beer, good service.
$ Milan restaurant, small, clean and well
cared for place just before the fort bridge.
Serves a range of cuisines and lives up to its
name serving 'real' Expresso coffee, not so
easy to find in these parts. Great breakfast.
Recommended.

Khajuraho *p89, map p91*
Chai and *parathas* cooked fresh at stalls in
the market square on Jain Temples Rd make
a good quick breakfast before the temples.
Good atmospheric start to the day.
$$ Garden View Restaurant, inside Hotel
Surya, Jain temple Rd. Western, Fantastic
Indian local recipes served in pleasant
garden surroundings, family-run, friendly
and inviting. Recommended.
$$ Mediterraneo, opposite Hotel Surya.
Good bruschetta, fresh pasta dishes, tasty
pizza, good desserts, Indian chefs. Beware of
imitators – a "branch" has opened in Orchha
but has nothing to do with this great place.

$$ Raja's Café, Main Rd, near Western
Temples entrance. Probably the best food you
will get in Khajuraho and great coffee too all
with the backdrop of the temples. There's a
nicely designed a/c room downstairs on days
that swelter or head up the spiral staircase
for great views. Highly recommended.
$ Agrawal, near Hotel Surya. The only
local-feeling place in town, good *thalis*
(vegetarian only), not too oily.

🎭 Entertainment

Khajuraho *p89, map p91*
Shilpgram, Airport Rd. Interesting
programme of cutural performances in
season, 1900-2100, often free. A more
rustic, less commercial experience than
the similarly named cultural centre across
the street, which attracts tour buses.

✴ Festivals

Orchha *p86*
Nov/Dec Ram Vivah (Rama's marriage).
Colourful processions draw crowds
particularly as superbly trained horses
perform extraordinary feats where one
removes a horseman's eye make-up with
a hoof.

Khajuraho *p89, map p91*
Feb-Mar Dance Festival. Many of the
country's most accomplished dancers
perform in the spectacular setting of the
Western Group. Ask at the tourist office
for details.

🛍 Shopping

Gwalior *p82, map p82*
Ganpatlal Krishna Lal, Sarafa Bazar.
Jewellery and antiques. Closed Tue.
Kothari, Sarafa Bazar. Brocade, *chanderi* (light
and flimsy cotton and silk material), silk saris.
Loyal, near High Court, Nai Sarak. Books.
MD Fine Arts, Subhash Market. Paintings
and objets d'art.

MP Emporium, Sarafa Bazar. Handlooms.
MP Khadi Sangh, Sarafa Bazar. Handlooms.
Mrignayani's, an MP State Emporium,
in Patankar Bazar also recommended.

Khajuraho *p89, map p91*
Gift shops sell cheap stone and bronze
sculptures, handicrafts and gems in the
bazar near the Western Group (**Panna
diamond mines**, the largest in the country,
are nearby).
Chandela Emporium, near Sibsagar.
Large selection of gifts, crafts and jewellery.
Ganesh Garments, Jain Temples
Rd. Reasonable Western clothes
(quick alterations).
Karan Jewellers, for diamonds.

What to do

Gwalior *p82, map p82*
Travel Bureau. 6/788 Devasheesh Enclave,
near Kailash Vihar, T0751-223 3765,
www.travelbureauagra.com. Branch of
this extremely efficient travel agency
with head office in Agra. Tours to Orchha
and Shivpuri, Rs 1600 (car for 5), same day
return. City sights, Rs 600, contact tourist
office at Tansen Hotel.

Orchha *p86*
River rafting trips (Oct-Feb) can be organized
by **MP Tourism**, or contact manager of
Betwa Retreat or **Sheesh Mahal** (see Where
to stay, page 98). Scenic 90-min and 3-hr
trips on the Betwa with a few fairly gentle
rapids (around Rs 1200/ 2000). The Jamuni
River has more adventurous runs (Rs 3000).

Khajuraho *p89, map p91*
Touraids, Bamitha Rd, near Shilpgram,
T07686-274125. Reliable cars with drivers.
Travel Bureau, Hotel Ramada, T07686-
274037, www.travelbureauagra.com.

Transport

Gwalior *p82, map p82*
Air At the time of writing there were no
flights to Gwalior.
Bus Bus stand, Link Rd, T0751-234 0192.
Frequent buses to **Agra**, **Bhopal**, **Indore**
and **Shivpuri**. Daily to **Khajuraho**.
Rickshaw Prepaid auto-rickshaw stand
at the railway station. Cycle-rickshaw
charge around Rs 25 for rides within town.
Tempos on fixed routes, Rs 3-8.
Train Tickets for the *Shatabdi Express* are
usually sold in the separate, 'non-
computerized' queue. Gwalior is on the
main Delhi–Mumbai and Delhi–Chennai
lines. Enquiries T131, reservations T135.
For **Agra Cantt**, take any Delhi train, 1¾ hrs.
Bhopal: *Shatabdi Exp 12002*, 0930 (Fri
0945), 5 hrs; **Delhi**: *Lakshadweep Exp 12617*,
0815, 5 hrs (**HN**); *Punjab Mail 12137*, 1605,
5½ hrs (**ND**); *Taj Exp 12279*, 1655, 5 hrs (**HN**).
Jabalpur (for **Kanha** and **Bandhavgarh**):
M P Smprk Krnti 12122 2142, 10½ hrs. **Jhansi**:
see Bhopal, journey time 1-1½ hrs. **Mumbai**
(**CST**): *Punjab Mail 12138*, 1040, 21¼ hrs.
Varanasi: *Bundelkhand Exp 11107*, 2040,
14½ hrs (calling at **Allahabad** 4 hrs earlier).

Khajuraho *p89, map p91*
Air The airport is 5 km south of the village
centre, T07686-274041. Flights are heavily
booked in season: confirm onward flight
on arrival. Transport to town: taxi Rs 200,
auto-rickshaw Rs 100 (overpriced; difficult
to bargain). **Indian Airlines**: Temple Hotel,
T07686-274035, Airport T07686-274036;
no credit cards. **Jet Airways**: T07686-274406
(airport). Both fly daily to/from **Delhi** and
Varanasi. **Bicycle** Cycle hire in Gole Market
behind museum and along Jain Temples Rd;
recommended mode though not allowed in
temple complex.
Bus Long-distance buses arrive at a newish
bus stand 1.5 km south of the main bazar on
Airport Rd, with a computerized counter for
reservations on buses and trains elsewhere.
Daily buses to **Agra** 391 km, 0700, 0800,

0900, 1800 (an exhausting 10-12 hrs via Jhansi and Gwalior); **Bhopal** 350 km, 0600, 0700; **Indore** 480 km, 0600; **Jhansi** 176 km, several 0500-1800 (4½-5 hrs), semi-deluxe via Orchha 1115; **Mahoba** (stops 3 km from the railway station), several 0600-1700 (3 hrs); **Satna** (for rail connections to **Jabalpur**, **Allahabad** and **Kolkata**), 0745, 0830, 0930, 1400, 1500, 4 hrs (very uncomfortable).
Car Car hire with driver to **Jhansi**, Rs 2000-3500, arranged through hotels or by **Touraids** and Travel Bureau, 4 hrs. **Satna**, Rs 2400. **Agra** or **Varanasi**, Rs 7000-10000, 8-9 hrs.
Rickshaw and taxi Cycle-rickshaws try to charge Rs 30 for shortest journey; approx local price from bazar to bus stand, Rs 15. Rs 75-100 per half day. Taxis are from MP Tourism or Touraids near Usha Hotel, but overpriced. To Satna, cheaper fares can be had from drivers who have dropped off passengers in Khajuraho.
Train **Agra** *Kurj Udz Exp 19665*, 0910, 8½ hrs and goes onto **Jhansi** (5hrs) and **Udaipur** (21hrs). **Delhi** *Kurj Nzm Exp 22447*, 1820, 11hrs (HN) also stops in **Agra** but at ungodly hour. **Varanasi** *Kurj Bsb Link E 21107*, T, F, Su, 2340, 11 hrs Computerized reservations at bus stand, T07686-274416.

Kanha National Park *p96*
Air Air India, Indigo and Jet Airways fly to Nagpur (226 km) from **Mumbai**, **Kolkata** and **Bhubaneswar**, **Hyderabad**, **Delhi** and **Bhopal**.
Bus Kanha is connected with **Jabalpur**, **Nagpur** and **Bilaspur** by motorable, but often poor roads. From Jabalpur buses daily to **Kisli** (via Mandla and Chiraidongri, 0800, 1100) and **Mukki** (0900).
Jeep Private hire to **Jabalpur** around US$65.

Train **Jabalpur** (173 km) is on the **Mumbai–Allahabad–Kolkata**, **Delhi–Jabalpur** and **Chennai–Varanasi** main lines; or via **Raipur**, 230 km. A wonderful narrow gauge (diesel) train runs between **Mandla** and **Jabalpur**.

Bandhavgarh National Park *p97*
Air Jabalpur is the nearest airport.
Bus From Tala buses go to **Umaria**, **Rewa**, **Satna** and **Katni**, all with rail connections.
Jeep From Tala it's possible to get a jeep seat to **Satna** (insist on your full seat); poor road, bumpy and dusty 3-hr ride. From **Umaria**: jeep to Tala for park, Rs 700, good for sharing. From **Jabalpur** drive to Shajpura (144 km) then take a country road (fairly hilly) to Umaria. From **Khajuraho** (237 km) 6-7 hrs.
Taxi Available from **Satna** (129 km) 3 hrs, **Katni** and **Umaria**.
Train **Umaria** (35 km) is the nearest station, on the Katni-Bilaspur sector (1 hr by road). Rickshaw to bus stand (Rs 50), from where you can get a bus to Tala. Direct train from Umaria to **Delhi**: *Utkal Express 18477*, 2050, 17¼ hrs. **Varanasi**, *Sarnath Exp 15160*, 0427, 12 hrs (book well ahead for a berth). If you are trying to get from **Khajuraho** to **Bandhavgarh**, get to to **Satna** for a train to **Katni**, Mahakoshal Exp 12190, 0650, 1 hr and change to **Umaria**, *Narmada Express 182330920*, 1¼ hrs.

Directory

Kanha National Park *p96*
Medical services Basic hospitals are Mandla Civil Hospital and Katra Mission Hospital. Only basic first aid at Mukki, Mocha and Baihar. **Post** At Mocha and Mukki.

Varanasi and around

Perhaps the holiest of India's cities, Varanasi defies easy description. A highly congested maze of narrow alleys winds behind its waterfront ghats, at once highly sacred yet physically often far from clean. As an image, an idea and a symbol of Hinduism's central realities, the city draws pilgrims from around the world, to worship, to meditate, and above all to bathe. It is a place to be born and a place to die. In the cold mists of a winter's dawn, you can see life and death laid bare. For an outside observer it can be an uncomfortable, albeit unmissable experience, juxtaposing the inner philosophical mysteries of Hinduism with the practical complications of living literally and metaphorically on the edge.

More holy places surround Varanasi: Sarnath, one of Buddhism's major centres, Jaunpur, a city with a strong Islamic history, and Allahabad, a sacred place for Hindus due to its position at the confluence of the Ganja and Yamuna rivers.

Varanasi → *For listings, see pages 114-119.*

The riverside city, and the focus for most tourists and pilgrims, extends from Raj Ghat in the north to Assi Ghat in the south. At dawn the riverbank's stone steps begin to hum with activity. Early risers immerse themselves in the water as they face the rising sun, boatmen wait expectantly on the waterside, pilgrims flock to the temples, flower sellers do brisk business, astrologers prepare to read palms and horoscopes while families carry the dead to their last rites by the holy river. A few steps away from the ghats, motorbikers speed through the lanes past wandering *sadhus*, hopeful beggars, curious visitors and wandering cows, while packs of stray dogs scavenge among the piles of rubbish.

Arriving in Varanasi
Getting there Airlines link Varanasi with Delhi, Kolkata, Kathmandu, Mumbai and other cities. From Babatpur airport, 22 km away, there is an unreliable airport bus to the Indian Airlines office in the Cantonment area. Better to take a taxi from the prepaid booth. Most trains stop at Junction Station near the Cantonment, about 5 km northwest of the Old City and the budget hotels. Some trains (eg Delhi–Kolkata *Rajdhani* and *Expresses* to New Jalpaiguri and Guwahati) do not pass through Varanasi itself but stop at Mughal Sarai, 17 km away, which is accessible by road from Varanasi. Shared jeeps cost Rs 25 between the two stations, or a taxi is Rs 300. Most long-distance buses arrive at the bus stands near Junction Station.

Note On arrival at Junction Station, you will be accosted by rickshaw-wallahs who are desperate to get you to a hotel which pays them commission. It can be stressful; don't

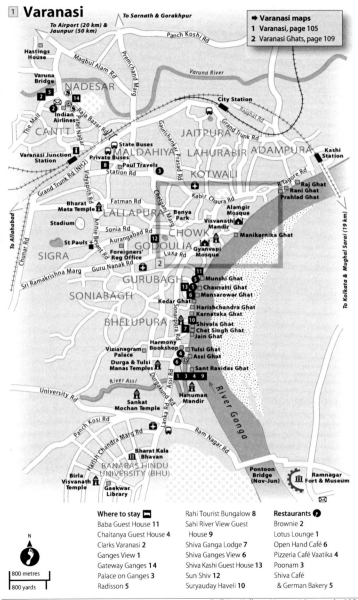

1 Varanasi

To Sarnath & Gorakhpur

To Airport (20 km) & Jaunpur (50 km)

Panch Koshi Rd

➡ **Varanasi maps**
1 Varanasi, page 105
2 Varanasi Ghats, page 109

Hastings House

Maqbul Alam Rd

Premchand Marg

Varuna River

Varuna Bridge

NADESAR

City Station

Raighat Rd

The Mall

Indian Airlines

Raja Bazar Rd

Hiralal Nagar

JAITPURA

LAHURABIR

ADAMPURA

Kashi Station

CANTT

Varanasi Junction Station

State Buses
Private Buses

MALDAHIYA

Paul Travels

Station Rd

KOTWALI

Grand Trunk Rd (NH2)

Vidyapith Rd

Fatman Rd

Cheragi Marg

Gaurishankar Prasad Rd

Kabir Chaura Rd

R Tagore Rd

Raj Ghat
Rani Ghat
Prahlad Ghat

Bharat Mata Temple

LALLAPURA

Benya Park

Alamgir Mosque

Visvanath Mandir

Annie Besant Rd

Stadium

St Pauls

Sonia Rd

Aurangabad Rd

CHOWK

GODOULIA

Manikarnika Ghat

SIGRA

Chunar Rd

Foreigners' Reg Office

Luxa Rd

Gyanvapi Mosque

Sri Ramakrishna Marg

Guru Nanak Rd

GURUBAGH

Munshi Ghat

SONIABAGH

Sonapura Rd

Kedar Ghat

Chauvalti Ghat
Mansarowar Ghat

Harishchandra Ghat
Karnataka Ghat

BHELUPURA

Shivala Ghat
Chet Singh Ghat
Jain Ghat

Harmony Bookshop

Vizianagram Palace

Tulsi Ghat
Assi Ghat

Durga & Tulsi Manas Temples

Durgakund Puri Rd

Sant Ravidas Ghat

River Assi

University Rd

Sankat Mochan Temple

PD Puri Rd

Hanuman Mandir

River Ganga

Panch Kosi Rd

Harish Chandra Marg Rd

Ram Nagar Rd

Bharat Kala Bhavan

BANARAS HINDU UNIVERSITY (BHU)

Birla Visvanath Temple

Gaekwar Library

Pontoon Bridge (Nov-Jun)

Ramnagar Fort & Museum

To Kolkata & Mughal Sarai (19 km)

N

800 metres
800 yards

Where to stay 🛏	Rahi Tourist Bungalow **8**	**Restaurants** 🍴
Baba Guest House **11**	Sahi River View Guest	Brownie **2**
Chaitanya Guest House **4**	House **9**	Lotus Lounge **1**
Clarks Varanasi **2**	Shiva Ganga Lodge **7**	Open Hand Café **6**
Ganges View **1**	Shiva Ganges View **6**	Pizzeria Café Vaatika **4**
Gateway Ganges **14**	Shiva Kashi Guest House **13**	Poonam **3**
Palace on Ganges **3**	Sun Shiv **12**	Shiva Café
Radisson **5**	Suryauday Haveli **10**	& German Bakery **5**

Ganga

The magnificent River Ganges is the spiritual heart of Hinduism and the blood that flows through its veins. Running from a high mountain glacier in Uttarakhand and flowing out at the Bay of Bengal, the river, worshipped as the goddess Ganga, sweeps across northern India attracting people from all over the world to pray and make purification *pujas*.

The story goes that when the goddess Ganga came to earth she fell upon the head of Lord Shiva, the first man of yoga, was caught in his hair and was let out in small streams to spread across the earth. Lord Shiva sat and received her at Gangotri in Uttarakhand, which was considered to be the source of the Ganges, and is now one of the most sacred places to dip in the holy waters. (Over the years the source has receded a further 18 km to the Gaumukh glacier).

Other auspicious places to dip are at Rishikesh, Haridwar, Allahabad and Varanasi. They are seen as *tirthas* – places where the veil between the physical and spiritual world is at its thinnest. People come to pray, to leave offerings of flowers and to bring the ashes of their dead. Haridwar and Allahabad both play host to the **Kumbh Mela**, the largest spiritual gathering on earth, attracting some 30 million people. The most recent *mela* was in Allahabad in 2013. If you cannot face 30 million people, there are spectacular Ganga Arti fire *pujas* performed by Brahmin priests every evening in Rishikesh, Haridwar and Varanasi.

The Ganges river basin – the most heavily populated in the world – is inhabited by 37% of India's mighty 1.2 billion population and this has evidently impacted on the river itself. This is a place where people bathe, perform *pujas*, do their laundry and bring the ashes of the dead. On top of that are the contamination of municipal and industrial waste and the impact of dams. Indeed, the pollution is shocking, with coliform bacteria levels reaching 5500, far too high to be safe for agricultural use, let alone drinking and bathing. While the Ganga as a celestial being enjoys immortality, the river itself is struggling.

An action plan is in place targeting industry, but progress is slow. Individuals are reacting too: Nagnath, a 52-year-old *sadhu* (holy man) who lives and works on the burning ghat Marnikarnika in Varanasi, has been on a fast since 2008 to protest against the environmental devastation of the Ganges. In India, the spiritual and material, the sacred and the profane are tightly bound together.

If you want to explore more of the river than is covered in this book, head west to Allahabad and north to Haridwar and Rishikesh, and maybe beyond to Gangotri. In Rishikesh, you can stay at **Rainforest House** (www.rainforest-house.com) and camp on the banks of the Ganga itself during the summer at **Camp Silver Sands** (www.aquaterra.in), or you can experience ashram life at **Parmath Niketan** (www.parmath.com). For information on trekking to the source of the Ganga go to www.euttaranchal.com.

believe touts who say your chosen hotel is closed or full – such things rarely change in Varanasi. Several budget hotels offer free pick-up from the station (call on arrival), or try to get at least 50 m outside of the station area before bargaining for an auto (Rs 80) or cycle-rickshaw (Rs 50). Shared autos leave from the far side of the main road outside the station to Godoulia (Rs 10) near Main Ghat. Note that autos are not permitted into the narrow lanes near the main ghats, and you will have to walk the last stretch (15-25 minutes to hotels). However, autos can get close to Assi Ghat (one of the ghats further south), from where it's a two-minute walk to hotels.

Getting around The only way to see the heart of the Old City is on foot, though no visit is complete without an early-morning boat trip along the ghats. Varanasi is quite spread out: the university to the south is nearly 7 km from the spacious Cantonment area and the Junction Station to the north. Around town, cycle-rickshaws and autos are plentiful. Shared autos run along main routes, though it is difficult (as a tourist) to avoid being pressured into private hire. Unmetered taxis are best for longer sightseeing trips. The city has some of the disadvantages of pilgrimage centres, notably rickshaw drivers who seem determined to extort as much as possible from unsuspecting visitors. ⏩ *See Transport, page 118.*

Tourist information Tourist Information Counter ① *Junction Railway Station, near 'Enquiry', T0542-250 6670, 0600-2000*, provides helpful maps and information. **Government of India Tourist Office** ① *The Mall, Cantt, T0542-2501784, Mon-Sat 0900-1630*, is well run, with helpful manager and staff; guides available at set rates. Also at Babatpur Airport.

History
Varanasi derives its name from two streams, the Varuna to the north and the Assi, a small trickle, on the south. **Banaras** is a corruption of Varanasi but it is also called **Kashi** (Siva's 'City of Light') by Hindus. As one of the seven sacred cities of Hinduism, it attracts well over one million pilgrims while about 50,000 Brahmins are permanent residents. The Jains too consider it holy because three *tirthankars* (seventh Suarsvanath, 11th Shyeyanshnath, 23rd Parsvanath) were born here.

Varanasi was probably an important town by the seventh century BC when Babylon and Nineveh were at the peak of their power. The Buddha visited in 500 BC and it was mentioned in both the *Mahabharata* and the *Ramayana*. It became a centre of culture, education, commerce and craftsmanship but was raided by **Mahmud of Ghazni's** army in 1033 and by Qutb-ud-din Ghuri in 1194. **Ala-ud-din Khalji**, the King of Delhi (1294-1316), destroyed temples and built mosques on their sites. The Muslim influence was strong so even in the 18th century the city was known briefly as Mohammadabad. Despite its early foundation hardly any building dates before the 17th century, and few are more than 200 years old.

The city stands as the chief centre of Sanskrit learning in North India. Sanskrit, the oldest of the Indo-European languages, used for Hindu ritual has been sustained here long after it ceased to be a living language elsewhere. The **Banaras Hindu University** has over 150,000 rare manuscripts. Hindu devotional movements flourished here, especially in the 15th century under Ramananda, and **Kabir**, one of India's greatest poets, lived in the city. It was here that **Tulsi Das** translated the Ramayana from Sanskrit into Hindi.

Old Centre
Visvanath Temple (1777) has been the main Siva temple in Varanasi for over 1000 years. Tourists have to enter by Gate 2, but can exit from any gate, and there is stiff security by

the entrances (take passport ID, bags not permitted). The original temple, destroyed in the 12th century, was replaced by a mosque. It was rebuilt in the 16th, and again destroyed within a century. The present **Golden Temple** was built in 1777 by Ahilya Bai of Indore. The gold plating on the roof was provided by Maharaja Ranjit Singh in 1835. Its pointed spires are typically North Indian in style and the exterior is finely carved. The 18th-century **Annapurna Temple** (*anna* food; *purna* filled) nearby, built by Baji Rao I, has shrines dedicated to Siva, Ganesh, Hanuman and Surya. Ask for directions as you make your way through the maze of alleys around the temples.

The **Gyan Kup** (Well of Knowledge) next door is said to contain the Siva lingam from the original temple – the well is protected by a stone screen and canopy. The nearby **Gyanvapi Mosque** (Great Mosque of Aurangzeb), with 71-m-high minarets, shows evidence of the original Hindu temple, in the foundations, the columns and at the rear.

The 17th-century **Alamgir Mosque** (Beni Madhav ka Darera), impressively situated on Panchganga Ghat, was Aurangzeb's smaller mosque. It was built on the original Vishnu temple of the Marathas, parts of which were used in its construction. Two minarets are missing – one fell and killed some people and the other was taken down by the government as a precaution. You can climb to the top of the mosque for fantastic views (donation expected); again, bags are prohibited and you may be searched.

Back lanes

The maze of narrow lanes, or *galis*, along the ghats through the old quarters exude the smells and sounds of this holy city. They are fascinating to stroll through though easy to get lost in. Some find it too over-powering. Near the Town Hall (1845) built by the Maharaja of Vizianagram, is the **Kotwali** (Police Station) with the Temple of **Bhaironath**, built by Baji Rao II in 1825. The image inside is believed to be of the Kotwal (Superintendent) who rides on a ghostly dog. Stalls sell sugar dogs to be offered to the image. In the temple garden of **Gopal Mandir** near the Kotwali is a small hut in which Tulsi Das is said to have composed the *Binaya Patrika* poem.

The **Bhelupura Temple** with a museum marks the birthplace of the 23rd Jain Tirthankar **Parsvanath** who preached non-violence. The **Durga Temple** (18th-century) to the south along Durga Kund Road, was built in the Nagara style. It is painted red with ochre and has the typical five spires (symbolizing the elements) merging into one (Brahma). Non-Hindus may view from the rooftop nearby. Next door in a peaceful garden, the **Tulsi Manas Temple** (1964) in white marble commemorates the medieval poet Tulsi Das. It has walls engraved with verses and scenes from the *Ramcharitmanas*, composed in a Hindi dialect, instead of the conventional Sanskrit, and is open to all (closed 1130-1530). Good views from the second floor of 'Disneyland-style' animated show. **Bharat Mata Temple**, south of Varanasi Junction Station, has a relief map of 'Mother India' in marble.

Riverfront

The hundred and more **ghats** on the river are the main attraction for visitors to Varanasi. Visit them at first light before sunrise (0430 in summer, 0600 in winter) when Hindu pilgrims come to bathe in the sacred Ganga, facing the rising sun, or at dusk when synchronized *pujas* are performed, culminating in leaf-boat lamps being floated down the river, usually from 1800 (later in summer). Large crowds gather at Dasasvamedha (Main) Ghat and Mir Ghat every night, or there's a more low-key affair at Assi Ghat. Start the river trip at Dasasvamedha Ghat where you can hire a boat quite cheaply especially if you can share (bargain to about Rs 200-250 per hour for two to eight people, at dawn). You may go either upstream (south) towards Harishchandra Ghat or downstream to Manikarnika Ghat. You may prefer to have a boat on the river at sunset and watch the lamps floated on the river, or go in the afternoon at a fraction of the price quoted at dawn. For photographs, visit the riverside between 0700-0900. The foggy sunshine early in the morning often clears to produce a beautiful light.

Kite flying is a popular pastime, as elsewhere in India, especially all along the riverbank. The serious competitors endeavour to bring down other flyers' kites and so fortify their twine by coating it with a mix of crushed light bulbs and flour paste to make it razor sharp. The quieter ghats, eg Panchganga, are good for watching the fun: boys in their boats on the river scramble to retrieve downed kites as trophies that can be re-used even though the kites themselves are very cheap. Cricket is also played on the ghats, particularly those to the north which are more spacious and less crowded.

Dasasvamedha Ghat Commonly called 'Main Ghat', Dasasvamedha means the 'Place of Ten Horse Sacrifices' performed here by Brahma, God of Creation. Some believe that in the age of the gods when the world was in chaos, Divodasa was appointed King of Kashi by Brahma. He accepted, on condition that all the gods would leave Varanasi. Even Siva

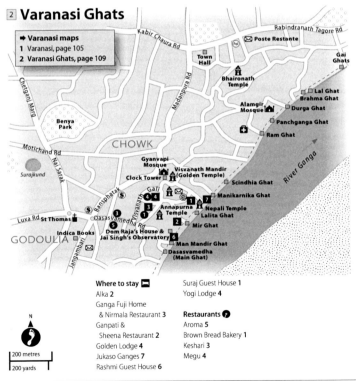

2 **Varanasi Ghats**

➡ **Varanasi maps**
1 Varanasi, page 105
2 Varanasi Ghats, page 109

Where to stay
Alka 2
Ganga Fuji Home
& Nirmala Restaurant 3
Ganpati &
Sheena Restaurant 2
Golden Lodge 4
Jukaso Ganges 7
Rashmi Guest House 6

Suraj Guest House 1
Yogi Lodge 4

Restaurants
Aroma 5
Brown Bread Bakery 1
Keshari 3
Megu 4

was forced to leave but Brahma set the test for Divodasa, confident that he would get the complex ceremony wrong, allowing the gods back into the city. However, the ritual was performed flawlessly, and the ghat has thus become one of the holiest, especially at eclipses. Bathing here is regarded as being almost as meritorious as making the sacrifice.

Moving south You will pass **Munshi Ghat**, where some of the city's sizeable Muslim population (25%) come to bathe. The river has no religious significance for them. Close by is **Darbhanga Ghat** where the mansion had a hand-operated cable lift. Professional washermen work at the **Dhobi Ghat**; there is religious merit in having your clothes washed in the Ganga. Brahmins have their own washermen to avoid caste pollution. The municipality has built separate washing facilities away from the ghat.

Narad Ghat and **Chauki Ghat** are held sacred since the Buddha received enlightenment here under a *peepul* tree. Those who bathe together at Narad, supposedly go home and quarrel! The pink water tower here is for storing Ganga water. High water levels are recorded at **Raj Ghat**. The flood levels are difficult to imagine when the river is at its lowest in January and February. **Mansarovar Ghat** leads to ruins of several temples around a lake. **Kedar Ghat** is named after Kedarnath, a pilgrimage site in the Uttarakhand, with a Bengali temple nearby.

The **Harishchandra Ghat** is particularly holy and is dedicated to King Harishchandra. It is now the most sacred *smashan* or cremation ghat although Manikarnika is more popular. Behind the ghat is a *gopuram* of a Dravidian-style temple. The **Karnataka Ghat** is one of many regional ghats which are attended by priests who know the local languages, castes, customs and festivals.

The **Hanuman Ghat** is where Vallabha, the leader of a revivalist Krishna bhakti cult was born in the late 15th century. **Shivala Ghat** (Kali Ghat) is privately owned by the ex-ruler of Varanasi. **Chet Singh's Fort**, Shivala, stands behind the ghat. The fort, the old palace of the Maharajas, is where the British imprisoned him but he escaped by climbing down to the river and swimming away. **Anandamayi Ghat** is named after the Bengali saint Anandamayi Ma (died 1982) who received 'enlightenment' at 17 and spent her life teaching and in charitable work. **Jain Ghat** is near the birthplace of Tirthankar Shyeyanshnath. **Tulsi Ghat** commemorates the great saint-poet Tulsi Das who lived here (see Tulsi Manas Temple, page 108). Furthest upstream is the **Assi Ghat**, where the River Assi meets the Ganga, one of the five that pilgrims should bathe from in a day. The order is Assi, Dasasvamedha, Barnasangam, Panchganga and Manikarnika. Upstream on the east bank is the Ramnagar Fort, the Maharaja of Varanasi's residence (see page 112). Here the boat will turn to take you back to Dasasvamedha Ghat.

Moving north Leaving Dasasvamedha Ghat, you come to **Man Mandir Ghat** dominated by a Rajput palace ① *open dawn till dusk, Rs100 foreigners, Rs 5 Indians*, built by Maharajah Man Singh of Amber in 1600 and one of the oldest in Varanasi. The palace was restored in the last century with brick and plaster. The beautiful stone balcony on the northeast corner gives an indication of how the original looked. Maharaja Jai Singh of Jaipur converted the palace into an **observatory** in 1710. Like its counterparts in Delhi, Jaipur and Ujjain, the rooftop observatory comprises a collection of instruments built of brick, cement and stone. At the entrance is the Bhittiyantra, or wall quadrant, over 3 m high and in the same plane as the lines of longitude. Similarly placed is the Samratyantra which is designed to slope upwards pointing at the Pole Star. From the top of the Chakra Yantra there is a superb view of the ghats and the town. Near the entrance to the palace is a small **Siva**

Temple whose shrine is a lingam immersed in water. During droughts, water is added to the cistern to make it overflow for good luck.

The **Dom Raja's House** is next door, flanked by painted tigers. The *doms* are the 'Untouchables' of Varanasi and are integral to the cremation ceremony. As Untouchables they can handle the corpse, a ritually polluting act for Hindus. They also supply the flame from the temple for the funeral pyre. Their presence is essential and also lucrative since there are fees for the various services they provide. The Dom Raja is the hereditary title of the leader of these Untouchables.

Mir Ghat leads to a sacred well; widows who dedicate themselves to prayer, are fed and clothed here. Then comes **Lalita Ghat** ① *entrance Rs 30*, with the distinctive Nepalese-style temple with a golden roof above and wood carvings decorating the exterior. Above **Manikarnika Ghat** is a well into which Siva's dead wife Sati's earring is supposed to have fallen when Siva was carrying her after she committed suicide. The Brahmins managed to find the jewel from the earring (*manikarnika*) and returned it to Siva who blessed the place. Offerings of *bilva* flowers, milk, sandalwood and sweetmeats are thrown into the tank where pilgrims come to bathe. Between the well and the ghat is *Charanpaduka*, a stone slab with Vishnu's footprint. Boatmen may try to persuade you to leave a 'private' offering to perform a *puja* (a ploy to increasing their earnings).

The adjoining **Jalasayin Ghat** is the principal burning ghat of the city. The expensive scented sandalwood which the rich alone can afford is used sparingly; usually not more than 2 kg. You may see floating bundles covered in white cloth; children, and those dying of 'high fever', or smallpox in the past, are not cremated but put into the river. This avoids injuring Sitala the goddess of smallpox. **Note** Photography is not permitted at the burning ghats, though travellers might be told that it is allowed and then a large fine demanded. Other scams involve conmen collecting 'donations' to provide wood for burning the poor. Beware of pestering individuals declaring they are "not a guide", they have the potential to ruin your experience.

Tourists are few and far between after the burning ghat. **Scindia Ghat**, originally built in 1830, was so large that it collapsed. **Ram Ghat** was built by the Maharaja of Jaipur. Five rivers are supposed to meet at the magnificent **Panchganga Ghat** – the Ganga, Sarasvati, Gyana, Kirana and Dhutpapa. The stone column can hold around 1000 lamps at festivals. The impressive flights of stone steps run up to the Alamgir Mosque (see page 108). At **Gai Ghat** there is a statue of a Nandi bull whilst at **Trilochana Ghat** there is a temple to Siva in his form as the 'Three-eyed' (*Trilochana*); two turrets stand out of the water. A beautiful little palace is found at **Rani Ghat**, then **Raj Ghat** is the last ghat you can reach before the path peters out. Excavations have revealed a site of a city from the eighth century BC on a grassy mound nearby. Raj Ghat was where the river was forded until bridges were built.

Other sights

Varanasi is famous for ornamental brasswork, silk weaving and for its glass beads, exported all over the world. *Zari* work, whether embroidered or woven, once used silver or gold thread but is now done with gilded copper or brass. You can watch weavers at work in Piti Kothi, the Muslim area inland from Raj Ghat. The significance of **silk** in India's traditional life is deep-rooted. Silk was considered a pure fabric, most appropriate for use on ceremonial and religious occasions. Its lustre, softness and richness of natural colour gave it precedence over all other fabrics. White or natural coloured silk was worn by the Brahmins and others who were 'twice born'. Women wore bright colours and the darker hues were reserved for the lowest caste in the formal hierarchy, few of whom could afford it. Silk garments were worn for ceremonials like births and marriages, and offerings of finely woven silks were made to deities in temples. This concept of purity may have given impetus to the growth of silk-weaving centres around ancient temple towns like Kanchipuram, Varanasi, Bhubaneswar and Ujjain, a tradition that is kept alive today.

Banaras Hindu University (BHU), to the south of the city, is one of the largest campus universities in India and enjoys a pleasant, relaxed atmosphere. Founded at the turn of the 19th century, it was originally intended for the study of Sanskrit, Indian art, music and culture. The **New Visvanath Temple** (1966), one of the tallest in India, is in the university semicircle and was financed by the Birla family. It was planned by Madan Mohan Malaviya (1862-1942), chancellor of the university, who believed in Hinduism without caste distinctions. The marble Siva temple modelled on the old Visvanath Temple, is open to all.

Bharat Kala Bhavan ① *BHU, Mon-Sat 1030-1630 (Jul-Apr), 0730-1300 (May-Jun) closed holidays, foreigners Rs 100, camera Rs 50 (lockers at entrance).* This peaceful museum contains a wealth of sculptures from Mathura and Sarnath, and an excellent gallery of miniature paintings including Mughal and Company works. Don't miss the Nidhi Gallery (limited hours, 1200-1300 and 1500-1600) containing treasures such as Jahangir's opium cup and priceless pieces of jewellery. Upstairs is an interesting exhibition on Benares containing old prints and photos, and also the Alice Boner gallery showing the life and work of this Swiss painter/sculptor who immigrated to India in 1935.

Across the river in a dramatic setting on the edge of narrow crowded streets is the run-down 17th-century **Ramnagar Fort**, the former home of the Maharaja of Varanasi. The ferry costs Rs 10 return, or there are rickshaws from the main gate of BHU which cross a bone-jarring pontoon bridge to the fort (under water June to October), Rs 10 each way, or take a boat back or else walk over the pontoon bridge. The **museum** ① *T0542-233 9322, 1000-1700, Rs 16,* has palanquins, elephant *howdahs* and headdresses, costumes, arms and furniture gathering dust. Look out for the amazing locally made astrological clock and peer inside the impressive Durbar Hall, cunning designed to remain cool in the summer heat, with lifesize portraits lining one wall. Nearby Ramnagar village has *Ramlila* performances during Dasara (October to November) and has some quieter backalleys which make for a relaxing hours wandering.

Sarnath

Sarnath, 10 km northeast of Varanasi, is one of Buddhism's major centres in India. The museum houses some superb pieces, including the famed four-lion capital that is the symbol of the Indian Union. The *stupas*, monasteries and Buddha statues make an interesting contrast to nearby Hindu Varanasi.

Tourist information Modern Reception Centre ① *T0542-259 5965, T(0)9580-574420, Mon-Sat 1000-1700,* provides a map and information.

History
When he had gained enlightenment at Bodhgaya, the Buddha came to the deer park at Sarnath and delivered his first sermon (circa 528 BC), usually referred to as *Dharmachakra* (The Wheel of Law). Since then, the site has been revered. The Chinese traveller Hiuen Tsang described the *sangharama* (monastery) in AD 640 as having 1500 monks, a 65-m-high *vihara*, a figure of the Buddha represented by a wheel, a 22-m-high stone *stupa* built by Ashoka, a larger 90-m-high *stupa* and three lakes. The remains here and the

sculptures now at the Indian Museum, Kolkata and the National Museum, Delhi, reveal that Sarnath was a centre of religious activity, learning and art, continuously from the fourth century BC until its abandonment in the ninth century AD and ultimate destruction by Muslim armies in 1197.

Archaeological Museum

The **Archaeological Museum** ① *Sat-Thu 0900-1700, entrance Rs 5, cameras and bags must be left outside*, has a well-displayed collection of pieces from the site, including the famous lion capital from the Ashokan Column. The four lions sitting back to back are of highly polished sandstone and show Mauryan sculpture at its best. Also on display are a Sunga period (first century BC) stone railing, Kushana period (second century AD) Boddhisattvas and Gupta period (fifth century AD) figures including a magnificent seated Buddha.

Enclosure

① *Open sunrise-sunset, foreigners Rs 100, video Rs 25.*

The **Dhamekh Stupa** (Dharma Chakra) dating to fifth to sixth century AD, is the most imposing monument at Sarnath, built where the Buddha delivered his first sermon to his five disciples. Along with his birth, enlightenment and death, this incident is one of the four most significant. The *stupa* consists of a 28-m-diameter stone plinth which rises to a height of 13 m. Each of the eight faces has an arched recess for an image. Above this base rises a 31-m-high cylindrical tower. The upper part was probably unfinished. The central section has elaborate Gupta designs, eg luxuriant foliation, geometric patterns, birds and flowers. The Brahmi script dates from the sixth to ninth centuries. The *stupa* was enlarged six times and the well-known figures of a standing Boddhisattva and the Buddha teaching were found nearby.

The **Dharmarajika Stupa** was built by the Emperor Ashoka to contain relics of the Buddha. It was enlarged on several occasions but was destroyed by Jagat Singh, Dewan of the Maharaja of Benares, in 1794, when a green marble casket containing human bones and pearls was found. The British Resident at the maharaja's court published an account of the discovery thereby drawing the attention of scholars to the site.

The **main shrine**, marking the place of the Buddha's meditation, is attributed to Ashoka and the later Guptas. To the rear is the 5-m lower portion of a polished sandstone **Ashokan Column** (third century BC). The original was about 15 m high and was topped by the lion capital which is now in the Archaeological Museum (see above). The column was one of many erected by Ashoka to promulgate the faith and this contained a message to the monks and nuns not to create any schisms and to spread the word. The monastery (fifth century onwards) in the southwest corner is one of four (the others are along the north edge of the enclosure). All are of brick, with cells off a central courtyard that are in ruins.

Other sights

The site is also holy to Jains because **Shyeyanshnath**, the 11th Tirthankar, was born near the Dhamekh *stupa*. The word 'Sarnath' may be derived from his name. A large temple and (on the opposite side of the road) a statue have been built to commemorate him. The modern **Mulagandhakuti Vihara** ① *open 0400-1130, 1330-2000* (1929-1931), contains frescoes by the Japanese artist Kosetsu Nosu depicting scenes from the Buddha's life. An urn in the ground is supposed to hold a Buddha relic obtained from Taxila (Pakistan). The wall around the **Bodhi tree** (*pipal, Ficus religiosa*) is thick with prayer flags. The tree, planted in 1931, is a sapling of the one in Sri Lanka that was grown from a cutting taken there circa 236 BC by

Mahinda's sister Princess Sanghamitta. Past the Mulagandhakuti temple is the **deer park/ zoo** ① *open 0800-dusk, Rs 20,* where you can see birds, deer and crocodiles.

The colourful and peaceful **Burmese monastery** is worth the detour from the road. The **Chinese monastery** has a map showing Hiuen Tsang's route to India during AD 629-644, as well as old photos on display. Tibetan, Japanese, Cambodian, Korean and Thai monasteries have also been built around the old complex. The 24-m-high **standing statue** of Lord Buddha, next to the Thai monastery, was completed in March 2011.

Chaukhandi, 500 m south, has a fifth-century *stupa*. On top of this is an octagonal brick tower built by Akbar in 1588 to commemorate the visit his father Humayun made to the site. The inscription above the doorway reads "As Humayun, king of the Seven Climes, now residing in paradise, deigned to come and sit here one day, thereby increasing the splendour of the sun, so Akbar, his son and humble servant, resolved to build on this spot a lofty tower reaching to the blue sky".

Varanasi and around listings

For hotel and restaurant price codes and other relevant information, see pages 12-15.

⊖ Where to stay

Varanasi *p104, maps p105 and p109*
Off-season discounts are available May-Aug. Be prepared for power cuts and carry a torch at night. Some rickshaw drivers insist on taking you to hotels where they get a commission; check whether your hotel arranges pick-up from the station to avoid this hassle. Hotels on the riverfront can be difficult to locate, particularly at night when walking along the minor ghats is not advisable. Auto- and cycle-rickshaws cannot go down the narrow lanes of the old city, which are a confusing maze on first arrival. Look for hotel signs (with arrows) painted on walls to find your way, or ask shopkeepers. Rooms with river view are worth the extra. Staying in the Cantonment area can be more comfortable and better value for money but it means missing out on the atmosphere of the city.

$$$$ Jukaso Ganges, Guleria Ghat, near Manikarnika Ghat, T0542-240 6666, www.welcomeheritagehotels.in. Beautiful newly renovated old palace with 15 comfortable rooms (mostly river-facing, some with delightful private balconies), great bathrooms, around an inner courtyard.

Roof terrace for dining, lovely seating out the front on the ghats, and charming public spaces in an amazingly elegant building. Breakfast included. Located on the northern ghats by among stunning ancient buildings – the less touristed part.
$$$$ Suryauday Haveli, Shivala Ghat, Nepali Kothi, T0542-654 0390, www.suryaudayhaveli. com. Newly opened hotel directly on the ghats in a renovated century-old stone edifice built by the Nepali kings. Some rooms river-facing, there's a fabulous roof deck, lovely courtyard, and yoga in mornings/sunset boat ride (free). Candlelit dinner accompanied by live Indian music in evenings should be special, although the quality of food isn't up to scratch (yet). Rooms are spacious with traditional elements of decor. An excellent location, and a characterful and swish place to stay right on the Ganga, but don't expect 5-stars. Rates drop by almost 50% May-Sep, breakfast included.
$$$ Clarks Varanasi, The Mall, T0542-250 1011-20, www.clarkshotels.com. In the quieter Cantonment area, not as plush as other high-end options, with rooms that feel a bit dated, but the facilities are good and it has some character. The pool itself is uninviting but the surroundings of established trees and plants is pleasing (non-residents, Rs 300 includes food), restaurant and nice bar. Discounts available (10%).

$$$ Ganges View, Assi Ghat, T0542-231 3218, www.hotelgangesview.com. Old patrician home converted into a welcoming guesthouse with a tastefully decorated range of small rooms, more expensive on the upper level with the better views, very pleasant atmosphere, interesting clientele, lovely riverside verandas, beautiful artwork adorns the public spaces, vegetarian restaurant (guests only), Wi-Fi Rs 25 per hr. Deservedly popular so book ahead.

$$$ Gateway Ganges, Nadesar Palace Ground, T0542-250 3001-19, www.thegate wayhotels.com. 130 rooms (plus suites), those on the 3rd floor have walk-in showers, 2 good restaurants serve alcohol, pool is the nicest in town, busy but formal efficient service.

$$$ Palace on Ganges, B-1/158 Assi Ghat, T0542-231 5050, www.palaceonganges.com. Set in a converted former palace, each room is decorated in the style of a different Indian state (the Punjab and Colonial rooms are best, facing the river; some rooms are getting faded). Restaurant with live Indian classical music plus a small rooftop dining area.

$$$ Radisson, The Mall, Cantonment, T0542-250 1566, www.radisson.com/varanasi.in. The grandest rooms in town, large with quality furnishings, wide white beds, sofas and good bathrooms. Good health facilities, disappointing pool (small with few loungers), excellent restaurant and modern bar.

$$$-$$ Rashmi Guest House, Manmandir Ghat, T0542-240 2778, www.palaceon river.com. This modern tower has an excellent location close to Main Ghat, rooms are clean and modern (but the cheapest lack windows), a good place for families. The rooftop restaurant is reliable and hygienic. A/c, hot water, TV, free Wi-Fi, advisable to book in advance.

$$$-$$ Shiva Ganges View, Mansarovar Ghat, T0542-245 0063, www.varanasi guesthouse.com. In a British-built old family house, 8 large spotless rooms with high ceilings, multiple windows, mosquito nets and coolers – but somewhat strange furniture and clashing decor. Great views

from the front upstairs rooms, which share a balcony and have a/c; lower rooms have air-coolers and are cheaper. Very chatty owner.

$$-$ Alka, Mir Ghat, T0542-240 1681, www.hotelalkavns.com. Wide variety of clean rooms in a modern building, though some are in need of a lick of paint. Expect towels, a/c and TV in the more expensive rooms, cheaper end share bathrooms. The prime riverside location means it is often full, book ahead. Handy access down to the ghats from the pleasant courtyard.

$$-$ Ganga Fuji Home, Shakarkand Gali, near Golden Temple, T0542-239 7333, www.gangafujihomevaranasi.com. An excellent choice with a wide range of price categories, from very cheap with shared bath up to comfortable deluxe rooms with a/c and TV. Free Wi-Fi, hot water, decent pillows and mattresses, competent management, **Nirmala** restaurant on rooftop (see Restaurants, page 117). A new 3-star building next door will be completed in 2012, with swimming pool and elevator. They can pick up from the train station – call on arrival.

$$-$ Ganpati, next to **Alka** on Mir Ghat, T0542-239 0059, www.ganpatiguesthouse. com. Atmospheric old building, 20 rooms range from cubby holes sharing bathrooms to spacious doubles with TV and river-fronting private balconies, some rooms have a/c. Great views from rooftop, good restaurant (see page 117), but the booking system can be hit-and-miss.

$$-$ Rahi Tourist Bungalow (UP Tourism), off Parade Kothi, opposite railway station, T0542-220 8545, www.up-tourism.com. A/c, air-cooled or fan rooms and dorm in barrack-style 2-storey building, restaurant, bar, shady veranda, pleasant garden, simple, clean and efficient, popular – definitely wise to phone ahead. Can arrange good-value cars for the day.

$ Baba Guest House, D20/15 Munshi Ghat, T0542-245 5452, www.babaguesthouse.com. Basic, freshly painted rooms, some with bath, dorm, huge Korean menu, food served in downstairs café when it's too hot to use rooftop restaurant. A cheery budget choice. Recommended.

$ Chaitanya Guest House, B1/158-A, Assi Ghat, T0542-231 3686, knpsahi@yahoo.com. A cosy family place with only 4 rooms, attached bathrooms, in an old building with moulded ceilings, coloured glass windows and tiny terrace at the front. Sadly views are over a car park rather than the Ganga. Rooms with a/c cost significantly more, or air coolers provided in summer. Good choice.

$ Golden Lodge, Kalika Lane, near Golden Temple, T0542-239 8788, www.goldenlodge. canalblog.com. Small clean rooms are very good value, those on the lower 2 floors are older but have character, common or private bath, some doubles with TV and a/c, triples available, 24-hr hot water, enthusiastic proprietor, a/c restaurant (Fagin's) is OK, Wi-Fi. Recommended.

$ Sahi River View Guest House, Assi Ghat, T0542-236 6730, sahi_rvgh@sify.com. 12 rooms of all standards, great views from balcony and rooftop, food from spotless kitchen, free local and received calls, owner eager to please, no commission given to touts.

$ Shiva Ganga Lodge, Niranjani Ghat, T0542-227 7755. Super little budget place, 10 rooms with common bath around a sweet courtyard, fabulous views from a nearby terrace, friendly owner. They have rooms with private bath in a hotel nearby (same name) but it lacks the atmosphere.

$ Shiva Kashi Guesthouse, Chausatti Ghat, T(0)9235-512294, shivakashiguesthouse varanasi@gmail.com. Very respectable rooms, quite modern, some with balcony, not on the river but very close, free Wi-Fi, peaceful and comfortable. Good choice.

$ Sun Shiv, D 54/16-D Ravi Niketan, Jaddumandi Rd (off Aurangabad Rd), T0542-241 0468, hotelsunshiv@rediffmail.com. 16 modest but charming rooms with balconies in unusual, art deco-inspired 1960s family home, room service, quiet, no commission to rickshaws. Highly engaging, multi-lingual owner.

$ Suraj Guest House, Lalita Ghat near Nepali Temple, T0542-239 8560. Tucked away behind a tiny temple, quaint simple rooms owned by eccentric family, extremely cheap, nice vibe.

$ Yogi Lodge, D8/29 Kalika Gali, near Golden Temple, T0542-240 4224, yogilodge@ yahoo.com. Simple rooms, shared bath, dorm (Rs 80), meals on roof terrace or in pleasant courtyard, open kitchen, internet, friendly staff, recommended.

Restaurants

Varanasi p104, maps p105 and p109
Restaurants outside hotels tend to be vegetarian and are not allowed to serve alcohol (though a couple do). Dry days are on the 1st and 7th of each month, and on some public holidays. Many tourist-oriented eateries are on Bengali Tola (large alley running from Main Ghat to Assi Ghat), and there are some excellent and cheap South Indian places at its southern end.

$$ Poonam, Pradeep Hotel, Jagatganj, T0542-220 4963/220 4994. Good variety of fabulous Indian dishes, served by professional staff in classy surroundings. Eden restaurant on the roof is equally good – and has a garden.

$$-$ Brown Bread Bakery, Tripura Bhairavi (near Golden Temple) and newer branch on Bengali Tola. Excellent salads and diverse menu (Thai, Italian, etc) in *haveli*-style setting, with cushions for lounging and live sitar music every evening. Organic ingredients used where possible. The service can be abominable, however, and food comes in long drawn-out stages – never expect to eat all together. Usually packed, nonetheless.

$$-$ Brownie, Bungalow No 53-1, between TV tower and India Tourism, Cantonment, T0542-251 1500. Open 0730-2230. If you find yourself in the area, head here for good mix of Indian and international menus (attentive to Western tastes), coffee, live music in the evenings, free Wi-Fi. The wicker booths are cosy.

$-$ Lotus Lounge, Mansarovar Ghat, T(0)9838-567717. Top spot for Ganga views from chilled-out terrace, prices are reasonable for inventive Asian and Western dishes, interesting salads and decent breakfasts. A perfect place if you need to get away from the bustle, plus a clean toilet. Closed in summer.

$$-$ Open Hand Cafe, Dumraun Bagh Colony, nr Assi Ghat, www.openhand.in. Excellent coffee, great pastries and food, and a relaxing cosy place to hang out with free Wi-Fi. Fair-trade. The shop is worth checking out (see Shopping, page 118).

$$-$ Pizzeria Café Vaatika, Assi Ghat. Wonderful shady plant-filled terrace on the Ganga, friendly staff, Italian (OK pizza) and Indian food, excellent cold coffee. A perfect place to relax.

$ Aroma, Dasasvamedha Rd, Godoulia, T0542-326 4564. Bland pastel decor and low ceilings but a clean a/c environment off the tourist circuit, best for south Indian meals. Free delivery 0800-2200 on orders over Rs 200.

$ Keshari, Teri Neem, Godoulia (off Dasasvamedha Rd), T0542-240 1472. Excellent vegetarian *thalis* (around Rs 150) plus north and south Indian dishes and some Chinese, "the longest menu in town" but not every item is available, efficient service, generous portions. Recommended.

$ Sheena, Ganpati Hotel (see Where to stay, page 115). Rooftop restaurant with sublime river views and lower balcony with Mediterranean feel, serving quality food, especially good *shakshuka*. Great place for hanging out, plus there's clandestine beer.

$ Megu, Kalika Lane near Golden Temple. Lunchtimes only, 1000-1600, closed Sun. This tiny restaurant specializes in Japanese food and is popular with those in the know. Fantastic ginger chicken, and the Korean *bibimbap* is a winner.

$ Nirmala, Ganga Fuji Home (see Where to stay, page 115). Hygienic kitchen, food tempered down for Western palate, live classical music every evening at 1930.

Recommended for the exceptional city views, ambiance and hospitality, serves beer.

$ Shiva Café and German Bakery, Bengali Tola near Naraol Ghat. Open from 0800. Very popular, especially for breakfasts which are excellent (proper porridge). Spartan decor on the ground floor but the 2nd storey is a bit jazzier with low seating and a Nepalese theme. Staff are delightful and prices very sensible. Free Wi-Fi.

❀ Festivals

Varanasi *p104, maps p105 and p109*
Feb Ganga Water Rally, organized by UP Tourism, is an international and national kayak get-together from Allahabad to Chunar Fort. A 40-km race from Chunar to Varanasi takes place on the final day. Also International Yoga Week.
Late Feb/early Mar 3 days at Sivaratri, festival of Dhrupad music attracts performers from near and far, beginners and stars, in a very congenial atmosphere, a wonderful experience, many *naga babas* (naked *sadhus*) set up camp on ghats.
Mar/Apr Holi is celebrated with great fervour.
Apr Pilgrims walk around 'Kashi', as laid down in the scriptures. Jain Mahavir Jayanti.
Apr/May Sankat Mochan Music Festival, Sankat Mochan Mandir. Non-stop temple music, open to all.
May Ganga Dasara celebrates the day the waters of the Ganga reached Haridwar.
Jul/Aug Month-long carnival with funfair opposite Monkey Temple, monsoon fever makes it particularly crazy.
Oct/Nov Dasara Ramlila at Ramnagar. Ganga Festival is organized by UP Tourism alongside a 10-day craft fair. Nagnathaiya draws up to 50,000 worshippers to Tulsi Ghat, re-enacting the story of Krishna jumping into the Yamuna to overcome Kalija, the King of the Serpents. Nakkataiya A fair at Chetganj recalling Rama's brother, Lakshmana, cutting off Ravana's sister's nose when she attempted to force him into a marriage.

At Nati Imli, **Bharat Milap**, the meeting of Rama and Bharat after 14 years' separation is celebrated – the Maharaja of Varanasi attends in full regalia on elephant back.
Dec-Feb Music festivals.

O Shopping

Varanasi *p104, maps p105 and p109*
Varanasi is famous for silks including brocades (Temple Bazar, Visvanath Gali), brassware, gold jewellery, sitar making and hand-block printed goods. The main shopping areas are Chowk, Godoulia, Visvanath Gali, Gyanvapi and Thatheri Bazar.

Books
Harmony, B1/158 Assi Ghat. Best selection in town (some say in India), excellent regional fiction, coffee-table books and religious/spiritual tomes.
Indica Books, D 40/18 Godoulia, near crossing. Specialist Indological bookshop.

Handloom and handicrafts
Benares Art Culture, 2/114 Badhaini Assi. Aims to promote local artists, interesting selection of sculpture, paintings and silks at fixed prices.
Ganga Handlooms, D10/18 Kohli Katra, off Viswanath Gali, near Golden Temple (ask locally). 1100-2000. Large selection of beautiful cotton fabrics, *ikats*, vegetable dyes, good tailors, great patterns (Western).
Open Hand Café & Shop (see Restaurants, page 117). Home furnishings, textiles, crafts, jewellery, and a good place to buy silk. Fair-trade credentials.

O What to do

Varanasi *p104, maps p105 and p109*
Body and soul
Panch Mandir, Assi Ghat. Drop-in classes each morning 0600-0930, reasonably priced.
Satya Foundation, B-37/54B Rukma Bhawan, Birdopur, T(0)9336-877455, www.satya foundation.com. Music,

meditation and yoga, highly authentic teachings. Recommended.
Siddhartha Yoga Centre, below Lotus Lounge, Mansarowar Ghat, T(0)9236-830966. 2-hr classes at 0800 and 1530, Rs 300, you can 'drop-in' but better to call ahead as there is only room for 4-5 people.

Language courses
'Tourist Hindi' courses are advertised in several hotels and restaurants.

Swimming
Pools at hotels **Radisson**, **Gateway Ganges**, and **Clarks Varanasi**.

Tour operators
Many small travel agents in laneways of Old City, usually charge Rs 50-100 commission on railway tickets.
TCI, Sri Das Foundation, S20/51-5 and S20/52-4, The Mall, T0542-250 0866, www.tcindia.com. Recommended.
Tiwari Tours and Travel, Assi Ghat, T0542-236 6727, www.tiwaritravel.com. Good service, bus tickets to high-end tours.

O Transport

Varanasi *p104, maps p105 and p109*
Air Transfer from the airport by taxi, a/c Rs 500, non-a/c Rs 400. Some taxis offer free transfer and claim a commission from hotel on arrival. A minibus to the airport runs from Assi Ghat for Rs 200 per person, contact **Tiwari Tours** (see above).

Indian Airlines flies daily to **Delhi**, Kolkata; to **Khajuraho** (via Agra) Mon, Wed, Sat. **Jet Airways**, **Jet Konnect** and **Spicejet** fly to Delhi, Kolkata and Mumbai.
Bicycle Enquire at your guesthouse about bicycle hire.
Boat This is the best way to enjoy Varanasi. It is necessary to bargain especially for an early-morning ghats visit; shared boat, Rs 50 per person per hr is the official rate for a boat carrying up to 10 people, ask around for others to share; 1-2 persons per boat

will cost about Rs 150 per hr; river crossing about Rs 80 return. A boat ride at dusk is also recommended, as well as the obligatory dawn ride.

Bus UP Roadways Bus Stand, Sher Shah Suri Marg, is opposite Junction Station, open 24 hrs, T(0)9415-049623. Buses to **Sarnath**, 10 km (Rs 5). To **Gorakhpur**, hourly from 0400-0030 (7 hrs, Rs 145. For **Delhi** go via **Kanpur**, frequent service from 0700 (8 hrs, Rs 172). **Agra**, at 1230, 1700 and 2000 (14 hrs). **Gaya**: better by rail.

Rickshaw *Tempos* and auto-rickshaws run on fixed routes; those near hotel gates overcharge (fix the fare before hiring). They are not allowed in the narrow streets of the old city but will go to **Godoulia** in the centre near Dasasvamedha Ghat, Rs 70 from station, or Rs 80 to **Assi Ghat**. There is a pre-paid taxi and rickshaw booth near the station reservations office.

Taxi Private taxis from agents and hotels. Uttar Pradesh Tourist Bungalow, Parade Kothi, T0542-220 6638, is a good place to start.

Train The official Reservations office is outside the station on the left as you exit. Be extra careful with your possessions on trains bound for Varanasi as theft is common.

Most trains stop at the **Junction** (or Cantonment) Station, T0542-234 8031 or T131, with 24-hr left luggage; to reach a Cantonment hotel on foot, use the back exit. Mughal Sarai station, T0542-225 5703, has the **Delhi/Kolkata** *Rajdhani Exp* (though some go via Patna); see below. Get your tickets (preferably a day in advance) from the Foreign Tourist Assistance inside the main hall which is very helpful and efficient, passport required (0800-2200, Sun 0800-1400). When it is closed use the computerized railway reservations (0800-1400, 1430-2000).

Agra Fort: *Marudhar Exp 14853/14863/14865*, 1720/1815/1745, 12½/11¾/12¼ hrs (book ahead); or frequent service from Mughal Sarai Station (see below).

Gaya many, including: *Doon Exp 23010/13010*, 1735, 3½ hrs. **Gorakhpur** (for Nepal): *Chaurichaura Exp 15003*, 0050,

6¼ hrs; *Manduadih Gorakhpur Exp 15104*, 0555, 5½ hrs. Several to **Kolkata** (**H**) including: *Kolkata 12322*, 0010, 11½ hrs; *Doon Exp 23010/13010*, 1615, 14½ hrs. **Mahoba** (for **Khajuraho**): *Bundelkhand Exp 11108*, 1805, 9¼ hrs (take onward bus). Several to **Satna** (for **Khajuraho**) including: *BSB LTT Superfast Exp 12168*, 1025, 5 hrs (from Satna, bumpy bus, 4-5 hrs). **New Delhi**: *Shiv Ganga Exp 12559*, 1915, 12½ hrs.

Mughal Sarai Station (with retiring rooms and left luggage). Take a connecting train from Varanasi (45 mins)Easiest to take a taxi from Varanasi, although shared autos leave from the railway station; allow plenty of time as you need to cross the Ganga and there are huge jams. Mughal Sarai has several trains to **Gaya**; a good one is *Purushottam Exp 12802*, 1040, 3 hrs. Also to: **Kolkata** (**H**): *Rajdhani Exp 12302/12306*, 0155, 8-11 hrs; *Kalka Howrah Mail 12312*, 2040, 10¾ hrs. **New Delhi**: *Poorva Exp 12381/12303*, 1837/1937 (12¼ hrs/11½ hrs); *RJPB Rajdhani Exp 12309*, 2235, 9 hrs. *Rajdhani Exp 12301/12305*, 0100, 9 hrs.

Sarnath *p112*

Bus/taxi Infrequent bus service from the Roadways bus stand; also included in coach tours. From Varanasi, autos from opposite railway station (Rs 100), *tempo* seat (Rs 10), you might have to change to another *tempo* halfway. Taxis take 30 mins (Rs 800 including wait).

❻ Directory

Varanasi *p104, maps p105 and p109*
Banks State Bank of India ATM at Godoulia (near Indica Books), many in Cantonment area. **Hospitals** Heritage Hospital, Lanka (near BHU main entrance), T0542-236 8888. Private hospital, out-patients 0830-2000. Many hotels, even budget ones, have a doctor on call. **Post** Head Post Office: Bisheshwarganj (parcel packing outside). Post office in Cantt, Mon-Sat 1000-1800. Also a small post office on Bengali Tola.

Bihar

Bihar, which takes its name from the word *vihara* (monastery), was the early home of Buddhism and the birthplace of one of India's most revered emperors, Asoka. His Buddhist legacy has left its imprint in some of the state's most visited pilgrimage sites, for while it may be on the outskirts of modern Patna, Kumrahar still has fragmentary remains of the early Mauryan capital; in Bodhgaya and Nalanda, Buddhism's tradition is powerfully visible.

Travellers intending to visit or travel through should be aware that this is one of India's poorest regions, and should strictly avoid travelling by night on rural roads. Nevertheless, most travellers who adopt the necessary precautions emerge unscathed.

Patna and around → *For listings, see pages 130-133.*

Bihar's straggling capital, Patna, has the air of a semi-rural provincial town in its more attractive areas, despite its size. It is one of India's poorest cities, stretching along the south bank of the Ganga for about 15 km. Divided in two by the large open Maidan, to the west are many administrative buildings of the British and to the east lies the chaotic old Chowk area. The central city is crowded and dusty; scant evidence remains of its earlier wealth and political supremacy. However, the new Buddha Smriti Park by the station, illuminated at night, is a sign of regeneration in the city. It is be interesting to take a cycle-rickshaw round by day. Many tribal people come into the town, often working on roads or building sites.

Arriving in Patna
Getting there and around Patna airport, 7 km west of the centre, has coaches and taxis for the transfer into town. State buses arrive at Gandhi Maidan Bus Stand, 15-25 minutes' walk from most budget hotels. These are strung out along Fraser Road towards Patna Junction railway station. Chaotic Mithapur Bus Stand (with private buses serving Gaya, Bodhgaya, Varanasi and Nepal) is located 2.5 km from Junction station; shared autos run between the two. The centre is compact enough to walk around, though shared rickshaws are available along all main routes. Hire an unmetered taxi from major hotels for longer trips.➤➤ *See Transport, page 132.*

Tourist information India Tourism ① *Kranti Marg (near PNT Club), R Block, T0612-250 6032. Mon-Fri 0930-1800*, provides excellent service from their office on the first floor. Nearby **BSTDC** ① *Hotel Kautilya Vihar, Bir Chand Patel Marg, T0612-250 6219, Mon-Sat 1000-1700* can help with car hire for day trips (minimum Rs 1300, 200 km, Rs 6.5 per km thereafter), also has counters at the airport and Patna Junction Railway Station. **ITDC** ① *Pataliputra Ashok, T0612-222 6270*, can also help with car hire. **Tourism Department** ① *Government of Bihar, 9D Hutment, Secretariat, T0612-222 4531.*

History

At the confluence of the rivers Son, Punpun, Gandak and Ganga, Patna's history can be traced back 2500 years. Ajatasatru, the second Magadha king who ruled from Rajgir, built a small fort at Pataligrama. Later Chandragupta Maurya founded the Mauryan Empire with Pataliputra as its capital. Buddhist histories suggest that it was here that Asoka usurped the throne of his father, Bindusara, murdering all his rivals and starting a reign of terror, before a conversion eight years later. It marked the beginning of perhaps the greatest reforming kingship the world has known. The Greek ambassador Megasthenes was deeply impressed by the efficiency of the Chandragupta administration and the splendour of the city. Ruins can be seen at Kumrahar, Bhiknapahari and Bulandhi Bagh with its 75 m wooden passage. Excavations date the site back to the pre-Mauryan times of 600 BC. In the 16th century the Pathan Sher Shah Suri established the foundations of a new Patna, building a majestic mosque in 1540 which dominates the skyline.

Places in Patna

Patna's buildings reflect its administrative and educational functions. The Collectorate, Court and educational institutions are all in the western part of the city, along with the Raj Bhavan, the High Court and the better residential areas (Sinha Library Rd, near the State Musuem, has a fine collection of old bungalows). To the east is Old Patna with its bazars, godowns, old mosques, Har Mandir and St Mary's Church.

The central area The restful **Buddha Smriti Park** ① *Fraser Rd, Tue-Sun 0900-1300 and 1600-1900, Rs 10, leave bags at the entrance*, opened in March 2011. The central *stupa* and surrounding buildings are fashioned from modernist slabs of grey stone; water features, grass, a meditation hall and Bo trees planted by the Buddhist countries of the world make it one of the city's most peaceful spots.

The glorious facade of the **State Museum** ① *Buddha Marg, Tue-Sun 1030-1600, entrance a shocking Rs 250, or Rs 500 to also see the relics of the Buddha*, houses a collection of exquisite stone sculptures, including the famous (and very voluptuous) life-size Didarganj Yakshi (Mauryan period) and the oldest known Jain image, a smoothed torso dating from the 3rd century BC). Noteworthy is a carving showing the birth of Buddha and a realistic image of a turbaned Buddha from Afghanistan (first century AD). Also on the ground floor is a gallery of moth-eaten stuffed animals and 'freaks of nature'. The first floor galleries are better lit with one of the most extensive collections *thangkas* outside of Tibet. Some random tribal artefacts (from throughout India) are worth a look, and a gallery displays a wealth of bronze statuary including some ancient naked Jain figurines. The miniature paintings include works on ivory and Patna Kalam paintings, which were commissioned by Company officials at the time when court-painting went into its final decline. Further galleries show artefacts found at Pataliputra and the Rajendra room has a curious small ivory map of India with Queen Victoria superimposed over the topography.

The **Golghar** (*Gola*, round house) is an extraordinary ovoid dome near the Maidan, built of stone slabs in 1786 by Captain John Garstin of the Bengal Engineers, who planned this grain store for the army in case of a repeat of the 1770 famine. It has a base 125 m wide, where the wall is 3.6 m thick, with two staircases that spiral up the outside; the workforce were to carry the grain up one and descend by the other. It was never completed so the last line of the inscription "First filled and publicly closed by ..." remains unfinished. Occasionally, it is possible to go inside and listen to the remarkable echo. It is well worth climbing the steps for an excellent view of the city and the Ganga. From July to September the river can be more than 5 km wide at this point.

To the east of the centre is **Khuda Bakhsh Oriental Public Library** ⓘ *Ashok Raj Path, T0612-230 0209, www.kblibrary.nic.in, Sat-Thu 0930-1700, entrance free*, inaugurated in 1891, with one of the largest collections of books and rare Persian and Arabic manuscripts in the world, in addition to Patna Qalam paintings and Moghul miniatures on ivory. The value and rarity of these objects means permission to view the originals (which are under double custody) is difficult to obtain. A slide-show of important pieces is offered instead; otherwise a selection of the manuscripts are exhibited each year from 1-5 August. It is now a national library bustling with Muslim scholars.

Kumrahar Excavations at the site of the ancient capital of Pataliputra have revealed ruins enclosed within a high brick wall. These date back to 600 BC, the first of four distinct periods of settlement over the following 1200 years. The buildings, mainly of wood, were devastated by a fire and lay hidden in the silt. The more recent fifth phase dates from the early 17th century. The most important finds are rare wooden ramparts and a large Mauryan three-storeyed assembly hall, with 15 rows of five highly polished sandstone pillars dating back to 400-300 BC. The garden has little to show today other than the single 6 m intact pillar. The tiny museum has its small collection of valuable finds almost invisibly shut away in a dark room. Shared autos leave from Junction Station and pass by the site.

Patna City

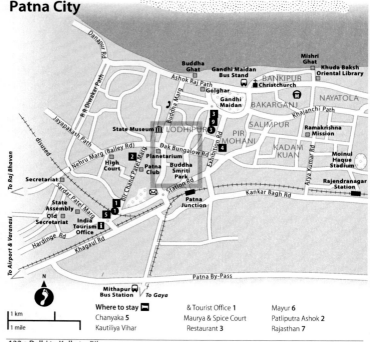

Where to stay 🛏	& Tourist Office 1	Mayur 6
Chanyaka 5	Maurya & Spice Court	Patliputra Ashok 2
Kautiliya Vihar	Restaurant 3	Rajasthan 7

Gulzarbagh Some 8 km east the centre (near the ASP's bungalow and Old City Court) are the former East India Company's main opium *godowns* (warehouses), now home to a government printing press. The three long buildings with porticoes on each side were strategically placed by the river for boats to carry the opium to Kolkata. The old *godowns*, ballroom and hall are open to visitors.

Har Mandir and around Har Mandir is in the Chowk area of old Patna, accessible by shared auto from Gandhi Maidan (Rs 15). The *gurudwara* built by Maharaja Ranjit Singh is the second of the four great *takhts* (thrones) of the Sikhs and consecrates the birthplace of the 10th Guru, Gobind Singh, in 1660. The shrine of white marble has kiosks on the terrace. Singers and musicians add to the beauty of the interior (heads must be covered before entering). There is a museum on the second floor of the gatehouse, which consists of panels telling the Sikh history.

Quila House (Jalan Museum) ⓘ *advance permission required from the family; contact Mr Aditya Jalan, Hira Place, Dak Bungalow Rd, Patna 1, T0612-265 5479/264 1121, visit@ quilahouse.com;. advisable to arrange 48 hrs in advance, preferred timings for visits Mon-Sat 0900-1100, Sun 100-1600; take a copy of your passport and visa pages,* is about 400 m from Har Mandir (locals will direct you). The private mansion was built over the ruins of Sher Shah's fort, and its setting by the Ganga is most tranquil and atmospheric. The diverse collection is particularly noteworthy for its Chinese porcelain and valuable jade pieces.

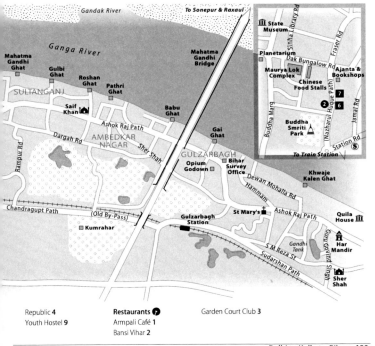

Republic **4**
Youth Hostel **9**

Restaurants 🍴
Armpali Café **1**
Bansi Vihar **2**

Garden Court Club **3**

Other highlights include Napoleon's bed and Tipu Sultan's palanquin, while panels in the hallway open up to reveal a set of George III Crown Derby. There are also beautiful ivory pieces, Toby jugs, French tapestries, Chinese paintings and a collection of silver filigree work of the Mughal period.

Saif Khan's Mosque (Pathar-ki-Masjid), on the river bank, was built in 1621 by Parwez Shah, the son of the Mughal Emperor Jahangir.

Around Patna

Sonepur ① *Sonepur and Vaishali can be visited comfortably in a day. You can hire a taxi or take a tour.* Sonepur is situated at the confluence of the Ganga and the Gandak and has a station on the Northeast Railway. Sonepur has Asia's biggest cattle market, beginning on the full moon of the Hindu month of **Kartik Purnima** (October/November). The fair lasts for two weeks to one month and draws thousands to the magic shows, folk dances, contests, handicrafts stalls and handlooms. Mark Shand's *Travels on my Elephant* gives a colourful account of the fair. Not just cattle but camels, horses, chimpanzees, birds and more are bought and sold (though numbers are dwindling); however, it is the large number of elephants, decorated for sale, which are the main attraction.

Vaishali Vaishali – derived from King Visala, from the *Ramayana* – dates back to the sixth century BC when it was a flourishing city of the Lichchavis, reputedly one of the first cities in the world to adopt a republican form of government. This is where the Buddha preached his last sermon and announced his approaching Nirvana. In 383 BC, 100 years later, it was the venue of the second Buddhist Council, when two *stupas* were erected. Jains of the Svetambara sect believe that Mahavir was born in Vaishali in 599 BC. Today, the district is part of the Mithila region, famous for Madhubani paintings on village houses.

The **Asoka Pillar** at **Kolhua**, also known as *Bhimsen-ki-Lathi* (stick), is a single 18 m piece of highly polished red sandstone with a bell-shaped inverted lotus capital and a life-sized lion carved on top. Asoka *stambhas* (pillars) were unornamented, with a circular section tapered like a palm tree trunk. They may have been forerunners of temples developed from the ancient form of worshipping in the forest. This is one of two Asoka pillars that remain in situ. The Wheel of Law on top of many pillars, which appears on the Indian flag, is the mark of the social and political order laid down by the emperor.

Patna to Bodhgaya → *For listings, see pages 130-133.*

The area to the south of Patna has many major Buddhist sites, and also some Muslim, Jain and Hindu places of pilgrimage. A route to the southwest of Patna visits the ruins of Nalanda, one of the world's oldest universities, Rajgir, royal capital of the Magadh Empire and Bodhgaya. Once out of Patna the countryside is often very attractive, early morning being particularly crisp and inviting. From March to the monsoon it gets extremely hot during the day.

Nalanda

Nalanda has the ruins of one of the world's oldest universities, founded in the fifth century AD on an ancient site of pilgrimage and teaching which had been visited by the Buddha and Mahavir (who spent '14 rainy seasons' in the area). Hiuen Tsang ascribed its name, which means 'charity without intermission', to the Buddha's liberality in an earlier birth. From the bus stand, *tongas* take passengers to the site 2.5 km away for Rs 50. There is a tourist information centre and good government cafeteria near the entrance, as well as numerous stalls selling food and souvenirs.

History Nalanda was hidden under a vast mound for centuries. Its archaeological importance was only established in the 1860s with most of the excavation taking place over about 20 years from 1916. The monasteries went through varying periods of occupation, and in one case nine different levels of building have been discovered. The Buddhist monastic movement resulted in large communities withdrawing into retreats. Even in the seventh century, according to Hiuen-Tsang, Buddhism was declining except in Bihar and Bengal where it enjoyed royal patronage and the support of the laity. The sanctuaries were often vast, as is the one here (500 m by 250 m).

The site ① *Ticket office open 0900-1600 (Oct-Feb), 0900-1700 (Mar-Sep), site open until sunset, entrance Rs 100. Note: Museums are closed on Fri.* The remains of 11 monasteries and

Nalanda

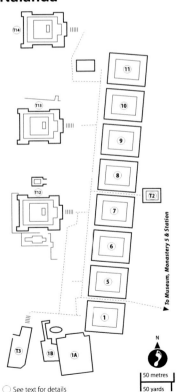

several *chaityas* (temples) built mainly in red brick have been found, as well as a large stairway, a library, lecture halls, dormitories, cells, ovens and wells. The buildings are in several storeys and tiers on massive terraces of solid brick, with stucco decorations of the Buddha as well as Hindu deities, and secular figures. Several of the monasteries have a guarded entrance on the western wall; the monks' cells are around a central courtyard with a wide veranda

The monasteries are numbered one to 11, from south to north. The path from the gate enters the complex between monasteries one and five and leads across an open space to **Temple No 3**, the largest here and the focal point for pilgrims' worship. Almost certainly this was originally built by Asoka. The earliest temples were small structures, completely incorporated into the successively larger mounds you see today. The north facing shrine chamber on top may have once contained an enormous Buddha image. Staircases lead up, but access is not allowed.

Returning east, **monasteries 1, 1A** and **1B** are the best restored and most important of the monastery group. It is possible to walk around all three of these southern monasteries and get a true sense of the scale of Nalanda past.

There are several interesting features in the other monasteries: double rows of cells in **monastery 5**, brick courtyards and

Monastic University for the Buddhist world

It is assumed that the Gupta emperors were responsible for Nalanda's first monasteries. In the seventh century Hiuen-Tsang spent 12 years, both as a student and a teacher, at Nalanda which once had over 3000 teachers and philosophers. The monks were supported by 200 villages, and a library of nine million manuscripts attracted men from countries as far flung as Java, Sumatra, Korea, Japan and China. Great honour was attached to a Nalanda student and admission was restricted with seven or eight out of 10 applicants failing to gain a place.

I-Tsing, another Chinese scholar, arrived here in AD 673 and also kept detailed records, describing the severe lifestyle of the monks. The divisions of the day were measured by a water clock, and the syllabus involved the study of Buddhist and Brahmanical scriptures, logic, metaphysics, medicine and Sanskrit grammar.

The university flourished until 1199 when the Afghan Bhaktiar Khalji sacked it, burning, pillaging and driving the surviving residents into hiding. It was the end of living Buddhism in India until the modern revival.

two sets of double ovens in the upper courtyard of **6**, and evidence of three successive monasteries built on the same site at **7**. There are the remains of arched doorways in **10** and the fragments of the 25 stone pillars that lined the veranda were found in the ruins of **11**, which stood 1 m apart and 2 m high.

In addition to the monasteries and the main temple, four other temples have been excavated. **Temples 12, 13** and **14** are in a line stretching north from the main temple. They all have a square outline and originally had large Buddha images, now destroyed. **Temple 2** (signed) is worth the short detour to see the sculpted dado with over 200 panels showing a huge variety of Hindu deities.

The **Archaeological Museum** ① *Sat-Thu 0900-1645, Rs 5*, displays some fabulous stone and bronze statues, some of which are perfectly preserved, found at Nalanda and nearby sites. Jain and Hindu figures feature prominently alongside the Buddha, but look for the the legs of a Buddhist deity crushing Siva and Gauri that illustrate the triumph over the Hindu pantheon.

Nava Nalanda Mahavihar About 2 km from the principal site is a postgraduate Institute for Research into Buddhism and Pali literature set up by the Bihar government, which has many rare manuscripts; it is now the site of the Indira Gandhi Open University. There is a colourful **Thai Temple** built in the 1980s. **Kundalpur**, 1.5 km north of Nalanda, is believed by the Digambara sect of Jains to be the birthplace of Mahavir.

Rajgir

Encircled by low ranges of rugged hills, Rajgir is held sacred by Buddhists who have built several temples in the area. **Mahavir** spent "14 rainy seasons" teaching in Rajgir and the 20th Tirthankara was born here, so it is also a major Jain pilgrimage centre, with temples on most of the hilltops. You can still see parts of the 40 km cyclopean dry stone wall that once enclosed the ancient city and fort. Today, the *kund* (hot springs) with large open-air baths are a special attraction for local tourists. The Kund Market nearby, where buses stop, has shops, stalls and basic rooms. For an idea of the layout of sites around Rajgir, visit the Gautam Vihar Tourist Bungalow (a five-minute walk from the bus stand) which has a map outside and a tourist information office.

The site About 5 km south of Kund (take a *tonga*, Rs 100 one way) the **Gridhrakuta** ('Hill of Vultures') was one of the Buddha's favourite places where he delivered many important sermons, and was where he is believed to have converted the Magadhan King Bimbisara, who had built the old stone road up the hill. It was used by Hiuen-Tsang in the seventh century and still provides good access. Alternatively, you can take the 600-m **cable car** ① *usually 0900-1300, 1500-1700, Rs 40 (good for the views)*, to the **Visva Santi Stupa** built by the Japanese and dedicated to world peace, on top of Ratnagiri. From here it is an easy walk to Gridhrakuta.

The first Buddhist Council was held in the **Saptaparni Cave** on Vaibhara Hill, six months after the Buddha's death, and his teachings were written down for the first time. On the way to the cave is the large, 7-m-high **tone house**, an extraordinary 'watchtower' built of blocks of stone. On all sides there are small cells for guards which were later used by monks. Allow plenty of time for this walk, it takes about 40 minutes to reach Saptaparni Cave from the drop-off point.

Little survives of the fifth century BC **Ajatasatru Fort**. The outer wall was built with blocks of stone up to 1.5 m long, with smaller boulders in its core. In places it was 4 m high and over 5 m wide. Of the 32 large gates (and 64 small ones) mentioned in ancient texts, only one to the north has survived. Of the inner city wall, which was about 5 km long and roughly pentagonal, only a section to the south remains, with three gaps through which the old roads ran. In the valley, a 6-m-high circular brick structure, decorated with stucco figures, had an old Jain shrine called **Maniyar Math**.

Nearby **Venuvana**, the bamboo grove where the Buddha spent some time, where excavations revealed a room, some *stupas* and the Karanda Tank, is now a deer park with a small zoo. To the south of Venuvana there are Jain and Hindu temples. The ruins of Buddha's favourite retreat within the valley, called the **Jivakamarvana Monastery** (fourth to third century BC), have been found with four halls and several rooms.

The large white Nipponzan Myohoji *stupa* has four golden statues of the Buddha representing his birth, enlightenment, preaching and death.

Bodhgaya → *For listings, see pages 130-133.*

Bodhgaya, a quiet sprawling village near the River Niranjana (Phalgu), is one of the holiest Buddhist pilgrimage centres in India. It was under the Bo tree here that Gautama, the prince, attained Enlightenment to become the Buddha. During the winter months, monks from the Himalaya head down to sultry Bodhgaya to escape the cold.

Arriving in Bodhgaya
Getting there and around Travel in daylight only, for your own safety. Buses run from Patna, Nalanda and Rajgir. Most people arrive by auto-rickshaw (Rs 100-150) from Gaya. Most hotels and monasteries are an easy walk the bus/auto stands. ➤➤ *See Transport, page 132.*

Tourist information Bihar Tourism ① *in the BSTCD complex on Dumahan Rd, T0631-220 0445, Mon-Fri 1000-1700.* Not very useful.

The site
Declared a World Heritage Site in 2002, Bodhgaya was 'lost' for centuries until rediscovered by Burmese Buddhists in 1877, which led to restoration work by the British. Lamas,

Rimpoches and Buddhists from all over the world assemble here during the week-long *monlam* (December-January) when the area north of the bus station resembles a medieval encampment with tents serving as informal restaurants and accommodation. The food is smoky and there are long waits, but it is atmospheric and full of colour. The 'tourist season' draws to a close at the end of February when many restaurants close and most meditation courses stop running.

Mahabodhi Temple
ⓘ *0400-2100, entrance free.*

Asoka's original shrine near the Bodhi tree was replaced a temple in the second century, which in turn has been through several alterations. The temple on a high and broad plinth, with a soaring 52-m-high pyramidal spire with a square cross-section and four smaller spires, houses a gilded image of the Enlightened Buddha. The smaller spires may have been added when Burmese Buddhists attempted extensive rebuilding in the 14th century. An ornately carved stone railing in bas relief surrounds the temple on three sides and several carved Buddhist *stupas* depict tales from the Buddha's early life. The lotus pond where the Buddha may have bathed is to the south, with a seated Buddha statue at its centre. Adjacent to the north side of the temple is the *Chankramana*, a raised platform (first century) with lotus flowers carved on it, which marks the consecrated promenade used by the Buddha while meditating. Further north, the **Animeshlochana** is another sacred spot where the Buddha stood to gaze in gratitude at the Bodhi tree for a week, after his Enlightenment.

The original Bodhi tree (pipal or *Ficus religiosa*) was supposedly destroyed by Asoka before he was converted, and others which replaced it also died. The present tree behind the temple is believed to come from the original stock – Prince Mahinda carried a sapling

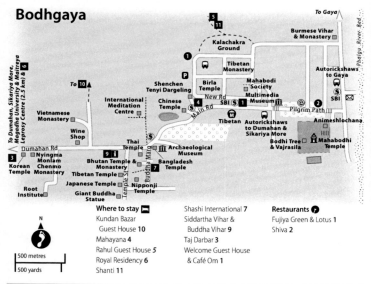

Bodhgaya

Where to stay 🛏
Kundan Bazar
  Guest House **10**
Mahayana **4**
Rahul Guest House **5**
Royal Residency **6**
Shanti **11**

Shashi International **7**
Siddartha Vihar &
  Buddha Vihar **9**
Taj Darbar **3**
Welcome Guest House
  & Café Om **1**

Restaurants 🍴
Fujiya Green & Lotus **1**
Shiva **2**

from the sacred Bo tree to Sri Lanka when he went to spread Buddhism there. This in turn produced a sapling which was brought back to Bodhgaya. The red sandstone slab, the **Vajrasila**, under the tree marks the place where Gautama sat in meditation.

The temple also attracts Hindu pilgrims since the Buddha is considered to be one of the *avatars* or incarnations of Vishnu. The candlelit ceremony at dusk is a particularly atmospheric time to visit, when pilgrims circle the outskirts of the temple among thousands of fairy lights.

Museums

Near the entrance to the Mahabodhi Temple is a **Multi-media Museum** ① *daily 0800-2000, Rs 100*, which gives a 3D history of Bodhgaya lasting one hour. More worthwhile is the **Archaeological Museum** ① *T0631-220 0739, Sat-Thu 0900-1700, Rs 10, photography not permitted*, which houses the original 2-m-high sculptured railings and pillars from the Mahabodhi Temple. The lighter proportions and the quality of the carving date the sandstone railings to the Sunga period (first century BC), while the less-weathered granite railings are from the Gupta period (sixth to seventh century AD). There are also many fine statues of the Buddha and Hindu deities, dating from the eighth-12th centuries, on display.

Other temples

Pilgrims from many lands have built their own temples. You can start at the giant 20-m stone **Buddha statue** which was built in 1989. Next door, the modern two-storey, spotless **Japanese Temple** ① *0700-1200, 1400-1800*, has beautiful polished marble floors and gold images of the Buddha. The **Tibetan Temple** and **Monastery** next to this (1938) is ornately painted and has a *Dharma Chakra* (Wheel of Law) which must be turned three times when praying for forgiveness of sins. A large 2-m metal ceremonial drum in red and gold is also on display. Opposite is the **Nipponji Temple** complex with a free clinic, monastery and a Peace Bell (rung from 0600-1200 and at 1700). Returning to the Mahabodhi Temple you will pass the colourful **Bhutan Temple** protected by carved Himalayan deities, a glittering pagoda-style **Thai Temple** and a **Bangladesh Temple**. The **Chinese Temple** houses an enormous, revolving ceremonial prayer drum.

Teaching centres

Meditation courses varying from a week to a month are available (most only during the Oct-Mar season), following both the Mahayana and Hinanyana traditions; enquire at the Burmese, Tibetan and Thai monasteries. The **Root Institute** ① *off Dumahan Rd, office hrs 0830-1130 and 1330-1630, T0631-220 0714, www.rootinstitute.com*, offers popular Vipassana courses from October-March (dates listed on the website, usually bi-monthly), rooms for personal retreats (year round) and is involved in community self-help schemes; the accommodation and setting is lovely and payment is by donation. **Insight Meditation** ① *www.bodhgayaretreats.org*, has been running 10-day retreats since 1975, during January and February in the Thai monastery. The **International Meditation Centre** ① *T0631-220 0707*, holds a variety of courses throughout the year.

Bihar listings

For hotel and restaurant price codes and other relevant information, see pages 12-15.

🛏 Where to stay

Patna *p120, map p122*
Some streets have been renamed:
Bir Chand Patel Path (or Marg) has replaced Gardiner Rd. Some old names continue to be used, eg Bailey Rd (J Nehru Marg), Fraser Rd (Nazharul Huque Path), Exhibition Rd (Braj Kishore Path).
Avoid the Railway Retiring Rooms.

$$$$ Maurya, South Gandhi Maidan, T0612-220 3040, www.maurya.com. 80 a/c rooms and very expensive suites (up to Rs 25,000). Swankiest in town geared towards business people, modern rooms have polished stone surfaces, but there are some cracks in standards. Excellent restaurant, café and bar (see Restaurants, page 132), nice pool.

$$$ Chanakya, Bir Chand Patel Marg, T0612-222 0590, www.chanakyapatna.com. Inviting rooms feel fresh and well-lit, with flatscreen TV, walk-in showers, good views from the higher levels, nice restaurants/bar, gym.

$$$ Patliputra Ashok (ITDC), Bir Chand Patel Path, T0612-250 5270-6, www.ashokpatna. com. 46 modern rooms, freshly decorated in muted colour schemes, fridge, bathrooms are better (walk-in showers) in the slightly pricier 'club' rooms, good restaurant, travel desk and tourist office, Wi-Fi. Bar 1000-2200. Pool (Rs 180 non residents). Breakfast and airport transfer included.

$$ Republic, Lauriya Bagh, Exhibition Rd, T0612-232 0021, www.hotelrepublicpatan. co.in. Old building but some of the 44 rooms recently renovated, a/c, good veg meals, roof garden, safe middle-range choice.

$$-$ Rajasthan, Fraser Rd, T0612-222 5102. 20 rooms some a/c, great vegetarian meals, very welcoming, gets full so book ahead, not much to look at from the outside.

$ Kautilya Vihar (Bihar Tourism), Bir Chand Patel Path, T0612-222 5411, http://bstdc. nic.in. 44 rooms of different categories, all clean and acceptable (cheapest double Rs 650), some a/c, dorm beds (Rs 100), multi-cuisine restaurant, tourist information on site. Book ahead.

$ Mayur, Fraser Rd, T0612-222 4149. Large rooms recently painted with clean sheets and towels, though bathrooms could be better maintained, it is still good value for the standard rooms. Quite pricey with a/c, good restaurant and a dark bar that is somehow funky (beer very reasonably priced, open 0700-2200).

$ Youth Hostel, Fraser Rd, T0612-221 1486, T(0)9973-174837. A cheap bed and acceptable enough, dorms Rs 120, doubles Rs 250, restaurant.

Nalanda *p124, map p125*
Nalanda is small and accommodation is available in the Chinese monastery, though it is recommended to stay in Rajgir.

Rajgir *p126*
There are several Jain *dharamshalas* near the bazar plus a host of unpleasant cheapies by the bus stand (many will not accept foreigners).

$$$ Indo Hokke, near Viraytan, 3 km from Kund Market, T06112-255245, www.theroyal residency.net/rajgir. The best hotel in town, 44 attractive rooms in an austere brick edifice, with lots of space, wide beds and East Asian influences, primarily catering to Japanese pilgrims, excellent restaurant with Indian, Thai and Japanese food, reserve well ahead in high season, 35% discounts in low season, check breakfast is included in the price. Located 3 km from the centre of town.

$ Mahalaxmi, Kund Market, T(0)9431-487646. Of the very cheap options near the bus stand, this is the best choice with clean sheets provided and airy terraces. Not much English spoken.

$ Siddharth, near Kund Market, T06112-255616. Good rooms with bath (Western toilets), TV and decent food.

$ Tathagat Vihar, near Viragtan, T06112-225176, http://bstdc.bih.nic.in. 32 rooms that are a standard government offering in that they are simple but clean, with TV, tiled floors and bathrooms. Slightly smaller rooms with Indian toilets are a bit cheaper, or pay more for a/c, plus some **$$** suites, Indian restaurant. Nice location at the foot of the hills, with a garden.

Bodhgaya *p127, map p128*

Budget hotels often quote higher rates so bargain; good off-season (Mar-Oct) discounts are available.

$$$ The Royal Residency, Dumahan Rd, T0631-220 0181, www.theroyalresidency.net/bodhgaya. The most attractive rooms of the higher-end hotels, though the exterior is typically blank and it's at least 1 km from the centre. Flatscreen TVs, a/c, quality furniture, wide inviting beds and large marble bathrooms with walk-in showers and tubs. Restaurant is featureless, as is the bar (1000-2200, beer Rs 250). Some suites.

$$$ Taj Darbar, Dumahan Rd, T0631-220 0053, www.hoteltajdarbar.com. A popular place with Thai pilgrims, white-walled rooms are modern and quite trendy, with flatscreens TVs, duvets, a/c, hair dryers. There's a multi-cuisine restaurant, no bar but staff will send out for alcohol.

$$ Shashi International, Buddha Marg, T0631-220 0459, www.hotelshashi.com. Small rooms are starting to fade, but if you want a/c and flatscreen TV then it is one of the cheaper options.

$$-$ Mahayana, Main Rd, T0631-220 0756, mahayanagt@yahoo.com. Huge bright rooms, a/c and TV, in an airy building with courtyards, peaceful vibe and charming staff, a good choice. Worth haggling over the price.

$ Siddartha Vihar, Bodhgaya Rd, T0631-220 0445. The state tourism department runs 3 adjacent lodgings, by far the best is the Siddartha with decent and reasonably priced

a/c and non-a/c rooms with balconies and TVs in a quirky circular building; next door **Buddha Vihar** and **Sujata Vihar** have dorm beds.

$ Welcome Guest House, above Café Om (see Restaurants, page 132), T0631-220 0377, T(0)9934-221943, welcomeguest_house@yahoo.co.in. Caters to backpackers, cheaper rooms share bathrooms (hot water), some have TV, also very cheap 5-bed mixed dorm, good central location. A string of similar guesthouses surround.

$ Kundan Bazar Guest House, Bhagalpur village, T0631-220 0049, www.kundanbazar.com. This guesthouse with bright super-clean rooms fulfils all travellers' needs, with free Wi-Fi in the rooms, a community kitchen, free bicycles, use of the washing machine, bookshop, clothes for sale and rooftop café with amazing views. 20 mins' walk from the Mahabodhi temple. Great value.

$ Rahul Guest House, behind Kalachakra Ground, T0631-220 0709, T(0)9934-463849, rahul_bodhgaya@yahoo.com. Bright and cheery rooms (some with attached bath), spotless sheets, fans, clean paintwork, towels, plus great front terraces with views to paddies. Although new buildings are fast encroaching, it remains a more peaceful location and is the best value choice among the small cluster of guesthouses here.

$ Shanti Guest House, behind Kalachakra Ground, T0631-220 0129, T(0)9934-153387, www.shanti-guesthouse.com. Very clean rooms, white linens, attached or shared baths, some with a/c, communal front balconies; only downside might be the children running around.

Monasteries

Some monasteries provide spartan accommodation primarily for pilgrims; contact the monk in charge. They expect guests to conform to certain rules of conduct.

$ Bhutan Monastery, Buddha Rd. 18 rooms in guesthouses, shared facilities.

$ Burmese Vihar, Gaya Rd. Simple rooms (some newer) with nets, dorm, no fan, garden (eat at **Pole Pole** opposite).

🍴 Restaurants

Patna *p120, map p122*
Hotels on Fraser Rd usually have a restaurant. There is a row of stalls selling excellent and cheap Chinese food (seating) next to the Maurya Lok Complex.
$$ Spice Court, Hotel Maurya (see Where to stay, page 130). Open 1230-1530 and 1930-2330. Pan Asian cuisine (Vietnamese, Malaysian satay, etc), alcohol available, mains Rs 250-500, lovely staff. Adjacent Vaishali Cafe is also very pleasant.
$$-$ Amrpali Cafe, Bir Chand Patel Path (next to Kautilya Vihar), T0612-222 9272. Open 0900-2300. Indian, Chinese, international veg and non-veg dishes. Bright and modern, tablecloths and TV, with a/c.
$$-$ Garden Court Club, Fraser Rd, T0612-320 2279. Open 24 hrs, but best to go 1500-2300. Though there is not much of view from this rooftop restaurant, the plants and open air make it a pleasant escape and the menu is varied.
$ Bansi Vihar, Fraser Rd. Daily 0800-2230. Fantastic South Indian menu, plus some Chinese, served by white-clad efficient waiters, has a/c. Highly recommended.

Rajgir *p126*
Food is not brilliant in the *dhabas* near the bus stop, for a decent meal you will have to try one of the higher-end hotels.

Bodhgaya *p127, map p128*
$ Café Om, Main Rd. Decent Western fare draws in most backpackers in town.
$ Fujiya Green, near Kalachakra Ground. Extensive vegetarian/non-vegetarian menu, specializes in Tibetan but it has every continent covered. Attractive interior lives up to the name, recently refurbished, friendly service.
$ Lotus, next to Fujiya Green, near Kalachakra. Delicious food, covers all bases from *thukpa* to Mexican, relaxing and friendly place.
$ Shiva, diagonally opposite entrance to Mahabodhi temple. Japanese and simple Western food.

🛍 Shopping

Patna *p120, map p122*
Patna and its surrounding villages are known for wooden toys, inlay work, *tussar* silk, lacquerware, leather shoes and *Madhubani* paintings. The run-down Bihar State Export, Udyog Bhawan, East Gandhi Maidan, near the Mona Cinema Hall, has cheap *Madhubani* paintings, textiles and handicrafts, as do Khadi Gramudyog, Bihar Emporium and Sonali State Emporium at Maurya Lok Complex (items are priced though 30% discount is customary, shops open Mon-Sat 1100-2000). Better quality *Madhubani* paintings are found at Ajanta, Fraser Rd, Mon-Sat 1030-2030.
There are 2 good bookshops in the Hotel Satkar Arcade on Fraser Rd, Readers Library and Tricel, both closed on Sun.

🎯 What to do

Patna *p120, map p122*
Ashok Travels & Tours, Hotel Pataliputra Ashok, T0612-222 6270-9, www.ashokpatna. com/att/?ashokpatna.com/att/?. Reasonably priced car hire for half- or full-day tours.
Bihar Tourism (BSTDC), www.bstdc.bih.nic. in/patna.htmbstdc.bih.nic.in/patna.htm. Runs city sightseeing Oct-Mar, Rajgir, Nalanda and Pawapuri, usually 0800-2200. Also to Vaishali, Bodhgaya, Buxar and Sasaram.

🚎 Transport

Patna *p120, map p122*
Air Transport to town is by taxi, auto-rickshaw or Indian Airlines coach to their City Office via some hotels. **Indian Airlines**, East Gandhi Maidan, T0612-222 2554, www.indian airlines.nic.in. Daily to **Delhi**. Jet Airways, www.jetairways.com, also flies to **Delhi**.
Bus Mithapur private bus stand is 2.5 km from Junction railway station, with Luxury and Express services between Patna and regional centres including **Kolkata**, **Siliguri**, **Bodhgaya** and **Ranchi**.

Taxi Private unmetered taxis available from the airport, some hotels and important tourist sites. Fix rates beforehand.

Train Patna Junction railway Station, enquiries, T131/0612-242 7812, reservations, T0612-222 2197. Several trains daily to **Delhi (ND)** including: *Vikramshila Exp 12367*, 170, 14½ hrs; *Rajdhani Exp 12423*, 2150, 10½ hrs. **Delhi (OD)**: *Brahmaputra Mail 14055*, 1310, 17 hrs. Several daily to **Gaya** including: *Patna Hatia Exp 18625*, 1140, 2 hrs. **Kolkata**: *Toofan Exp 13008*, 0635, 13 hrs; *Rajdhani Exp 12306*, 0500, Sat, 7½ hrs; *Poorva Exp 12304*, 0805, Mon, Thu, Fri, Sun, 8½ hrs (and others with longer journey times). **Varanasi**: *Farraka Exp 13413/13483*, 0530, 5½ hrs; *Shramjeevi Exp 12391*, 1050, 3½ hrs.

Nalanda *p124, map p125*
Regular buses from Patna to **Bihar Sharif** where you change to **Rajgir** (15 km) with the nearest railway station or **Nalanda**. Cycle-rickshaw and *tonga* (Rs 50) between the bus stop to the site.

Rajgir *p126*
Bus to **Bihar Sharif** then change for **Patna** (105 km), 3½ hrs total journey time; to **Gaya** (78 km) 2 hrs.

Bodhgaya *p127, map p128*
Air There is an airport 8 km away (T0631-221 0129), with daily flights.
Bus There are daily buses to **Patna** run by BSTDC at 0700 and 1400 (Rs 65) leaving from outside the Hotel Buddha Vihar. More frequent services (and buses for **Rajgir**) leave from Gaya.

Rickshaw Auto-rickshaws take 30 mins to Gaya; the last shared one leaves 1800, then private hire (Rs 150) until 2100.

Train Gaya (16 km) has the nearest train station. **Delhi**: *Rajdhani Exp 12301*, 2239, except Sun, 11½ hrs; *Rajdhani Exp 12421*, 2313, Wed, Sat, Sun, 11½ hrs; *Purushottam Exp 12801*, 1405, 15 hrs; **Kolkata (H)**: *Howrah Superfast 12308*, 2018, 7½ hrs; *Kalka-Howrah Mail 12312*, 2328, 8 hrs; *Rajdhani Exp 12302*, 0404, except Sat, 6 hrs; plus others. **Patna**: *Palamau Exp 13347*, *Hatia Patna Exp 18626*, 1310, 2½ hrs. **Varanasi**: *Doon Exp 13009*, 0510, 5 hrs; *Poorva Exp 12381*, 1455, Wed, Thu, Sun, 3½ hrs; plus lots that arrive/depart in middle of night, and others that go to **Mughal Sarai**, with transfer by auto-rickshaw to Varanasi.

⊙ Directory

Patna *p120, map p122*
Banks State Bank of India have an ATM at the station and on Gandhi Maidan; there are many other ATMs in the central area.
Internet Plenty of cafes in the centre, Rs 20 per hr. **Hospitals** Patna Medical College Hospital, Ashok Raj Path E, T0612-267 0132. Nalanda Medical College Hospital, T0612-263 1159, By-Pass Rd. **Post** GPO: Station Rd, in a splendid Raj-era building.

Bodhgaya *p127, map p128*
Banks State Bank of India has an ATM.
Internet There are many internet cafes all over Bodhgaya, Rs 30 per hr, decent connection. **Post** Close to the entrance to Mahabodhi Temple.

Contents

Kolkata

Kolkata (Calcutta)

To Bengalis Kolkata is the proud intellectual capital of India, with an outstanding contribution to the arts, services, medicine and social reform in its past, and a rich contemporary cultural life. As the former imperial capital, Kolkata retains some of the country's most striking colonial buildings, yet at the same time it is truly an Indian city. Unique in India in retaining trams, and the only place in the world to still have hand-pulled rickshaws, you take your life in your hands each time you cross Kolkata's streets. Hugely crowded, Kolkata's Maidan, the parkland, give lungs to a city packed with some of the most densely populated slums, or *bustees*, anywhere in the world.

Arriving in Kolkata

Getting there
Subhas Chandra Bose Airport at Dum Dum serves international and domestic flights with the new 'integrated terminal' (opened 2013). Taxis to the city centre take 45-60 minutes and there is a pre-paid taxi booth before exiting the airport (to Sudder Street, the backpacker hub, costs Rs 270). There are air-conditioned buses which leave from outside Terminal 1, some of which go to Howrah and Esplanade (for Sudder Street), and cost about Rs 40. Arrival at **Howrah Train Station**, on the west bank of the Hugli, can be daunting and the taxi rank outside is often chaotic; the pre-paid taxi booth is to the right as you exit – check the price chart near the booth, note that Sudder Street is less than 5 km. Trains to/from the north use the slightly less chaotic **Sealdah Terminal** east of the centre, which has pre-paid taxis. Long-distance buses arrive at Esplanade, 15 minutes' walk from most budget hotels. ▸▸ *See Transport, page 163.*

Getting around
You can cover much of Central Kolkata on foot. For the rest you need transport. You may not fancy using hand-pulled rickshaws, but they become indispensable when the streets are flooded. Buses and minibuses are often jam packed, but routes comprehensively cover the city – conductors and bystanders will help you find the correct bus. The electric trams can be slightly better outside peak periods. The Metro, though on a limited route and very crowded, is the easiest way of getting from north to south. Taxis are relatively cheap (note that the meter reading is not the true fare – they have conversion charts which work out at about double the meter) but allow plenty of time to get through very congested traffic. Despite the footpath, it is not permitted to walk across the Vidyasagar Bridge (taxi drivers expect passengers to pay the Rs 10 toll).

Tourist information
India Tourism ⓘ *4 Shakespeare Sarani, T033-2282 5813, Mon-Fri 0930-1800, Sat 0900-1300*, can provide a city map and information for all India. More useful is **West**

Bengal Tourism Development Corporation (WBTDC) ⓘ *BBD Bagh, T033-2248 8271, www.westbengaltourism.gov.in, Mon-Fri 1030-1630, Sat 1030-1300; also a counter at the station in Howrah.*

Background

Calcutta, as it came to be named, was founded by the remarkable English merchant trader **Job Charnock** in 1690. He was in charge of the East India Company factory (ie warehouse) in Hugli, then the centre of British trade from eastern India. Attacks from the local Muslim ruler forced him to flee – first down river to Sutanuti and then 1500 km south to Chennai. However, in 1690 he selected three villages – Kalikata, Sutanuti and Govindpur – where Armenian and Portuguese traders had already settled, leased them from Emperor Aurangzeb and returned to what became the capital of British India.

The first fort here, named after King William III (completed 1707), was on the site of the present BBD Bagh. A deep defensive moat was dug in 1742 to strengthen the fort – the Maratha ditch. The Maratha threat never materialized but the city was captured easily by the 20-year-old **Siraj-ud-Daula**, the new Nawab of Bengal, in 1756. The 146 British residents who failed to escape by the fort's river gate were imprisoned for a night in a small guard room about 6 m by 5 m with only one window – the infamous '**Black Hole of Calcutta**'. Some records suggest 64 people were imprisoned and only 23 survived.

The following year **Robert Clive** re-took the city. The new Fort William was built and in 1772 Calcutta became the capital of British administration in India with **Warren Hastings** as the first Governor of Bengal. Some of Calcutta's most impressive colonial buildings were built in the years that followed, when it became the first city of British India. It was also a time of Hindu and Muslim resurgence.

Colonial Calcutta grew as new traders, soldiers and administrators arrived, establishing their exclusive social and sports clubs. Trade in cloth, silk, lac, indigo, rice, areca nut and tobacco had originally attracted the Portuguese and British to Bengal. Later Calcutta's hinterland producing jute, iron ore, tea and coal led to large British firms setting up headquarters in the city. Calcutta prospered as the commercial and political capital of British India up to 1911, when the capital was transferred to Delhi.

Central Kolkata → *For listings, see pages 151-164.*

BBD Bagh (Dalhousie Square) and around

Many historic Raj buildings surround the square, which is quietest before 0900. Renamed Benoy Badal Dinesh (BBD) Bagh after three Bengali martyrs, the square has an artificial lake (tank) fed by natural springs that used to supply water to Kolkata's first residents. On Strand Road North is the dilapidated **Silver Mint** (1824-1831). The **Writers' Building** (1780), designed by Thomas Lyon as the trading headquarters of the East India Company, was refaced in 1880. It is now the state Government Secretariat. The classical block with 57 sets of identical windows was built like barracks inside. The white domed **General Post Office** (1866) was built on the site of the first Fort William. Around the corner, there is a quaint little **Postal Museum** ⓘ *Mon-Sat 1100-1600, free*, which displays shabby maps, original post boxes and has a philatelic library. Facing the Hooghly (also spelt Hugli) on Strand Road is colonnaded **Metcalfe Hall** ⓘ *Mon-Sat 1000-1700, entrance from rear*, modelled on the Palace of Winds in Athens. This was once the home of the Imperial Library, and still contains the journals of the Asiatic Society in the ground floor **library** ⓘ *Mon-Fri 0945-1815 (allegedly),*

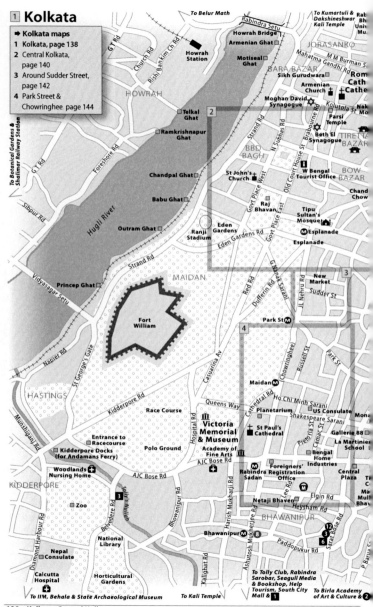

1 Kolkata

➡ **Kolkata maps**
1 Kolkata, page 138
2 Central Kolkata, page 140
3 Around Sudder Street, page 142
4 Park Street & Chowringhee page 144

plus a small exhibition on the first floor including glazed tiles from Gaur and Pandua, and a gallery of bricks. Unsurprisingly, the visitors' book shows an average of two tourists per month. Elegant **St Andrew's Kirk** ① *0900-1400* (1814), like the earlier St John's Church (1787), was modelled partially on St Martin-in-the-Fields, London. **Mission Row** (now RN Mukherjee Road) is Kolkata's oldest street, and contains the **Old Mission Church** (consecrated 1770), built by the Swedish missionary Johann Kiernander. The **Great Eastern Hotel** (1841) was in Mark Twain's day "the best hotel East of the Suez", but from the 1970s it steadily declined. It is now undergoing major restoration by the Lalit group of hotels and was due to open in 2013 (though that looks unlikely from the present state of the building).

Directly south of BBD Bagh is the imposing **Raj Bhavan** (1799-1802), the residence of the Governor of West Bengal, formerly Government House. It was modelled on Kedleston Hall in Derbyshire, England (later Lord Curzon's home), and designed by Charles Wyatt, one of many Bengal engineers who based their designs on famous British buildings (entrance not permitted). The beautiful old **Town Hall** (1813) has been converted into the **Kolkata Museum** ① *Mon-Sat 1100-1800 (ticket counter closes 1700), foreigners Rs 10 (Rs 15 on Sat), bag deposit*, telling the story of the independence movement in Bengal through a panoramic, cinematic display, starring an animatronic Rabindranath Tagore. Visitors are sped through in grouped tours, however, and some of the videos drag on rather. There's a good life-size diorama of a Bengali street and some great film posters. The bright-red gothic **High Court** (1872) was modelled on the medieval cloth merchants' hall at Ypres in Flanders. It is possible to enter through Gate F: a fascinating glimpse into Bar Rooms crammed floor-to-ceiling with books, and bustling with black-robed lawyers (no cameras allowed). The **State Bank Archives and Museum** ① *11th Fl, SBI,*

1 Strand Rd, open Tue-Fri 1430-1700, free, in a recent building designed to look period, is a grand marble-floored repository of information; it also contains paintings of Raj India, furniture and memorabilia related to the early days of banking. The **Floatel** bar (see page 158), on the Hooghly, is a good place to relax after wanderings.

② Central Kolkata

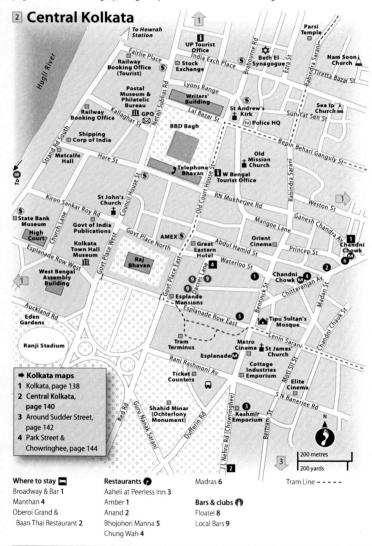

→ Kolkata maps
1 Kolkata, page 138
2 Central Kolkata, page 140
3 Around Sudder Street, page 142
4 Park Street & Chowringhee, page 144

200 metres
200 yards

Where to stay 🛏
Broadway & Bar 1
Manthan 4
Oberoi Grand & Baan Thai Restaurant 2

Restaurants 🍴
Aaheli at Peerless Inn 3
Amber 1
Anand 2
Bhojohori Manna 5
Chung Wah 4

Madras 6

Bars & clubs 🍸
Floatel 8
Local Bars 9

Tram Line - - - - -

Esplanade Mansions is a stunning Art Nouveau building on Esplanade Row East, built in 1910 by Jewish millionaire David Ezra. At the other end of the street, the minarets and domes of **Tipu Sultan's Mosque**, built by Tipu's son in 1842, poke above market stalls selling stationery and little kebab restaurants. The **Ochterlony Monument** (1828), renamed Shahid Minar (Martyrs' Memorial) in 1969, was built as a memorial to Sir David Ochterlony, who led East India Company troops against the Nepalese in 1814-1816. The 46-m-tall Greek Doric column has an Egyptian base and is topped by a Turkish cupola.

St John's Church (1787) ① *0800-1700, Rs 10*, was built on soft subsoil that did not allow it to have a tall spire and architecturally it was thought to be 'full of blunders'. Verandas were added to the north and south in 1811 to reduce the glare of the sun. Inside the vestry are Warren Hastings's table and chair, plus Raj-era paintings and prints. *The Last Supper*, by Johann Zoffany was restored in 2010 and shows the city's residents dressed as the apostles. Job Charnock is buried in the grounds. His octagonal mausoleum, the oldest piece of masonry in the city, is of Pallavaram granite (from Madras Presidency), which is named charnockite after him. The monument built by Lord Curzon to the **Black Hole of Calcutta** was brought here from Dalhousie Square (BBD Bagh) in 1940.

Eden Gardens ① *daily 1200-1700*, which are situated in the northwest corner of the Maidan, were named after Lord Auckland's sisters Emily and Fanny Eden. There are pleasant walks, a lake and a small Burmese pagoda (typical of this type of Pyatthat). Laid out in 1834, part forms the **Ranji Stadium** ① *usually open for matches only, a small tip at Gate 14 gains entry on other days*, where the first cricket match was played in 1864. Revamped in 2011 for the Cricket World Cup, massive crowds are attracted for IPL and Test matches.

Around Sudder Street

Conveniently close to Chowringhee and Esplanade, Sudder Street is the focus for Kolkata's backpackers and attracts touts, beggars and drug pushers aplenty. Beggars on Chowringhee and Park Street often belong to organized syndicates to whom they have to pay a large percentage of their 'earnings' for the privilege of working the area. Women asking for milk or rice for their baby is the most popular ploy on Sudder Street. Nearby is the vast and archaic shopping hub of **New Market**, opened in 1874 (largely rebuilt since a fire in 1985 and recently revamped), and originally called Sir Stuart Hogg Market. The clock tower outside, which strikes every 15 minutes, was imported from England. It used to be said that you could buy anything from a needle to an elephant (on order) in one of its stalls. Today it's still worth a visit; arrive early in the morning to watch it come alive (closed Sundays).

Around the corner from Sudder Street is the **Indian Museum** ① *27 Chowringhee (JL Nehru Rd), T033-2286 1679, www.indianmuseumkolkata.org, Mar-Nov Tue-Sun 1000-1700, Dec-Feb 1000-1630, foreigners Rs 150, Indians Rs 10, cameras Rs 50/100 with tripod; no bags allowed (there is a cloakroom)*, possibly Asia's largest. The Jadu Ghar (House of Magic) was founded in 1814 and has an enormous collection. The colonnaded Italianate building around a central courtyard has 36 galleries (though large sections are often closed off for restoration). Parts are poorly lit and gathering dust so it is best to be selective. Highlights include: the stone statutory with outstanding exhibits from the Harappa and Moenjodaro periods; the Cultural Anthropology room with information on India's tribes; and the excellent new Mask Gallery (hidden on the fourth floor, up the stairs past the ground floor coin collection and library). There are some lovely miniature paintings, the Egyptian room has a popular mummy and the Plant Gallery is curiously beautiful, with jars, prints and samples filling every inch of space. The animals in the Natural History Gallery have been

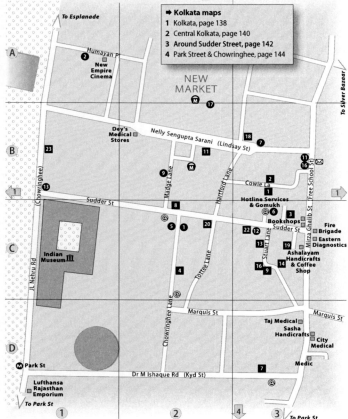

➡ **Kolkata maps**
1 Kolkata, page 138
2 Central Kolkata, page 140
3 Around Sudder Street, page 142
4 Park Street & Chowringhee, page 144

Where to stay 🛏
Afridi Guest House **1** B3
Ashreen Guest House **2** B3
Astoria **3** C3
Bawa Walson Spa'o'tel **22** C3
Capital Guest House **4** C2
Emirates **7** D3
Fairlawn **8** C2
Galaxy **9** C3
Lindsay and Blue &
Beyond **11** B2
Maria **13** C3
Modern Lodge **14** C3

Paragon **16** C3
Sapphire Suites **18** B3
Super Guest House **19** C3
Times Guest House **20** C2
YMCA **23** B1

Restaurants 🍽
Blue Sky Café **1** C2
Brothers Snacks **2** A1
Fresh & Juicy **5** C2
Jimmy's **7** B3
Kathleen's **16** B3
Khalsa **9** B2

Nahoum **17** B2
NV Stores **11** B3
Raj's Spanish Café **6** C3
Tirupati **12** C3
Zaranj & Jong's **13** B1

there since 1878 while the birds are so dirty they are all uniformly black in colour. The geological collection with Siwalik fossils is mind-bogglingly huge. Allow a couple of hours.

Park Street

Park Street Cemetery ① *daily 0800-1630, free, information booklet Rs 100, security guard opens gate and will expect you to sign the visitors' book,* was opened in 1767 to accommodate the large number of British who died 'serving' their country. The cemetery is a peaceful paradise and a step into history, located on the south side of one of Kolkata's busiest streets, with a maze of soaring obelisks shaded by tropical trees. The heavily inscribed decaying headstones, rotundas, pyramids and urns have been restored, and gardeners are actively trying to beautify the grounds. Several of the inscriptions make interesting reading. Death, often untimely, came from tropical diseases or other hazards such as battles, childbirth and even melancholia. More uncommonly, it was an excess of alcohol, or as for Sir Thomas D'Oyly, through "an inordinate use of the hokkah". Rose Aylmer died after eating too many pineapples! Tombs include those of Colonel Kyd, founder of the Botanical Gardens, the great oriental scholar Sir William Jones, and the fanciful mausoleum of the Irish Major-General 'Hindoo' Stuart. Across AJC Bose Road, on Karaya Road, is the smaller and far more derelict **Scottish Cemetery** ① *daily 0700-1730, free, pamphlet by donation to the caretaker,* established in 1820. The Kolkata Scottish Heritage Trust began work in 2008 to restore some of the 1600 tumbledown graves but the undergrowth is rampant and jungle prevails. It is also known as the 'dissenters' graveyard', as this was where non-Anglicans were buried. Also nearby, on AJC Bose Road, is the enormous **Lower Circular Road Cemetery** created in 1840 when Park Street Cemetery became full.

The **Asiatic Society** ① *1 Park St, T033-2229 0779, www.asiaticsocietycal.com, Mon-Fri 1000-1800, free,* the oldest institution of Oriental studies in the world, was founded in 1784 by the great Orientalist, Sir William Jones. It is a treasure house of 150,000 books and 60,000 ancient manuscripts in most Asian languages, although permission is required to see specific pieces. The museum includes an Ashokan edict, rare coins and paintings. The library is worth a visit for its dusty travelogues and titles on the history of Kolkata. The original 1804 building is to the rear; you can ask to view the impressive staircase adorned with statues and paintings. Here also is the manuscript restoration department, where staff are pleased to explain the work they undertake. Bring a passport, as the signing-in process to visit the building is (at least) a triplicate process.

The Maidan

This area, 200 years ago, was covered in dense jungle. Often called the 'lungs of the city', it is a unique green, covering over 400 ha along Chowringhee (JL Nehru Road). Larger than New York's Central Park, it is perhaps the largest urban park in the world. In it stands Fort William and several clubhouses providing tennis, football, rugby, cricket and even crown green bowls. Thousands each day pursue a hundred different interests – from early morning yogis, model plane enthusiasts, weekend cricketers and performers earning their living, to vast political gatherings.

The massive **Fort William** was built by the British after their defeat in 1756, on the site of the village of Govindapur. Designed to be impregnable, it was roughly octagonal and large enough to house all the Europeans in the city in case of an attack. Water from the Hugli was channelled to fill the wide moat and the surrounding jungle was cleared to give a clear field of fire; this later became the Maidan. The barracks, stables, arsenal, prison

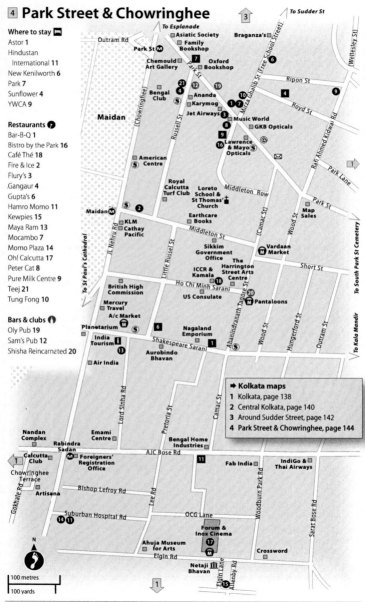

and St Peter's Church are still there, but the fort now forms the Eastern Region's Military Headquarters and entry is forbidden.

At the southern end of the Maidan is **Kolkata Race Course**, run by the Royal Calcutta Turf Club. The history of racing goes back to the time of Warren Hastings and the 1820s grandstand is especially handsome (see page 137 for more details).

Chowringhee and around

You can still see some of the old imposing structures with pillared verandas (designed by Italian architects as residences of prominent Englishmen), though modern high-rise buildings and a flyover have transformed the skyline of what was the ancient pilgrim route to Kalighat.

St Paul's Cathedral ① *0900-1200, 1500-1800, 5 services on Sun,* is the original metropolitan church of British India. Completed in 1847, its Gothic tower (dedicated in 1938) was designed to replace the earlier steeples which were destroyed by earthquakes. The cathedral has a fine altar piece, three 'Gothic' stained-glass windows, two Florentine frescoes and the great West window by Burne-Jones. The original stained-glass East window, intended for St George's Windsor, was destroyed by a cyclone in 1964 and was replaced by the present one four years later.

Academy of Fine Arts ① *2 Cathedral Rd, Tue-Sun 1500-2000 (ground floor galleries), 1200-1900 (museum), free,* was founded in 1933. The first floor museum has a newly restored gallery showing 33 pictures by Rabindranath Tagore, plus his writings and some personal effects. The textiles gallery and other sections have been closed for years, but may reopen soon. The ground floor galleries show changing exhibitions contemporary paintings and sculptures by Indian artists.

The **Victoria Memorial** ① *T033-2223 1889-91, www.victoriamemorial-cal.org; gardens open 0530-1815 (ticket counter closes at 1745), Rs 4; museum open Tue-Sun 1000-1700 (ticket counter closes at 1630, very crowded on Sun), foreigners Rs 150, cameras not permitted inside; son et lumière show, summer 1945, winter 1915, 45 mins, Rs 20 front seats, Rs 10 elsewhere* (1906-1921), was the brain-child of Lord Curzon. The white marble monument to Queen Victoria and the Raj, designed in Italian Renaissance/Indo-Saracenic style, stands in large, well-kept grounds with ornamental pools. A seated bronze Queen Victoria dominates the approach from the north, while a marble statue stands in the main hall where visitors sometimes leave flowers at her feet. The building is illuminated in the evening; the musical fountain is a special draw. The statues over the entrance porches (including Motherhood, Prudence and Learning), and around the central dome (of Art, Architecture, Justice, Charity) came from Italy. The impressive weather vane, a 5-m-tall bronze winged Angel of Victory weighing three tonnes, looks tiny from below. The principal gallery, covering the history of the city, is well presented and makes interesting reading. It includes some fascinating lithographs and illustrations of the city during the Raj period. The painting gallery has magnificent works by European artists in India from 1770-1835, including Zoffany, the two Daniells and Samuel Davis. Recently, the upper gallery of the Queen's Hall was reopened after more than a decade, and visitors can now walk around the inside of the rotunda again.

North Kolkata → *For listings, see pages 151-164.*

College Street

This is the heart of intellectual Kolkata with the **university** and several academic institutions, including the old **Sanskrit College** and the elite **Presidency College**.

Europeans and Indian benefactors established the Hindu College (1817) to provide a liberal education. In 1855, this became the Presidency College. A centre for 19th-century Bengali writers, artists and reformers, it spawned the early 20th-century Swadeshi Movement. The famous **Indian Coffee House** (opened in 1944), cavernous haunt of the city's intelligentsia, has tonnes of atmosphere and is always packed despite the average coffee and food. Along the pavements are interesting second-hand book stalls. The **Ashutosh Museum of Indian Art** ① *University Centenary Building, Mon-Fri 1100-1630, closed university holidays, Rs 10,* is well maintained and worth a visit. The ground floor is packed with eastern Indian sculptures and terracotta tiles depicting figures. The first floor has colourful Bengali and Orissan folk art, faded textiles, and a hoard of paintings including 14th- to 19th-century miniatures, Kalighat paintings, Nepalese art and Tibetan *thankas*. Also look out for the model of the Senate Hall (1873-1960) which was pulled down to make way for the concrete monster of the present Centenary block, in the days before heritage buildings were accorded any value.

Marble Palace

① *46 Muktaram Babu St, closed Mon and Thu, 1000-1600. Free pass from WBTDC (see page 137), 24 hrs ahead, or baksheesh (Rs 20 per person) to the security man at the gate and a further tip to the attendant who will accompany you around. Shoes must be removed, no photography allowed.*

Located in Chor Bagan ('Thieves' Garden'), the one-man collection of Raja Rajendra Mullick is in his ornate home (1835) with an Italianate courtyard, classical columns and Egyptian sphinxes. Family members still inhabit a portion of the house while servants' descendants live in the huts that encircle the grounds. Six sleeping marble lions and statuary grace the lawns and there is a veritable menagerie at the back of the garden. The galleries, disorganized and gathering dust, are crammed with statues, porcelain, clocks, mirrors, chandeliers and English (Reynolds), Dutch (Reubens) and Italian paintings. The pink, grey and white Italian marble floors are remarkable, as is the solid rosewood statue of Queen Victoria. Allow one hour to look round, or take a book and relax in the garden. The rambling two-floor museum has more than just curiosity appeal – it is one of Kolkata's gems.

Howrah Bridge area

Howrah Bridge (Haora), or Rabindra Setu, was opened in 1943. This single-span cantilever bridge, the quintessential image of Kolkata, replaced the old pontoon (floating) bridge that first joined the city of Kolkata with Howrah and the railway station. To avoid affecting river currents and silting, the two 80-m-high piers rise from road level; the 450-m span expands by a metre on a hot day. It is the busiest bridge in the world in terms of foot passengers, with more than 3.5 million pedestrians per day (many with improbable loads on their heads). Wrestlers can be seen underneath and there is a daily **flower market** beneath the eastern end at Mullik Ghat, with piles of marigolds glowing against the mud. At night the bridge is illuminated, which makes a fine sight – if waiting for a night train at Howrah station go to the first floor waiting rooms for a good view. The pedestrian-free **Vidyasagar Setu Bridge**, further south, has eased the traffic burden slightly.

Southeast of Howrah Bridge, the gorgeously well-kept **Armenian Church** of **Holy Nazareth** (1724) is a reminder of the important trading role the small Armenian community, who mostly came from Iran, played from the 17th century. The church is open 0600-1200 on weekdays or you can ask someone to open up in order to view the beautifully maintained interior. A gravestone in the compound is inscribed with the date 1630. The 150 or so Armenians in the city still hold a service in Armenian in one of their two churches in the city every Sunday. Their college on Mirza Ghalib Street (also the birthplace of William Makepeace Thackery in 1811) has boarding pupils from Armenia who are usually orphans. To the east of the Church of Holy Nazareth is the **Roman Catholic Cathedral** (1797), built by the Portuguese. The Jewish community, mostly Sephardic, of Baghdadi origin, was also once very prominent in commerce. Their two synagogues are well maintained with stained-glass windows. The grander of the two is the church-like and cavernous **Moghan David Synagogue** (1884) ① *Canning St, daily 0900-1700*, while the nearby **Beth El Synagogue** ① *26/1 Pollock St, Sun-Fri 1000-1700*, is smaller. Just around the corner from the Moghan David Synagogue, on Brabourne Road hidden behind market stalls, is the older and derelict **Neveh Shalome Synagogue** (now inaccessible). There are only around 30-40 elderly Jews left in the city (the community numbered about 6000 before the Second World War) who continue to congregate at **Nahoum & Son's bakery** in the New Market. The Jewish Girls School in Park Street no longer has Jewish pupils, in fact the vast majority of the girls are Muslims from a nearby neighbourhood. To view the interior of the synagogues, it is necessary to get signed permission either from Nahoum's Bakery (easiest) or from the office at 1 Hartford Lane.

A few reminders that there was once a Chinatown in Kolkata remain in the form of Chinese 'churches'. Seek out the **Sea Ip Church** (1905), which has an intricately carved wooden altar and the **Nam Soon Church**, with a school at the rear. The latter is gorgeously maintained with bright paint, a huge bell and drum, and a little courtyard with trees. Both are willingly opened by the custodians. At the top of Bentinck Street, where it meets BB Ganguly Street, are several tiny old-fashioned shoe shops run by aging members of the Chinese community.

Rabindra Bharati Museum

Trams run along Rabindra Sarani, previously known as the Chitpur Road and one of the oldest streets in the city. Rising above the street-level are the three green domes, 27 minarets and multiple archways of **Nakhoda Mosque** (1926), Kolkata's principal mosque holding 10,000 worshippers. A large brick gateway leads to **Rabindra Bharati Museum** ① *6/4 Dwarakanath Tagore Lane (red walls visible down lane opposite 263 Rabindra Sarani), Mon-Fri 1000-1700, Sat 1000-1330, Sun and holidays 1100-1400, www.museum.rbu.ac.in/about_rb*, in a peaceful enclave away from the teeming chaos of Rabindra Sarani, occupies the family home of Rabindranath Tagore, who won the Nobel Prize for Literature in 1913. It showcases Tagore's life and works, as well as the 19th-century Renaissance movement in Bengal. Be sure to explore along all the corridors, as it's easy to miss the galleries of Indian and European art, and the Japanese exhibition rooms.

Kumartuli

South of the Dakshineshwar Temple (see below) is Kumartuli. Off Chitpur Road, the *kumars* or potters work all year, preparing clay images around cores of bamboo and straw. For generations they have been making life-size idols for the *pujas* or festivals, particularly of goddess Durga on a lion, slaying the demon. The images are usually unbaked since they are immersed in the holy river at the end of the festival. As the time of the *pujas* approaches, you will see thousands of images, often very brightly painted and gaudily dressed, awaiting the final finishing touch by the master painter. There are also *shola* artists who make decorations for festivals and weddings. The potters' area of Kumartuli is being slowly rebuilt, and concrete structures are replacing the towering bamboo workshops that were so very photogenic.

Northeast of the city centre

Just north of the Belgachia Metro station is a cluster of three Digambar Jain temples, one of the most tranquil spots in the city. The meticulously maintained and ornate **Paresnath Temple** ① *0700-1200, 1500-2000, no leather*, is dedicated to the 10th Tirthankara. Consecrated around 1867, it is richly decorated with mirrors, Victorian tiles and Venetian glass mosaics.

Difficult to find (and perhaps not worth the effort unless you are a true aficionado of Raj history) is **Clive's House** ① *off Jessore Rd in Nagarbajar, Dum Dum*. This was the country home of the first Governor-General of the East India Company and is the oldest colonial monument in Kolkata. For years, Bangladeshi immigrants lived in and around the derelict property until it was restored in 2008. The brick walls are being re-consumed by plant life and it requires some imagination to envisage its former glory.

Belur Math and the Dakshineshwar Kali Temple

Some 16 km north of the city is **Belur Math** ① *0600-1200, 1600-1900*, the international headquarters of the **Ramakrishna Mission**, founded in 1899 by Swami Vivekananda, a disciple of the 19th-century Hindu saint Ramakrishna. He preached the unity of all religions and to symbolize this the *Math* ('monastery') synthesizes Hindu, Christian and Islamic architectural styles in a peaceful and meditative atmosphere.

On the opposite side of the river from Belur Math is the **Dakshineshwar Kali Temple** ① *0600-1200, 1500-1800, 1830-2100, no photography allowed inside*. This huge Kali temple was built in 1847 by Rani Rashmoni. The 12 smaller temples in the courtyard are dedicated to Siva and there are also temples to Radha and Krishna. Because of the Rani's low caste, no priest would serve there until Ramakrishna's elder brother agreed and was succeeded by Ramakrishna himself. Here, Ramakrishna achieved his spiritual vision of the unity of all religions. The temple is crowded with colourfully clad devotees, particularly on Sundays when there are lengthy queues, and is open to all faiths.

A boat (Rs 8) takes 20 minutes to/from Belur Math across the Hooghly. Buses from BBD Bagh go to Dunlop Intersection, from where it's a short auto ride to the temple; trains run from Sealdah to Dakshineshwar.

South Kolkata For listings, see pages 151-164.

Netaji Museum

① *Netaji Bhavan, 38/1 Elgin Rd, Tue-Sun 1100-1430 (last entry 1615), Rs 5, no photography*.
This museum remembers the mission of Subas Chandra Bose, the leader of the INA (Indian National Army), and is in the house where he lived before he had to flee the British oppressors. On the first floor, you can view his bedroom and study (where walls are painted with the tricolours of the Congress flag), although panes of glass prevent close inspection of his possessions. A detailed video is played in the second floor rooms showing old footage and giving a detailed explanation of his life's work. Interesting is the German Room, with a photo of Netaji meeting Hitler and information on Azad Hind and the Indo-German Friendship Society.

Kali Temple

① *Off Ashok Mukherjee Rd, 0500-1500, 1700-2200*.
This is the temple to Kali (1809), the patron goddess of Kolkata, usually seen in her bloodthirsty form garlanded with skulls. There was an older temple here, where the goddess's little toe

is said to have fallen when Siva carried her charred corpse in a frenzied dance of mourning, and she was cut into pieces by Vishnu's *chakra*. Where once human sacrifices were made (up until 1835, a boy was beheaded every Friday), the lives of goats are offered daily on two wooden blocks to the south of the temple. When visiting the temple, priests will attempt to snare foreigners for the obligatory *puja*. A barrage may start as far away as 500 m from the temple. Don't be fooled in to handing over your shoes and succumbing to any priests until you are clearly inside the temple, despite being shown 'priest ID' cards. An acceptable minimum donation is Rs 50. Books showing previous donations of Rs 3000 are doubtless faked. Having done the *puja*, you'll probably be left alone to soak up the atmosphere.

Mother Teresa's homes

Mother Teresa, an Albanian by birth, came to India to teach as a Loreto nun in 1931. She started her Order of the Missionaries of Charity in Kalighat to serve the destitute and dying 19 years later. **Nirmal Hriday** ('Pure Heart'), near the Kali Temple, the first home for the dying, was opened in 1952. Mother Teresa died on 5 September 1997 but her work continues. You may see nuns in their white cotton saris with blue borders busy working in the many homes, clinics and orphanages in the city.

Gariahat and Rabindra Sarobar

The southern neighbourhoods around Gariahat are more middle class and greener than Central Kolkata, but no less interesting, with plenty of good restaurants and small hotels. On Gariahat Road, the shiny white edifice of **Birla Mandir** ① *0600-1100 and 1630-2030*, pulls in a lot of devotees and it is particularly impressive when lit up at night. Taking 22 years to complete, another gift of the Birla family, it is modelled on the Lingaraj Temple at Bhubaneshwar and is covered with carvings both inside and out. No photos are permitted inside. Just north of the temple is the **CIMA Gallery** (see page 159) which is worth a look. South of the Birla Mandir, beyond the southeast corner of Gariahat Crossing, is **Gariahat Market** which specializes in fish and is a fascinating hive of activity, especially in the early morning. Running west from the crossing is Rash Behari Avenue, one of the city's liveliest streets: a 2-km stretch lined with sari stalls, *menhdi* (henna) artists, momo vendors and vegetable sellers. A couple of blocks south, housed in a modern high-rise, the **Birla Academy of Art and Culture** ① *108/109 Southern Av, T033-2466 2843, Tue-Sun 1600-2000*, concentrates on medieval and contemporary paintings and sculpture. The ground floor sculpture gallery has been recently remodelled, and displays some beautiful pieces including Buddhist and Hindu statues. It is well lit and worth visiting. The upper levels host changing art exhibitions.

The large and pleasant lake of **Rabindra Sarobar** is shaded by ancient trees and surrounded by a pathway perfect for joggers and walkers. There are several rowing clubs (the oldest dates from 1858), and Laughing Clubs meet in the mornings (around 0600) to mix yoga and group laughing. A road from the southwest corner of the lake leads to the trim little **Japanese Buddhist Temple** (1935) ① *Lake Rd*, the oldest temple of the Nichiren sect in India. Visitors are welcomed, and can join in the hypnotic prayers by beating handheld drums (at dawn and dusk). A slim congregation of ex-Ghurkhas, Nepali ladies and bemused Bengalis are drawn in. The interior is restful with an elaborate golden shrine, gaudy flowers, ornamental lanterns and origami birds which somehow come together to pleasing effect. It's possible to walk from the temple south, via Dhakuria Bridge, to the **Dakshinapan** shopping complex (handicrafts and handloom) and refresh at **Dolly's, The Tea Shop** (see pages 157 and 161).

Alipore

South of the Maidan, the elite address of Alipore is home to a couple of sights. On Belvedere Road the **National Library** was once the winter residence of the Lieutenant Governors of Bengal. Built in the Renaissance Italian style, with a double row of classical columns, it is approached through a triple arched gateway and a drive between mahogany and mango trees. The library itself, the largest in the country with over eight million books, is now mainly housed in an adjacent newer building (sadly the old building can no longer be entered). Opposite is the **zoo** ① *Fri-Wed 0900-1700, Rs 10.* Opened in 1876, the grounds house a wide variety of animal and bird life. The white tigers from Rewa and the tigon – a cross between a tiger and a lion – are the rarest animals. A reptile house and aquarium are across the road. There are restaurants and picnics are permitted, however it's often terrifyingly busy (particularly at the weekend). Nearby, on Alipore Road, the expansive **Agri Horticultural Gardens** ① *0600-1300 and 1400-1830, Rs 10,* are the most peaceful green space in the city. The Horticultural Society was started in 1820 by the Baptist missionary William Carey. Bring a book; you'll be the only visitor during the week.

State Archaeological Museum

① *Next to Behala tram depot, 1 Satyen Roy Rd, off Diamond Harbour Rd, Behala, Wed-Sun 1000-1630 (last entry 1600), Rs 5. Shared autos run from Kalighat metro to Behala, finishing close to the museum entrance.*

This little-visited yet well-presented museum has seven galleries over two floors, housed in a modern structure adjacent to the original colonial building. Galleries are devoted to West Bengal sites, such as the Buddhist remains of Nandadirghi Vihara near Malda, and the terracotta Hindu temples in Purulia. There's a meagre selection of local stone sculpture, intricate metal work, and a selection of Bengali paintings including Kalighat Pat (mostly religious in nature, but the famous *Two Women and a Rose* is a notable secular exception), and Murshidabad-style painting.

Botanical Gardens

① *20 km south from BBD Bagh, 0700-1700, Rs 50, avoid Sun and public holidays when it is very crowded, catch a bus from Esplanade; minibuses and CTC buses (No C-12) ply the route.*

Kolkata's Botanical Gardens, on the west bank of the Hugli, were founded in 1787 by the East India Company. The flourishing 250-year-old banyan tree, with a circumference of almost 400 m, is perhaps the largest in the world. The original trunk was destroyed by lightning in 1919 but over 2800 offshoots form an impressive sight. The avenues of Royal Cuban palms and mahogany trees are impressive and there are interesting and exotic specimens in the herbarium and collections of ferns and cactii. The gardens are peaceful and deserted during the week and make a welcome change from the city.

Kolkata listings

For hotel and restaurant price codes and other
relevant information, see pages 12-15.

🛏 Where to stay

Watch out for the 10% luxury tax and
10% service charge in the higher price
brackets. Medium price and budget hotels
attracting foreigners are concentrated in
the Sudder St area.

Central Kolkata *p137, map p140*

$$$$ Oberoi Grand, 15 Chowringhee
(JL Nehru), T033-2249 2323, www.oberoi
hotels.com. Atmospheric Victorian building
opposite the Maidan, exquisitely restored,
range of rooms and suites with giant
4-posters, all are spacious, those with
balconies overlooking the raised garden
and pool are charming, bathrooms a tad
old-fashioned but in keeping with the
colonial style, excellent Thai restaurant
and 24-hr La Terrasse with international
cuisine, billiards in the bar, lovely pool for
guests, wonderful spa. Reasonable prices
available online for a standard room.

$$ Manthan, 3 Waterloo St, T033-2248
9577, manthanhotel@gmail.com. Only 4
rooms, spacious and well appointed, TV, a/c
and pleasant furnishings. The bar/restaurant
and banquet service mean it's fairly bustling.
Bargaining is most certainly possible.

$ Broadway, 27A Ganesh Chandra Av,
T033-2236 3930, www.broadwayhotel.in.
Amazingly good-value hotel in a
characterful building that hasn't changed
much since it opened in 1937. Very clean
rooms are non-a/c but airy with powerful
fans, antique furniture and Bengali-red
floors, towels, some with common bath,
plus 24-hr checkout. Noisy on the lower
levels at the front. The bar is very appealing
(see Bars, page 158). Highly recommended.

Around Sudder Street

p141, maps p142 and p144

Kyd St has changed its name to Dr Md
Ishaque Rd and Free School St is now
called Mirza Ghalib St.

$$$ Lindsay, 8-A Lindsay St, T033-
2252 2237/8, www.hotellindsay.com.
Recently refurbished hotel towering over
Newmarket, mainly for business travellers,
Wi-Fi in rooms, good breakfast. **Blue
& Beyond** rooftop restaurant/bar has
panoramic city views and great food.

$$$ Sapphire Suites, 15 Lindsay St,
T033-2252 3052-4, www.sapphiresuites.in.
29 a/c rooms in a new hotel in an attractive
period building, right next to New Market.
Aimed at business travellers, rooms have
sleek black and white furnishings, flatscreen
TVs, bathrobes, tea/coffee facilities. Breakfast
included, good multi-cuisine restaurant and
fitness centre. A few teething problems,
however good deals available online.

$$$-$$ Bawa Walson Spa'o'tel, 5A Sudder
St, T033-2252 1512, www.bawahotels.com.
An unlikely situation for a Spa'o'tel, but the
Walson is immaculate with Thai accents
throughout. Rooms are wood and white,
swish shower rooms, free Wi-Fi, Arabic
restaurant. Huge discounts possible, also
when booking online.

$$ Astoria Hotel, 6 Sudder St, near fire
station, T033-2252 2241, www.astoria.in.
Offers 41 rooms of a good standard, after
being recently renovated. All have a/c,
hot water, and there's free Wi-Fi, it's a
good standard for the price. Great top-
floor room with a terrace.

$$ Fairlawn, 13A Sudder St, T033-2252
1510/8766, www.fairlawnhotel.com.
A Calcutta institution, the old-fashioned
but characterful rooms have a/c, TV, hot
water, and are comfortable. Semi-formal
meals at set times aren't the best, but
breakfast and afternoon tea are included.
The hotel and management provide
a throwback to the Raj, bric-a-brac

everywhere, photos cover all the communal spaces, quite a place and the garden terrace is great for a beer. Wi-Fi Rs 250 per day.

$ Afridi Guest House, opposite Ashreen Guest House (see below), calcutta_guest house@yahoo.com. A decent budget option, most rooms share bathrooms, some have a/c, most have TV, but many rooms are window-less. Sheets are clean and standards better than many Sudder St options. Try and book ahead, though that is easier said than done.

$ Ashreen Guest House, 2 Cowie Lane, T033-2252 0889, ashreen_guesthouse@ yahoo.com. Modern rooms with above-average facilities (for Sudder St) with TV and hot water, a suitable place to break yourself into Kolkata gently, however prices are ever escalating while standards slip. Pick-up for late night flights.

$ Capital Guest House, 11B Chowringhee Lane, T033-2252 0598. Tucked away from the road in a freshly painted old building, **Capital** is relatively quiet and all rooms have TV and private bath, though ones with windows are more expensive. Good value compared to nearby options but not a place to meet other travellers.

$ Emirates, 11/1 Dr Md Ishaque Rd (Kyd St), T033-2217 8487. Fresh, bright rooms in a building with character, some a/c, bathrooms are a bit jaded but there's a pleasant terrace.

$ Galaxy, 3 Stuart Lane, T033-2252 4565, hotelgalaxy@vsnl.net. 12 good tiled rooms with attached bath and TV, singles Rs 500, doubles Rs 700/900 without/with a/c, a decent choice but often full with long-stayers. Try at around 1030 just after checkout.

$ Maria, 5/1 Sudder St, T033-2252 0860. 24 clean, basic rooms (hard beds), some with bath, dorm, internet, TV in the 'lobby', hot water, water filter for guests' use. Popular budget place with a good atmosphere.

$ Modern Lodge, 1 Stuart Lane, T033-2252 4960. Very popular, 14 rooms, attached or shared bath, cheapest at ground level, prices rise as you go up to the breezy rooftop, pleasant lobby with plants but sinister 'lounge', quirky staff, no reservations so try at 1000.

$ Paragon, 2 Stuart Lane, T033-2252 2445. Textbook backpacker haunt with 45 rooms, some tiny and prison-like but it's clean just about (some doubles have attached bath) and mixed sex dorms (with shared/ private bath), rooftop rooms are better. Water heater to fill buckets. Open communal spaces, indifferent management.

$ Super Guest House, 30A Mirza Ghalib St, T033-2252 0995, super_guesthouse@ hotmail.com. This guesthouse has some of the cleanest rooms in the area for Rs 1200-1500 per double, all a/c with hot bath, tiled and simple box rooms. Be sure to ask for a room that does not suffer noise from the daily live music in **Super Pub Bar**. No single rates.

$ Times Guest House, 3 Sudder St, T033-2252 1796. Get a room at the front with balcony to view the action on the street below. Has character, jolly staff, very cheap singles with shared bath.

$ YMCA, 25 Jl Nehru Rd, T033-2249 2192, www.calcuttaymca.org. 17 rooms, some a/c, all with bath, geyser and TV, in large, rambling colonial building, clean linen, recently renovated but check room first as some are nicer than others. Helpful staff, rates include bed, tea and breakfast. The oldest YMCA in Asia.

Park St and Chowringhee
p143, map p144

$$$$ Park, 17 Park St, T033-2249 9000, www.theparkhotels.com. Trendy designer hotel, one of Kolkata's most reputable, good restaurants, nightclubs, health club, 24-hr café, service can be disappointing, entrance themed on underground car park. Go online for the best discounts.

$$$$-$$$ New Kenilworth, 1 & 2 Little Russell St, T033-2282 3939/40, www. kenilworthhotels.com. A very comfortable and attractive hotel, though overpriced at rack rates (good deals online). The foyer is all marble and chandeliers, but modern rooms are neutrally furnished with soft lighting, flatscreen TV, minibar, nice bathrooms. The older period building

contains suites and the **Big Ben** English-style pub, which has appeal as a dark den with a pool table and sports TV, plus there's a spa.
$$$ Astor, 15 Shakespeare Sarani, T033-2282 9957-9, www.astorkolkata.com. In a red-brick colonial building, comfortable a/c rooms with bath tubs, inferior annexe, have not retained original features, although public areas have fared better. The tiny blue-lit bar (**Cheers**, daily 1100-2300) is a nice place to be, and **Plush** lounge-bar is also fun (every night except Mon, liveliest on Wed, Fri and Sun). Breakfast included, minibar, off-season discounts, Wi-Fi (charge per 24 hrs).
$ Sunflower Guest House, 7 Royd St, T033-2229 9401, www.sunflowerguesthouse.com. An airy 1950s building with very clean well-maintained rooms, TV, hot water, more costly with a/c and newer bathrooms. Spacious lounge area, the numerous staff are kindly. Good location, near Sudder St but out of the backpacker scene. No single room rates.
$ YWCA, 1 Middleton Row, T033-2229 2494. Old colonial building with good atmosphere, airy verandas and tennis courts. Some rooms with bath (Rs 650) but doubles with shared bath have windows (Rs 350), dorm, all spotless, very friendly staff. Rates include breakfast, alcohol forbidden, a pleasant if shabby oasis in the city. A recommended alternative to Sudder St for female travellers.

South Kolkata *p148, map p138 and p144*
South Kolkata is a more salubrious area than elsewhere in the city, where quiet residential streets hide some good (mainly mid-range) guesthouses. Excellent little restaurants and vibrant markets are in plentiful supply.
$$$$ Chrome, 226 AJC Bose, T033-3096 3096, www.chromehotel.in. Space-age hotel with slick modern rooms dense with gadgetry, 'adrenalin' showers and trendy colour schemes. 6 categories, the 'Edge' suites being the zenith, but all are supremely comfortable. Good city-scapes from the higher levels. Minimalist **Khana Sutra** restaurant has huge set lunch/dinner North Indian menus as well as à la carte and

world cuisine, rooftop bar/club **Inferno** on the 7th floor, and **Nosh** café in the lobby is good for speciality coffee and global cuisine. Swimming pool is planned. Discounts possible, especially for stays of a few days.
$$$$ Hindusthan International, 235/1 AJC Bose Rd, T033-2283 0505, www.hindusthan. com. Comfortable quiet rooms on 8 floors are priced right, but staff are distracting with their demands for tips. The food is nothing special although there are a couple of quite cool bars/coffee shop and **Underground** nightclub is popular, pool (non-residents Rs 500). Big discounts are possible.
$$$ Samilton, 35A Sarat Bose Rd, T033-3051 7700/77, www.samiltonhotel.com. Modern business-like rooms with good amenities, free Wi-Fi and hot drinks. Decent restaurant/coffeeshop. Basement nightclub and rooftop with shishas.
$$$-$$ The Bodhi Tree, 48/44 Swiss Park (near Rabindra Sarovar metro, exit Swiss Park), T033-2424 6534, www.bodhitree kolkata.com. Simply beautiful little boutique hotel with just 6 rooms, each uniquely furnished in a different regional style (eg rural Bengal, with mud-plastered walls), flatscreen TVs, 1 penthouse. The owners are active promoters of young artistic talent, the in-house café is a delight (see Coffee shops, page 157), dinner is available, business centre, free Wi-Fi, small library, serves alcohol. Prices are entirely reasonable for the special experience. Discounts for single women travellers/social workers. A real oasis; recommended.
$$ 66/2B The Guest House, 66/2B Purna Das Rd, T033-2464 6422/1, www.662bthe guesthouse.com. On a tree-lined street with some great restaurants a 2-min walk away (2 of which are owned by **66/2B**), this cheerful place is well furnished, with decent baths, all rooms have a/c, geysers and flatscreen TV. A more relaxing area to stay in. Breakfast included, as is Wi-Fi. Recently refurbished.
$$ The Residency Guest House, 50/1C Purna Das Rd, T033-2466 9382, r_singla@vsnl. net. A very appealing mid-range hotel, with

clean tiled rooms, quality furnishings, a/c, TV, good bathrooms, comfortable beds. Close to Gariahat markets but on a quiet street.

$ Sharani Lodge, 71/K Hindustan Park, T033-2463 5717, gautam_sharani@ rediffmail.com. In a quiet area, yet very close to hectic Rash Behari Av, this well-maintained and well-run lodge has an old-fashioned Indian ambiance. The a/c rooms are not worth really worth the extra money, but non-a/c are a great deal (Rs 770-880), ones with common bath also share balconies at the front, all have TV, towels and plenty of space. Use of PC (Rs 20 per hr). They have a second building, across Rash Behari, with lovely little outdoor terrace (again, the non-a/c rooms are more spacious and attractive than a/c).

Other areas *map p138*
$$$$ Taj Bengal, 34B Belvedere Rd, Alipore, T033-2223 3939, www.tajhotels.com. Opulent and modern, restaurants are plush, imaginative, intimate, with good food (ground floor Indian cheaper than 5th floor), leisurely service, unusual Bengali breakfast, **Khazana** shop is excellent (see Shopping).
$$$$ Vedic Village, T033-2280 2071, www.thevedicvillage.com. In Rajarhat, 20 mins from the airport on the eastern edge of the city, but a world away from the rest of Kolkata. The appeal is the clean air and rural surrounds as much as the luxurious rooms, fabulous pool and of course the spa. Top-end villas and suites are stunning while studio rooms are not unreasonable when compared to other options in the city.
$$$ Tollygunge Club, 120 Deshapran Sasmal Rd, T033-2473 4539, www.thetolly gungeclub.org. On the south side of the city in 100 acres of grounds with an 18-hole golf course, swimming pool, tennis and other activities. Good bar and restaurants, one of which is open air. The place has charm and atmosphere which helps you overlook worn-out towels and casual service, ask for a renovated room, and enjoy the colonial feel. Interesting mid-range choice.

🍽 Restaurants

Licensed restaurants serve alcohol (some are unpleasant places to eat in since the emphasis is on drink). Be prepared for a large surcharge for live (or even recorded) music. This, plus taxes, can double the price on the menu. Many restaurants outside hotels do not accept credit cards. Special Bengali sweets are made fresh every afternoon at thousands of sweet shops (1600-1730): try *shingaras, kochuris* and *nimkis*.

Central Kolkata *p137, map p140*
$$$ Aaheli and **Oceanic**, at the Peerless Inn, 12 JL Nehru Rd, T033-2228 0301. **Aaheli** has an excellent menu of Bengali specialities, carefully selected from around the state by the chef, open from 1900. **Oceanic** has interesting seafood and is more pricey, open lunch and dinner. Both are comfortable with a/c and serve alcohol.
$$$ Baan Thai, Oberoi Grand (see Where to stay, page 151), T033-2249 2323. Excellent selection, imaginative decor, Thai-style seating on floor or chairs and tables.
$$$-$$ Amber, 11 Waterloo St, T033-2248 3477. Open 1100-2330. 2 floors of North Indian and continental gourmet delights (best for meat tandoori), generous helpings, fast service. **Essence** on 2nd floor fancies itself as a cocktail bar, but alcohol is served in both. There's also a functional bar on the ground floor (strictly no women). Also has a smaller restaurant on Middleton Row (T033-4000 7490), open 1200-1600 and 1900-2300.
$$-$ Anand, 19 Chittaranjan Av, T033-2212 9757. Open 0900-2130, Sun from 0700, closed Wed. Great South Indian food. Mammoth *dosas*, stuffed *idly*, all-vegetarian, family atmosphere and warmly decorated. Barefoot waiters are efficient. Queues at weekends.
$$-$ Bhojohori Manna, Esplanade. Open 1130-2130 (closed for cleaning 1630-1800). The newest branch of the **Bengali** chain, with budget prices for veg dishes and pricier fish items. Ticks on the whiteboard indicate availability, choice can be limited in the evenings as they sell out.

$$-$ Chung Wah, 13A Chittaranjan Av. Open 1100-2300. This hectic restaurant is functional and basic, with curtained-off booth seating down the sides. Hugely popular and with a large menu, it attracts a mostly male clientele, alcohol served. Recommended for the old-style atmosphere rather than the spicy Chinese food. Lone women are not encouraged.

$ Madras Restaurant, 25/B Chittaranjan Av, T033-2237 9764. A simpler setting than nearby **Anand** and slightly cheaper, but still has a/c. The list of *dosa* and *uttampams* is endless, plus there are a few Chinese dishes. Go between 1130-1530 for the South Indian thalis.

Coffee shops, sweets and snacks
Indian Coffee House, Albert Hall, just off College St (see page 145).

Around Sudder Street
p141, maps p142 and p144

$$$ Zaranj and **Jong's**, 26 JL Nehru Rd. Adjacent restaurants, both tasteful, stylish, subdued decor, excellent food. Try *pudina paratha*, *murgh makhani*, tandoori fish in Zaranj, or delectable Burmese fare in Jong's.

$$ Jimmy's, 14D Lindsay St. Chinese. Small, a/c, good *momos*, Szechuan dishes, ice cream. Alcohol served.

$ Blue Sky Café, 3 Sudder St. Chiefly Western. Very popular travellers' meeting place, a/c, always full and cramped, opinions on food vary.

$ Fresh and Juicy, Chowringhee Lane, T033-2286 1638. Newly renovated with a/c and 1st floor seating, good place for a sociable breakfast with reasonably authentic Indian meals and Western favourites, attracts a loyal following. Phone ahead for parcel-order.

$ Khalsa, 4C Madge Lane, T033-2249 0075. Excellent *lassis*, Western breakfasts, Indian mains all super-cheap, and beyond excellent service from the utterly charming Sikh owners.

$ NV Stores, T033-2252 9661, and Maa Kali, 12/2 Lindsay St. Closed Sun. Stand-up

street eateries making surprisingly good sandwiches (toasted are best) from any possible combination of ingredients; great *lassis* too.

$ Raj's Spanish Café, 7 Sudder St. Daily 0800-2200. Great Spanish nibbles, real coffee from a real machine, salads, pastries, pasta and sandwiches also good. Wi-Fi. A sociable spot. Recommended.

$ Tirupati, street stall next to **Hotel Maria**. A Sudder St institution; find a spot on the busy benches and enjoy enormous helpings of food from every continent. Closes out of season.

Coffee shops, sweets and snacks
Ashalayam, 44 Mirza Ghalib St. Peaceful oasis run by an NGO, sells handicrafts made by street children as well as coffee and snacks.

Kathleen's, several branches, including 12 Mirza Ghalib St, corner of Lord Sinha Rd.

Nahoum, Shop F20, New Market, T033-6526 9936. Good pastries, cakes, savouries and brown bread. The original 1930s till and some fixtures still in situ.

Kathi-rolls
Brothers Snacks, 1 Humayun Pl, Newmarket. Safe, tasty bet with outdoor seats. Kathi-rolls (tender kebabs wrapped in *parathas*) are hard to beat. Try mutton/chicken egg roll (if you don't want raw onions and green chillis, order *'no piaaz e mirchi'*) There are also plenty of great vegetarian options.

Park St *p143, map p144*
Visitors craving Western fast food will find plenty of familiar names in this area.

$$$ Bar-B-Q, 43 Park St, T033-2229 9916. Always popular, always delicious. 3 sections serving Indian and Chinese food, bar.

$$$ Bistro by the Park, 2A Middleton Row, T033-2229 494. It's near the park rather than 'by' it, but this attractive contemporary place serves world cuisine (including Southeast Asian, Middle Eastern) with the main focus on Italian fare (salads, pockets, pizzas, etc). Serves alcohol.

$$ Fire and Ice, Kanak Building, Middleton St, T033-2288 4073, www.fireandicepizza.com. Open 1100-2330. Pizzas here are the real deal, service is excellent, and the ambience relaxing. Decor is very much what you would expect from a pizza place at home.

$$ Flury's, 18 Park St. Classic Kolkata venue with hit-and-miss Western menu, but pastries and afternoon tea are winners and the bakery has brown bread. It's an institution.

$$ Gangaur, 2 Russell St. A wide menu of Indian delights, if you can resist the superb *thali* (1130-1530). Afterwards head next door for Bengali sweets.

$$ Mocambo, 25B Park St. International. A/c, pleasant lighting, highly descriptive menu. Long-standing reliable favourite.

$$ Peter Cat, 18A Park St (entrance on Middleton Row), T033-2229 8841. Chiefly Indian, with some international dishes. Good kebabs and sizzlers, hilarious menu of cheap cocktails, pleasant ambience but can rush you on busy weekend nights. No booking system, expect to queue outside.

$$ Teej, 2 Russell St, T033-2217 0730. Pure vegetarian Rajasthani delights washed down with cold beer, colourful *haveli*-esque setting.

$$ Tung Fong, Mirzah Ghalib St. Quality Chinese food for a reasonable price, the setting spacious and subtly Asian, white linens and Ming vases. Great Manchurian dishes, good fish and chilli garlic paneer, excellent desserts. Super-swift service.

$$-$ Gupta's, 53C Mirza Ghalib St, T033-2229 6541. Open 1100-2300. Excellent Indian and Chinese. More intimate and softly lit upstairs, low ceilings (beware of the fans), try fish *tikka peshwari* and *bekti tikka*, alcohol reasonably priced.

$ Hamro Momo, Suburban Hospital Rd (near Momo Plaza, see below). Open 1300-2100. Cheap and good Chinese and Tibetan dishes, in simple eat-and-run surroundings, always packed out and there's very little space.

$ Maya Ram, 1 Lord Sinha Rd, T033-6515 5837. Open 1100-2300. A good place to try 'snacks' such as *paw bhaji*.

$ Momo Plaza, 2A Suburban Hospital Rd, T033-2287 8260. Open 1200-2200. With black half-tiling and pastel pink walls accentuated by kitsch ornaments, which could be intentionally bohemian. Recommended for plentiful and delicious Tibetan and Chinese meals. Try the soups, chilli chicken, huge *momos* and *thukpa*.

Coffee shops, sweets and snacks

Café Thé, Tagore Centre, 9A Ho Chi Min Sarani, T033-4003 5878. Daily 0900-2100. Modern, clean cafe serving Western/ Indian/Chinese snacks and meals, with an interesting menu of hot/cold teas.

Pure Milk Centre, near Rafi Ahmed Kidwai St/Ripon St corner. Good sweet 'curd' (*mishti doi*), usually sold out by lunchtime. Excellent hot *roshogollas*.

South Kolkata p148, map p138 and p144

$$$ Mainland China, 3A Gurusaday Rd, T033-2283 7964; also at South City Mall, 3rd floor. Sublime Chinese. Unusual offerings, especially fish and seafood, tastefully decorated with burnished ceiling and evocative wall mural, pleasant ambience, courteous. Book ahead.

$$$ Oh! Calcutta, in the Forum Mall, 10/3 Elgin Rd, T033-2283 7161. Fantastic fish and seafood, plus many vegetarian options, this award-winning restaurant (branches across India, another in Kolkata on EM Bypass) re-creates Bengali specialities. It's an attractive venue; the only minor oddity is the location inside a mall.

$$$-$$ 6 Ballygunge Place, Ballygunge, T033-2460 3922. In a charming Raj-era bungalow, the intricate Bengali menu is as delightful as the ambiance. For more than a decade, this has been the perfect place for a special night out. Again, the fish dishes are a highlight.

$$ Kewpie's, 2 Elgin Lane (just off Elgin Rd), T033-2486 1600/9929. Tue-Sun 1200-1500, 1700-2245. Authentic Bengali home cooking at its best, add on special dishes to basic *thali*, unusual fish and vegetarian. Just a few tables in rooms inside the owners' residence, a/c, sells recipe book. Highly recommended, book in advance.

$$ Mirch Masala, 49/2 Gariahat Rd, Gariahat, T033-2461 8900. Lunch 1200-1500, dinner 1900-2230. This popular restaurant-bar has walls decorated with *pukkah* murals depicting Bollywood stars. Food can be a bit heavy (mainly Indian, non-veg) but the atmosphere is lively and staff competent.

$$-$ Bhojohori Manna, 13 PC Sorcar Sarani (aka Ekdalia Rd); also at JD Park. Budget prices and a perfect little place to sample pure Bengali cuisine, veg and non-veg. Ticks on the wall menu indicate availability, try *echor dalna* (jackfruit curry) and *bhekti paturi* (mustard-drenched fish steamed in banana leaves). 2 people should order 4-5 different dishes to share. Much better than the newer **Bhojohori 6** outlet on Hindustan Rd nearby. Decent toilet.

$ Banana Leaf, 73-75 Rash Behari Av, T033-2464 1960. Open 0730-2200. Vegetarian South Indian, top-notch *dosas* and *thalis* plus superb *mini-idli* and decent southern-style coffee.

$ Bliss, 53 Hindustan Park, T033-2463 5962. For Chinese in a fast-food environment, **Bliss** is ideal. Portions are generous, the soups delicious, it's tiny but there's seating.

$ South India Club, off Rash Behari Av. Daily 0700-2130. An authentic taste of the South in a canteen environment, full meals for under Rs 5, and a good place to experiment with less commonly seen dishes such as *pongal* or *upma*. Highly recommended.

Coffee shops, sweets and snacks

Art Café, at The Bodhi Tree (see Where to stay, page 153). Open Tue-Sat, 1400-1830. Half-inside/half-outside, this beautiful slate-floored café is lit by green lights and decorated with Buddhas, palm trees and original works of art (exhibitions are occasionally held). There's a tempting drinks menu (plus beer) in addition to light meals. Something quite out of the ordinary for Kolkata.

Dolly's, The Tea Shop, Dakshinapan market (just after Dhakuria Bridge). The quaintest place in the city for a variety of teas, refreshing iced-teas (try watermelon) and decent toasties. Tea-chest tables, low basket chairs, indoor and outdoor seating, even the walls are lined with old tea-crates. Dolly is a formidable lady.

Nepal Sweets, 16B Sarat Bose Rd. *Chandrakala*, almond *pista barfi*, mango *roshogolla*, *kheer mohan* (also savouries). Recommended.

Other areas *map p138*

$$$ Chinoiserie, Taj Bengal (see Where to stay, page 154), T033-2223 3939. Good for a splurge on excellent Chinese.

Chinese food fans also go to South Tangra Rd off EM bypass, east of the city centre. The approach is none too picturesque, past tanneries and open drains, but among the maze of lanes (in places lit by lanterns) many eateries are quite swanky.

$$ Beijing, 77/1A Christopher Rd, T033-2328 1001. Try garlic chicken, sweet and sour fish, chop suey, steamed fish, generous portions.

$$ Golden Joy, **Kafulok** and **Sin Fa**, to name but a few, offer excellent soups, jumbo prawns and honey chicken, best to go early (1200 for lunch, 2000 for dinner).

Kathi-rolls

Rehmania and **Shiraz Golden Restaurant**, on opposite corners of Park St/AJC Bose Rd crossing. Muslim joints famed for their mutton rolls and kebabs.

🎧 Bars and clubs

Kolkata *p136, maps p138, p140, p142, p144*
Bars

The larger hotels have pleasant bars and upmarket restaurants serve alcohol. The top hotels are well stocked, luxurious but pricey. In Sudder St, **Fairlawn's** pleasant garden terrace is popular at dusk attracting anyone seeking a chilled beer. The clientele is quite mixed, fairy lights set the greenery glowing and it's perfect for a 1st night drink to acclimatize – but beware the below-average food and stiff charges for snacks. **Super Pub Bar**, Sudder St, is always busy and sociable, but expect gruff service and check your change. The 1st floor has live music (Hindi and Bengali singing) every night from 1600-2400. (If you need a beer after hours, **Super Chicken** next door has take-away beers tucked in the fridge and is open later than the wine-shops). The 9th-floor bar **Blue & Beyond** at the Lindsay Hotel, is a rooftop bar/restaurant with great views over New Market and Kolkata and some excellent Indian and Chinese food (quite pricey), plus a few Western dishes. The 'ceiling' is composed of blue fairy lights, there is an indoor a/c section, but it's quite pricey. **Sam's Pub**, off Park St, is open later than most (last orders at 2330 on weekend nights) and still permits smoking in a curious indoor gazebo; football and cricket matches are shown on the flatscreen. For a sunset drink on the water, try the **Floatel**, a floating hotel on the Hooghly moored close to Babu Ghat. The simple bar is usually quiet, and has a small outdoor area, good for watching the river life.

'Local' bars, open usually from 1100-2230, often lack atmosphere or have deafening live singing; some are positively men only – there is a seedy choice down **Dacres Lane**, just north of Esplanade. Women also welcome in the **Broadway Bar** at the Broadway Hotel (last orders 2230), where marble floors, polished Art Deco seating, soft lighting, whirring fans and windows open to the street make it probably the best choice in the city. Lone women will feel comfortable as it's a busy and respectable place. The bar at the **New Empire Cinema**, between New Market and Chowringhee, is pleasant, blue-lit and efficiently staffed. **Oly Pub**, 21 Park St, is an institution: very noisy, serves steak and eggs, more airy downstairs, expect rats by the end of the night upstairs. Another classic is **Tripti's**, SP Mukerjee Rd (next to Netaji Bhavan metro), Mon-Sat 1100-2300, Sun 1100-2200. Established in 1935, Tripti's is styled like a canteen, sadly it's been tackily refurnished but 1950s flooring and shuttered windows remain, expect rowdiness and cheap booze. It's on the 1st floor up hidden steps, look for the sign; take a wander round sprawling and atmospheric **Jadu Babu Bazar** to the rear while in the area.

Discos and nightclubs

At hotels: **Incognito** (Taj Bengal), closed Mon, understated, relaxed ambience, 30-plus crowd, good food, taped music, fussy dress codes. **Someplace Else** (Park Hotel). Pub, live bands play loud music to the same crowd each week. **Tantra** (Park Hotel). Taped music, large floor, young crowd, no shorts or flip-flops, cover charge. Next door **Roxy** is less popular, but has free entry and is more relaxed, with slouchy sofas upstairs. **Underground** (Hindusthan International). Good live band, young crowd, good sizzlers, pool tables. The noisy dance-bar beneath **Ginger** restaurant (106 SP Mukerjee Rd, T033-2486 3052/3, near JD Park metro) accommodates same-sex couples, open 1130-2330. You can hear a variety of live music (Wed-Fri) at pub/club **The Basement** (Samilton Hotel), 35A Sarat Bose Rd, where there's also a shisha place on the rooftop. **Shisha Reincarnated**, Block D, 6th floor, 22 Camac St, T033-2281 1313, www.shisha reincarnated.com. Open 1800-2400, Wed, Fri and Sat -0200. Dark and stylish with a chilled atmosphere and low red lights, huge bar lined with spirits, and DJs every night (varying music styles) and a decent sized dancefloor. Hookahs cost Rs 300, the roof-deck is the best place to hang out.

⊕ Entertainment

Kolkata *p136, maps p138, p140, p142, p144*
The English-language dailies (*Telegraph*, *Times of India*, etc) carry a comprehensive list.

Cinema

A/c and comfortable cinemas showing English-language films are a good escape from the heat, and many are still very cheap. Check the newspapers for timings; programmes change every Fri. **Elite**, SN Banerjee Rd, and **New Empire Cinema**, New Market St, are conveniently close to Sudder St. **Nandan Complex**, AJC Bose Rd, T033-2223 1210, shows classics and art house movies; the **Kolkata International Film Festival** is held here in Nov, an excellent event. Swish **Inox** multiplexes (www.inox movies.com) are scattered around town (Forum, City Centre); tickets for these are Rs 100-150 and can be booked by credit card over the phone. **Fame cinema**, www.fame cinemas.com, Rs 100-250, in South City Mall is open 1000-0100, ticket line T4010-5555.

Dance, music, theatre and art

Regular performances at **Rabindra Sadan**, Cathedral Rd. **Kala Mandir**, 48 Shakespeare Sarani. **Gorky Sadan**, Gorky Terrace, near Minto Park. **Sisir Mancha**, 1/1 AJC Bose Rd. **ICCR**, 9A Ho Chi Min Sarani, has a lovely new concert hall. You can see Bengali theatre of a high standard at **Biswaroopa**, 2A Raja Raj Kissen St, and **Star Theatre**, 79/34 Bidhan Sarani. **Girish Mancha**, government theatre complex, 76/1 Bagbazar St, T033-2554 4895.

Galleries

Ahuja Museum for Arts, 26 Lee Rd (Elgin Rd crossing with AJC Bose), T033-2289 4645, www.ahujaptm.com/museum. The private collection of Mr SD Ahuja contains over 1200 works of art, which are displayed here in rotation.
Academy of Fine Arts, Cathedral Rd (see page 145).
Chemould Art Gallery, 12F Park St. One of the big names in contemporary art, and worth keeping an eye on.
CIMA Gallery, 2nd floor, Sunny Towers, 43 Ashutosh Chowdhury Av, T033-2485 8717, www.cimaartindia.com. Tue-Sat 1100-1900, closed Sun, Mon 1500-1900. The best exhibition space in the city and the shop has a good stock in wall-hangings, metalwork, clothes, stoles, ornaments, etc.

Experimenter, 2/1 Hindustan Rd, Gariahat. A trendy contemporary space with great exhibitions by Indian and international artists.
The Harrington Street Arts Centre, 2nd Floor, 8 Ho Chi Minh Sarani. Cool white space in an old apartment, hosting quality photography and art exhibitions.
Bengal Gallery, ICCR, 9A Ho Chi Min Sarani. Has a large space showing established artists.
Seagull Arts and Media Centre, 36C SP Mukherjee Rd (just off Mukherjee on a sidestreet), T033-2455 6492/3, www.seagull india.com. Holds regular photography exhibitions (see listings in the daily papers) from 1400-2000. Also has a bookshop on the opposite side of SP Mukherjee.
Studio 21, 17/L Dover Terrace (off Ballygunge Phari), T033-2486 6735, studio21. gallery@gmail.com. A minimalist new space for emerging artists from all disciplines, art/ photography exhibitions change regularly.

Performing arts

English-language productions are staged by the British Council and theatre clubs. **Sangeet Research Academy**, near Mahanayak Uttam (Tollygunge) Metro station, a national centre for training in Indian Classical music, stages free concert on Wed evenings. **Rabindra Bharati University**, 6/4 Dwarakanath Tagore Lane, holds performances, particularly during the winter, including singing, dancing and *jatras*. *Jatra* is community theatre, highly colourful and exaggerated both in delivery and make-up, drawing for its subject romantic favourites from mythology or more up to date social, political and religious themes.

✪ Festivals

Kolkata *p136, maps p138, p140, p142, p144*
Jan Ganga Sagar Mela at Sagardwip, 105 km south of Kolkata, where the River Hugli joins the sea, draws thousands of Hindu pilgrims.
Mar/Apr Holi (*Dol Purnima*) spring festival.
Jun-Jul Ratha Yatra at Mahesh, nearby.

Worship of the clay goddess

Durga Puja, the 17th-century festival in honour of the clay goddess, precedes the full moon in late September/early October, when all offices and institutions close down and the Metro only operates from the late afternoon.

Images of the 10-armed, three-eyed goddess, a form of Shakti or Kali astride her 'vehicle' the lion, portray Durga slaying Mahisasura, the evil buffalo demon. Durga, shown with her four children Lakshmi, Sarasvati, Ganesh and Kartik, is worshipped in thousands of brightly illuminated and beautifully decorated *pandals* (marquees). Traditionally these are made of bamboo and coloured cloth, but often modern *pandals* are veritable works of art constructed to complex designs and tapping into current themes or re-creating popular Indian landmarks. The priests perform prayers at appointed times in the morning and evening. On the fourth and last day of festivities, huge and often emotionally charged processions follow devotees who carry the clay figures to be immersed in the river at many points along the banks. The potters return to collect clay from the river bank once again for the following year.

You can see the image makers in Kumartuli (see page 147) a few days earlier and visit the *pandals* early in the day, before they become intensely crowded. Local communities are immensely proud of their *pandals* and no effort is spared to put on the most impressive display. The images are decorated with intricate silver, golden or *shola* (white pith) ornaments, there are moving electric light displays and huge structures are built (sometimes resembling a temple) in order to win competitions.

Sep-Oct Durga Puja, Bengal's celebration of the goddess during **Dasara**. See box, above.
Oct-Nov Diwali (*Kali Puja* in Bengal) is the festival of lights.
Dec Christmas. Many churches hold special services, including Midnight Mass, and the New Market takes on a new look in Dec as **Barra Din** (Big Day) approaches with stalls selling trees and baubles. Other religious festivals are observed as elsewhere in India.

O Shopping

Kolkata *p136, maps p138, p140, p142, p144*
Most shops open Mon-Sat 1000-1730 or later (some break for lunch). New Market stalls, and most shops, close on Sun.

Books

College St, a thicket of second-hand pavement bookstalls along this street mainly for students but may reveal an interesting 1st edition for a keen collector (see page 145).

Crossword, Elgin Rd. Deservedly popular chain store, with 2 floors of books, CDs, good selection of magazines and films and a busy coffee shop.
Earthcare Books, 10 Middleton St (by Drive Inn), T033-2229 6551, www.earthcare books.com. Excellent selection of children's books, Indian-focussed titles, socially conscious books, plenty of fiction, has small photo exhibitions.
Kolkata Book Fair, Milan Mela Prangan, EM Bypass, www.kolkatabookfair.net. End of Jan for a fortnight, stalls sell paperback fiction to antiquarian books.
Mirza Ghalib St. Has a string of small shops selling new, used and photocopied versions of current favourites. Bargaining required.
Oxford Book Shop, Park St. Huge selection of English titles, postcards and films, nice café upstairs where you can browse through titles. Excellent for books on Kolkata, and a children's bookshop next door.

Seagull, 31A SP Mukherjee Rd, T033-2476 5869/5, www.seagullindia.com. Large and unusual stock of art-related books, coffee-table tomes, etc.

Starmark, top floor, Emami Centre, 3 Lord Sinha Rd, T033-2282 2617-9; also City Centre and South City Mall. The best selection of fiction in Kolkata, plus imported magazines, films.

Clothes and accessories

Ananda, 13 Russell St. Fancy saris.
Anokhi, Shop 209, Forum Shopping Mall, 10/3 Lala Lajpat Rai Sarani, near AJC Bose Rd. Beautiful block-print bed-linens, floaty bed-wear, scarves, accessories, clothes and more. Made in Jaipur, mid-range prices.
Biba, South City Mall, Prince Anwar Shar Rd, www.bibaindia.com; also has franchises in **Pantaloons** department stores. Chic cotton print dresses, tasteful *salwar*.
Fabindia, 16 Hindustan Park (also branches at Woodburn Park Rd, near AJC Bose Rd, and City Centre Mall in Salt Lake). Clothes, textiles, toiletries, rugs and home furnishings from fair-trade company. Hugely successful due to their tasteful and high-quality selection. Well worth a visit.
Gomukh, next to **Raj's Spanish Café**, 7 Sudder St. Traveller wear, plus a range of scarves and wall-hangings, cheap and well stocked.
Monapali, 15 Louden St. Designer *salwar*.
Ritu's Boutique, 46A Rafi Ahmed Kidwai Rd. *Kurtas* and saris.
Khazana, Taj Bengal (see Where to stay, page 154). For pricey textiles, Baluchari saris, *kantha* embroidery, etc, and souvenirs.

Government emporia

Government emporia are mainly in the town centre and are fixed-price shops. All the Indian states are represented at **Dakshinapan**, near Dhakuria Bridge, Mon-Fri 1030-1930, Sat 1030-1400, excellent selection of handloom and handicrafts. **Central Cottage Industries**, 7 JL Nehru Rd, is convenient as is **Kashmir Art**, 12 JL Nehru Rd. **Phulkari**,

Punjab Emporium, 26B Camac St. **Rajasthali**, 30E JL Nehru Rd. **Tripura**, 58 JL Nehru Rd. **UP**, 12B Lindsay St.

Handicrafts and handloom

There are many handicraft shops around Newmarket St, selling batik prints, handloom, blockprints and embroidery, but starting prices are usually excessive so bargain hard. Shops listed below are all either fair trade-based or associated with self-help groups.

Artisana, 13 Chowringhee Pl (off Gokhale Rd), T033-2223 9422. Handloom and handicrafts, traditional hand-block textiles, designer jewellery, metalware and more.
Ashalayam Handicrafts, 1st floor, 44 Mirza Ghalib St. Products made by street children who have been trained and given shelter by the **Don Bosco Ashalayam Project**. Proceeds are split between the artisans and the trust.
Calcutta Rescue Handicrafts, Fairlawn Hotel. Thu 1830. Medical NGO sells great selection of cards, bags and trinkets made and embroidered by former patients.
Kamala, 1st floor, Tagore Centre, 9A Ho Chi Min Sarani, T033-2223 9422. Outlet shop for the Crafts Council of West Bengal; great selection of textiles, jewellery, gifts and trinkets at very reasonable prices (sourced directly from the artisans).
Karmyog, 12B Russell St. Gorgeous handcrafted paper products.
Sasha, 27 Mirza Ghalib St, T033-2252 1586, www.sashaworld.com. Attractive range of good-quality, fair trade textiles, furnishings, ceramics, metalwork, etc, but not cheap, welcome a/c.

Jewellery

Bepin Behari Ganguly St (Bow Bazar) is lined with mirrored jewellers' shops; **PC Chandra**, **BB Dutt**, **B Sirkar** are well known. Also many on Rash Behari Av. **Silver market** (*Rupa bajar*) is off Mirza Ghalib St opposite Newmarket. Gold and silver prices are listed daily in the newspapers.

Markets

The **New Market**, Lindsay St, has more than 2500 shops (closed Sun). You will find mundane everyday necessities to exotic luxuries, from fragrant florists to gory meat stalls. Be prepared to deal with pestering basket-wallahs.

Kolkata has a number of bazaars, each with a character of its own. In **Bentinck St** are Muslim tailors, Chinese shoemakers plus Indian sweetmeat shops and tea stalls. **Gariahat market** early in the morning attracts a diverse clientele (businessmen, academics, cooks) who come to select choice fresh fish. In **Shyambazar** the coconut market lasts from 0500 to 0700. **Burra Bazar** is a hectic wholesale fruit market held daily. The colourful **flower market** is on Jagannath Ghat on the river bank. The old **China Bazar** no longer exists although **Tiretta Bazar** area still retains its ethnic flavour; try an exceptional Chinese breakfast from a street stall.

Music and musical instruments

Braganza's, 56C Free School (Mirza Ghalib) St, T033-2252 7715. An institution; with an extensive collection.
Music World, 18G Park St, T033-2217 0751. Sells a wide range of all genres.

Also head to the southern end of Rabindra Sarani for musical instruments (sitars, tablas, etc).

Tailors

Garments can be skilfully copied around New Market and on Madge Lane. Tailors will try to overcharge foreigners as a matter of course.

◆ What to do

Kolkata p136, maps p138, p140, p142, p144
Body and soul
Look out for adverts around Sudder St for yoga classes held on hotel rooftops.
Aurobindo Bhavan, 8 Shakespeare Sarani, T033-2282 3057. Very informal yoga classes,

women on Mon/Wed/Fri 1530-1930, men on Tue/Thu/Sat 130-1930 (Rs 200). Bring a copy of your passport and visa.

Cricket

Occasional Test matches and One-Day Internationals and regular IPL fixtures at Eden Gardens, see page 141, 100,000 capacity; get tickets in advance.

Golf

Royal Calcutta Golf Club, 18 Golf Club Rd, T033-2473 1352. Founded in 1829, the oldest golf club in the world outside the UK.
The Tollygunge Club, 120 Despran Sasmal Rd, T033-2473 5954. The course is on land that was once an indigo plantation.

Horse racing

Royal Calcutta Turf Club, T033-2229 1104, www.rctconline.com. Racing takes place in the cool season (Nov to early Apr) and monsoon season (Jul-Oct). The Derby is in the 1st week of Jan. It's a fun, cheap day out in the public stands, better still if you can access the members enclosure to get up close to the racehorses and enjoy a drink in the bar with antlers mounted on the wall.

Sightseeing tours

Calcutta Walks, www.calcuttawalks.com. Run interesting walks through the city and also do cruises on the Hooghly.
WBTDC, departure point is Tourism Centre, 3/2 BBD Bagh E, 1st floor, T033-2248 8271. Daily tours, 0830-1730. Tour stops at: Eden Gardens, High Court, Writers' Building, Belur Math, Dakshineswar Kali Temple, Jain Temple, Netaji Bhavan, Kolkata Panorama and Esplanade, Victoria Memorial, St Paul's Cathedral and Kali Ghat. Entry fees not included. Private tour operators also offer city tours. Approved guides from **Govt of India Tourist Office**, T033-2582 5813.

Swimming

Wet 'O' Wild, at Nicco Park, HM Block, Salt Lake City. Kolkata's best waterpark with a truly enormous pool and wave machine. The **Hindustan International Hotel** pool is open to non-residents (Rs 500).

Volunteer work

Many people come to Kolkata to work with one of the many NGOs. The following organizations accept volunteers, though it's wise to contact them in advance (except for the **Missionaries of Charity**, where you only need to attend one of the registration days). **Don Bosco Ashalayam Project**, T033-2643 5037, www.ashalayam.org. Rehabilitates young homeless people by teaching skills. **Hope Kolkata Foundation**, 39 Panditya Pl, T033-2474 2904, www.hopechild.org. An Irish charity focussing on the needs of disadvantaged children. **Missionaries of Charity (Mother Teresa)**, The Mother House, 54A AJC Bose Rd, T033-2249 7115. The majority of volunteers work at one of the Mother Teresa homes. Induction/registration sessions are at 1500 on Mon, Wed and Fri in various languages.

⊖ Transport

Kolkata *p136, maps p138, p140, p142, p144*
Kolkata is at the eastern end of the Grand Trunk Rd (NH2). Many city centre roads become one way or change direction from 1400 to 2100 so expect tortuous detours.
Air Enquiries T033-2511 8787, www.calcuttaairport.com. The spacious terminals are well organized and have been recently renovated. A reservation counter for rail (same-day travel only) is found in the Arrivals hall. There are money changers by the exit of the terminal.

For transport into town, pre-paid taxis (office closes at 2200) to the city centre cost about Rs 350 (deluxe cars Rs 550-700). From the city centre to the airport costs the same or less if you bargain hard. New a/c buses leave from directly outside Arrivals, going to Howrah station (via the city centre) and Esplanade (from where it is a 15-min walk to Sudder St), taking at least 1 hr and costing

Rs 40. They also go to Tollygunge. The old public bus is not recommended for new arrivals as it's a 400-m walk across the car park to main the road, and then changing for the nearest Metro station which is at Dum Dum (Rs 8 to city centre); auto-rickshaws to the Metro cost about Rs 80.

Domestic: For schedules and prices it's best to visit a 3rd-party booking site such as www.yatra.com or www.makemytrip.com. Airlines include: **Air India**, 50 Chowringhee Rd, T033-2282 2356, airport T033-2248 2354. **Jet Airways**, 18D Park St, T033-3989 3333, airport T033-2511 9894. **IndiGo**, Crescent Tower, 229 AJC Bose Rd, T033-4003 6208, www.goindigo.com; and **Spicejet**, T1800-180 3333, www.spicejet.com.

Bicycle Bike hire is not easy; ask at your hotel if a staff bike is free. Spares are sold along Bentinck St, north of Chowringhee.

Bus **Local**: State transport services run throughout the city and suburbs from 0500-2030; usually overcrowded after 0830, but very cheap (minimum Rs 5 on the big blue-yellow buses, which are noteworthy for their artwork) and a good way to get around. Maroon minibuses (little more expensive, minimum Rs 6) cover major routes. Newer a/c buses are becoming commonplace.

Long distance: An extensive hub and spoke bus operation from Kolkata allows cheap travel within West Bengal and beyond, but long bus journeys in this region are gruelling as roads are generally terrible, and are a last resort when trains are full. The tourist office, 3/2 BBD Bagh, has timetables. Advance bookings at computerized office of **Calcutta State Transport Corp (CSTC)**, Esplanade, T033-2248 1916.

Ferry **Local**: to cross the Hugli, between Howrah station and Babu Ghat, Rs 5, except Sun. During festivals a ferry goes from Babu Ghat to Belur Math, 1 hr.

Metro The Metro is usually clean, efficient and punctual. The recently extended Metro line runs for 25 km from Dum Dum in the north to Kavi Subhash in the south from 0700-2145, Sun 1400-2145, every 7-12 mins;

fare Rs 4-14. Note that Tollygunge has been renamed 'Mahanayak Uttam Kumar' on station signs, but is still commonly referred to as Tollygunge. There are women-only sections interspersed throughout the train. A further 5 metro lines are planned for the future.

Rickshaw Hand-pulled rickshaws are used by locals along the narrow congested lanes. Auto-rickshaws operate outside the city centre, especially as shuttle service to/ from Metro stations along set routes. Auto-rickshaws from Sealdah station to Sudder St cost about Rs 70.

Taxi Car hire with driver: Gainwell, 8 Ho Chi Minh Sarani, T033-2454 5010; Mercury, 46 JL Nehru Rd, T033-2244 8377. Tourist taxis from India Tourism and WBTDC offices. Local taxis are yellow. Ambassadors: insist on the meter, then use conversion chart to calculate correct fare.

Train Kolkata is served by 2 main railway stations, Howrah and Sealdah. Howrah station has a separate complex for platforms 18-21. Enquiries, Howrah, T033-2638 7412/3542, 'New' Complex, T033-2660 2217, Sealdah, T033-2350 3535. Reservation, T138 (computerized). Foreign tourist quota is sold at both stations until 1400, at which point tickets go on general sale. Railway reservations, Fairlie Place, BBD Bagh; 1000-1300, 1330-1700, Sun 1000-1400 (best to go early), tourists are automatically told to go to the Foreign Tourist Counter to get Foreign Tourist Quota. It takes 10-30 mins. You will need to show your passport and complete a reservation form. Payment in rupees is accepted; you can also pay in US dollars, sterling or euros, but expect a poor exchange rate.

Trains listed depart from Howrah (**H**), unless marked '(**S**)' for Sealdah. **Agra Fort**: *Jodhpur Exp 12307*, 2320, 20 hrs; (**S**) *Sealdah Ajmer Exp 12987*, 2320, 19 hrs, *Howrah Mumbai Mail 12321*, 2200 (**Gaya**, 7½ hrs). **New Delhi** via **Gaya** and **Allahabad**: *Rajdhani Exp 12301*, 1655 (except Sun), 17 hrs; *Rajdhani Exp 12305*, 1405 (Sun), 20 hrs, via **Patna**; (**S**) *Rajdhani Exp 12301*,

1655 (daily except Sun), 17 hrs. **Varanasi**, *Vibhuti Exp 12333*, 2000, 13½ hrs

Tram Kolkata is the only Indian city to run a tram network. 0430-2300. 2nd-class carriage Rs 4, front '1st class' Rs 4.50, but no discernible difference. Many trams originate at **Esplanade depot** and it's a great way to see the city – ride route 1 to Belgachia through the heart of North Kolkata's heritage, or route 36 to Kidderpore through the Maidan. Route 26 from the **Gariahat depot** in the south all the way to Howrah, via Sealdah and College St. Services run from 0430-2230, with a restricted service at the weekends.

❶ Directory

Kolkata *p136, maps p138, p140, p142, p144* **Banks** There are 24-hr ATMs all over the city centre. Money changers proliferate on Sudder St. **Cultural centres and libraries** British Council, Information Centre, L&T Chambers, 16 Camac St, T033-2282 5370. Mon-Sat 1100-1900. Good for UK newspapers, reference books. French Association, 217 AJC Bose Rd, T033-2281 5198. Goethe Institut, Max Mueller Bhavan, 8 Pramathesh Barua Sarani, T033-2486 6398, www.goethe.de/kolkata. Mon-Fri 0930-1730, Sat 1500-1700. **Internet** You will need your passport to register the first time you visit an internet café. Many across the city; lots in Sudder St area with Skype, printing, etc; standard charge is Rs 20 per hr. On Sudder St, very helpful and with good equipment are Hotline Services, daily 0830-2200. In the city centre, E-Shan Digital Services, 13B CR Av, T033-2225 5716, fast connection but no Skype, Rs 25 per hr, Mon-Sat 0900-2100. **Medical services** Apollo Gleneagles Hospital, 5B Canel Circular Rd, T033-2320 3040. Wockhardt Medical Centre, 2/7 Sarat Bose Rd, T033-2475 4320, www. wockhardt hospitals.net, reliable diagnostic centre. Woodlands Hospital, 8B Alipore Rd, T033-2456 7076-9. There are many chemists around Lindsay St and Newmarket. Angel, 151 Park St (24-hr). Dey's, 6/2B Lindsay St. Moonlight, 180 SP Mukherjee Rd (24-hr).

Contents

Footnotes

Index

Titles available in the Footprint *Focus* range

For the latest books, e-books and a wealth of travel information, visit us at:
www.footprinttravelguides.com.

footprinttravelguides.com

Join us on facebook for the latest travel news, product releases, offers and amazing competitions:
www.facebook.com/footprintbooks.